The Rising of the Women

The Rising
of the Women

Feminist Solidarity and
Class Conflict, 1880–1917

MEREDITH TAX

University of Illinois Press
Urbana and Chicago

First Illinois paperback, 2001
Manufactured in the United States of America
P 5 4 3 2 1

⊗ This book is printed on acid-free paper.

Library of Congress Cataloging-in-Publication Data
Tax, Meredith.
The rising of the women : feminist solidarity and
class conflict, 1880–1917 / Meredith Tax.
p.   cm.
Originally published: New York : Monthly Review
Press, 1980.
Includes bibliographical references and index.
ISBN 0-252-07007-0 (pbk. : alk. paper)
1. Women labor union members—United States—
History. 2. Feminism—United States—History.
3. Women and socialism—United States—History.
I. Title.
HD6079.2.U5T39   2001
331.4'78'0973—dc21   2001027439

University of Illinois Press
1325 South Oak Street
Champaign, IL 61820-6903
www.press.uillinois.edu

Contents

Twenty Years Later

The Rising of the Women is about the strategic necessity for and unavoidable difficulty of feminist coalitions, and how these coalitions change according to the character of the period. Twenty years after this book was first published, thirty years after I began to write it, its subject seems clearer and even more important than it did then.

Feminism is not a politically homogeneous movement. No significant popular movement is; all contain differences of interest, affiliation, and belief. Today, when the global women's movement is stronger than it has ever been, many countries have a national women's bureau or umbrella organization set up by the government, while others, like the United States, have a cluster of leaders and organizations recognized by the state and the media—we can call these the "official women's movement," as the Chinese did at the 1995 U.N. conference in Beijing. While the official women's movement is important, it is never more than the tip of the iceberg in any period where women's rights are actually on the agenda. This is because the emancipation of women is so fundamentally challenging to every established order that a broad and diverse mobilization is needed to win even small gains. The women's movement is therefore a coalition in itself, and it operates in coalition with other movements.

The Rising of the Women focuses on a subsection of the broad coalition that is the women's movement, a subsection that we can call, in the language of a socialist periodical of the day, "progressive feminism." The progressive feminists discussed here were trade union activists, industrial unionists, intellectuals; they were socialists, anarchists, and radical feminists of every shade from deep red to pale pink. This book looks at what they believed, the ways they dealt with one another, and the various kinds of arrangements they made with the men who controlled their organizations and the women of means who were their patrons. If *The Rising of the Women* still has a contribution to make, after twenty years during which many others have dug into the same material, this contribution lies in its complex, detailed approach to such issues of power and its emphasis on strategic question seldom addressed by academics. I wrote it as a way of teaching myself to think strategically about the emancipation of women—an antique phrase which I like to use because it reminds me how far we have come.

By the early 1970s, it had become clear that the women's liberation movement of which I was a part was too narrow in its social base, too white, and too politically immature to be able to reach its goals. We needed to broaden out and change, and we needed allies who understood things we didn't. Looking for ways we could become stronger and sink deeper roots into the people, trying to understand how we needed to transform, I zeroed in on the question of coalitions. Studying the long, tortuous progress of the organizations in this book, I learned that the political success of a movement is only partly determined by its members' hard work, motivation, and intelligence. Other factors, such as the relative strength of conservative and progressive organization and opinion, the state of the economy, and the level of unity among progressive movements, may be even more important. Today these points may seem too obvious to need mention, but history was for me an important corrective to the voluntarism of the 1960s, a time in which many seemed to think that the process of building a more just society could be sped up if they only attended enough meetings.

The ability to think strategically depends on seeing conditions in the present as they are, grasping their potential for transformation, and being able to map a route from the present to the desired future. This requires the intellectual ability and information to make a realistic estimate of a situation; the social sensitivity to observe when it is changing and how; and the imagination to see how one's own meager strength could become a lever to change it. How does one learn to think this way? It isn't taught in school. In the early 1970s, as Bread and Roses, my women's organization, begin to disintegrate, I felt like I was butting my head against a wall; I simply did not know how to think about what we needed to do to keep our movement alive, and neither did anyone else I knew.

Now I realize that economic and social segregation had made it impossible for most women, even activists, to learn how to think strategically. Men who became leaders in business, the military, politics, and social movements learned about strategy, tactics, and long-range planning by building organizations, serving in military campaigns, even leading sports teams. But, until very recently, most women were barred from such fields. Very few of us had the opportunity to accumulate capital or order armies. Centuries of work in subsistence agriculture and handicrafts, caring for children, managing the survival needs of a family, and engaging in low-level mercantile activity or small-scale garment or food production, shaped different habits of thinking that emphasized cultural transmission, frugality, the value of human life, and the importance of human relations.

I wanted to learn what "the boys" knew without losing what I already knew myself. To do so, I turned not only to history but to Marxism.[1] By this I mean a systematic way of analyzing history in terms of conflicts between opposing economic forces and the dialectical interplay between culture and economics. Because Marxist dialectics shaped the thinking in *The Rising of the Women,* some of its language sounds very dated now, particularly the phrase "united front of women," which I use to describe feminist coalitions. Today the term is probably more distracting than useful; it can be abandoned as long as one understands that the women's movement itself is a strategic coalition between women of different classes, racial and ethnic backgrounds, and politics.

The fall of the Berlin Wall in 1989, marking the disintegration of the communist bloc in Eastern Europe and the end of the cold war, seemed to signal the triumph of Western capitalism, at least momentarily. These events made Marxist language socially unacceptable. It has been replaced in the academy by the language of social construction; one of the ways this book now sounds peculiar is that it talks about women rather than gender. It remains to be seen whether poststructuralism has anything to offer activists who want to learn how to think strategically.

It is abundantly clear that Marxist thinking and practice had glaring limitations and flaws, not only in countries where Leninists actually ran the state, but even in the United States, where they never had significant power. In fact, one of the subjects of this book is the difficulty U.S. socialists had dealing with women's issues. But the inhumanities of socialist practice should not lead us to overlook those of capitalist practice; the economic brutality described in *The Rising of the Women* remains with us today, in the United States and everywhere else that globalization calls the tune. In 1896, the top

1 percent of the U.S. population had 50 percent of the nation's wealth; today they have 90 percent.[2] And historical materialism remains one of the few ways to learn how to think strategically about social change.

One of the main factors determining the success of feminist movements is the strength of other progressive movements at the time, and the degree of overlap between them. The feminist organizers in part II of this book, who built women's trade unions and the Illinois Women's Alliance into a powerful coalition between 1886 and 1894, had the support of a strong labor movement led by radicals and the help of a vibrant group of settlement-house reformers; and they were working in the context of a progressive movement that swept John Peter Altgeld into the Illinois governor's chair in 1892. This was an extremely good environment for feminist organization. (See figure 1.) The group of women at the heart of figure 1 were at

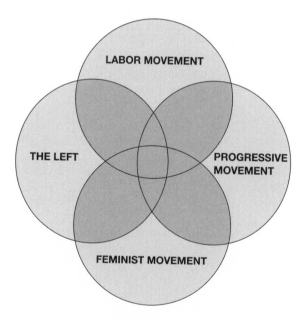

Figure 1: "Chicago Will Be Ours!"

the center of all these movements, linking them and overlapping with one another.

Despite efforts to remain democratic, even this strong coalition could not hold off the forces of conservatism and co-optation (in this case, the American Association of Manufacturers and the Chicago Democratic Party machine) for more than a few years, and eventually split. But their landmark work—the first eight-hour bill,

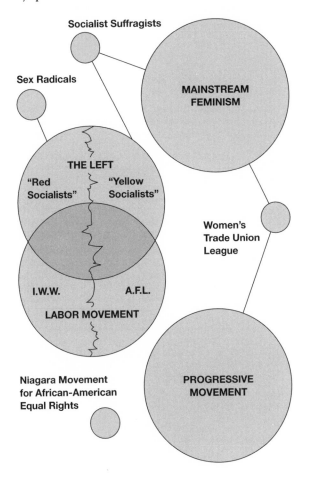

Figure 2: Fragmentation

the first strategy to end child labor through compulsory education—was like a prophecy, showing what could be achieved when
the labor movement and feminists, radicals and reformers worked
together. A similar though by no means identical picture could be
drawn of the overlapping movements of the late 1960s, another
good moment for feminist organizing.

Part III of the book shows what the same kind of women could
and could not achieve twenty years later, in a less favorable environment, when social change movements of all kinds, though still rela-

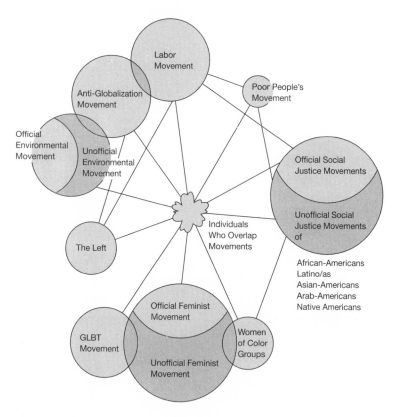

Figure 3: The Present

tively strong and vibrant, were split by political differences. (See figure 2.) A women's coalition like the one in Chicago, which brought together socialists and syndicalists, trade unionists and settlement workers, sex radicals and temperance workers, was not possible in a period when the mainstream women's movement had narrowed itself down to the single demand of suffrage and was interested in working women mainly as illustrations of the need for the vote, while the labor movement was split between the "pure-and-simple" trade unionists of the AFL, who had no interest in organizing women, and the syndicalists of the IWW, who disdained electoral politics, hoping to bring about a revolution through a general strike. In this context, working-class feminists like Leonora O'Reilly or Clara Lemlich could not bring together the various strands of their politics in any one organization.

Today the labor movement and the left have shrunk to the point that they would be almost unrecognizable to anyone time-traveling from 1912, while the movement for African American rights that began with W. E. B. DuBois and the Niagara Movement has not only grown enormously, but has inspired social justice movements of other ethnic minorities. (See figure 3.) Like the women's movement and the environmental movement, these have their official, recognized organizations, but are much larger than the membership of those organizations. And there is an important and growing new movement against globalization, largely labor and student based. Despite these hopeful signs, the picture is one of almost complete fragmentation, with little overlap between movements except in the persons of a few beleaguered and overstretched individuals.

While projecting a strategy to remedy this situation is beyond the scope of this introduction, a few observations may be permissible to update the questions considered in this book. Because we live in a period of globalization, the coalition that is the women's movement has today become international, to the point where activists in it have begun to work together on global campaigns and strategies for U.N. conferences. This is an extremely healthy development, as it enables U.S. feminists to learn from women in Africa, Asia, and Latin America like Patricia McFadden, program officer at the Southern African Research Institute for Policy Studies (SARIPS) in Zim-

babwe, whose analysis of the tasks facing African feminism is relevant
to any discussion of women's coalitions:

> I make a distinction between the women's movement and the femi-
> nist movement. The African women's movement grew out of women's
> activism in the nationalist movements and performs many of its func-
> tions as almost a wing of the government, concentrating on social
> welfare issues because of the need to alleviate the poverty of our
> people. The African feminist movement is much more on the edge,
> focussed on individual rights, and frequently under attack as
> inauthentically African. Feminists need to ally with the women's move-
> ment in order to help it redefine its relationship to the post-colonial
> state and respond to the new ideas of our civil society groups, in
> which women are major players, and which emphasize women's in-
> dividual rights to land, money, and power.[3]

In the United States, the position of the feminist movement and
the women's movement is reversed; here it is the feminists, especially the large Washington-based organizations, who see themselves
as almost a wing of the government, or at least of the Democratic
Party, while the broader if less visible movements of poor women,
women in the labor movement, and immigrant women are virtually
shut out. What could be more natural in the United States, where
class is a dirty secret, race colors every contradiction, and the corporate media assimilate and drain the transformational possibilities
from every new idea? Given these attributes, how does a women's
movement deal with the need to unite its scattered forces? Let us
take a look at the U.S. women's movement and see.

Imagine sitting in the upper balcony of Radio City Music Hall,
looking at the movement spread out upon the stage. In the center,
with big eye-catching organizational banners, are the mainstream
feminist groups: NOW, the National Women's Political Caucus, the
Feminist Majority. Surrounding them are the issues organizations
working on reproductive rights, breast cancer, violence against women;
the academic women and policy-oriented feminist think tanks; the
business and professional women's organizations; the religious women
of various denominations; and the old-line women's organizations
like the YWCA and the Girl Scouts, who pre-date contemporary
feminism but have adapted to it. Pushed to one side, though so numerous they can barely squeeze themselves in, are the feminists
active in movements for racial equality and environmental equity

and economic rights; movements against globalization, police brutality, and war; trade unions and welfare groups and community organizations. Then there are the U.S.-based international advocacy groups, some secular, some religious, most oriented to a single issue or slice of issues. And last, the progressive feminists of the 1960s along with groups of black feminists, Latina feminists, Asian American feminists, women of color, and LGBT groups.

All these people are potentially part of a vast coalition for the emancipation of women that could work with other movements for social and economic rights. Get out your binoculars; focusing on a few elements in the mix, closer up, may help us identify the barriers to such unity.

Official feminism could be observed at the Feminist Majority Expo in Baltimore, March 28–April 2, 2000, the purpose of which was to "showcase the power of the feminist Movement, its ideas and vision for the 21st Century!"[4] The Expo was an extravaganza with six thousand participants; a feminist trade fair with booths featuring everything from book signings to massage; and a conference with many workshops and four plenaries (on the themes of fighting the right, economic power, political power, and global fundamentalism), not to mention an opening tribute featuring a bevy of heavily scripted celebrities and female Democratic politicians.

The raison d'être of the event was to assert the women's movement's importance to the Democratic Party. "We are setting an agenda in the most powerful country militarily at this presidential election time," said Ellie Smeal in her keynote address. "We didn't invite candidates but we are sending them a message." And what was the message? "Elect more women. Save abortion rights. Pay equity. More women-owned businesses." Nothing about class or the need for unions. Nothing about poverty. Nothing about race—the obligatory rainbow onstage was belied by the whiteness of the audience and the narrow class perspective of the message.

None of this is news; class and race issues have been problems for the U.S. feminist movement since the 1960s, if not, indeed, since before the Civil War. But the influence of corporate ideology has never been stronger than it is today; this ideology has permeated the mainstream Washington organizations to the point that they could be described as corporate feminists. Corporate feminists assume that what is good for them personally is good for the movement, thus thinking like corporations, who do not build coalitions, but compete for a larger market share.

The Chicago coalition described in part II of this book was based on a perception of common purpose; working women, socialists, club women, and reformers could all unite to achieve goals they shared, in a process that gave all of them something they wanted. Everyone involved in such a coalition has to be willing to make some compromises: to meet in somebody else's neighborhood, to work with people who make them nervous, to let go of control and negotiate on wording, to share the photo ops. The payoff is a bigger, stronger movement with the kind of ties between groups that can only come from working together. Such a coalition could be built today between women in feminist organizations and women representing community groups, labor unions, civil rights organizations, and environmental groups. But this does not seem to be on anyone's agenda. Occasionally a mainstream Washington organization will put together a project or call a demonstration, get endorsements from a large list of groups without giving them any real input, and call this a coalition. But, unless it really builds a broader, stronger movement, this is not the kind of coalition I mean; it is, rather, a public relations gimmick by an organization that values hegemony more than diversity.

In the current corporate climate, such narrow choices seem almost inevitable. The mainstream women's organizations have big budgets to meet, they are looking for visibility that will help them raise money, and most have been utterly shaped by interaction with the state, so their perspective is always: what will help with lobbying, what will help in the next election. Of course building a broad-based, democratic, diverse women's movement would help with electoral and legislative goals, in the long run. But, even if one could leave aside issues of ego and control, corporate feminists are likely to see efforts to build a broader movement as competing with efforts to build their own organization. After all, soft drink companies do not see themselves as part of a soft drink movement where everyone works together for the good of the industry; they see themselves as competing for brand loyalty and consumer recognition. So do corporate feminists.

The Feminist Majority Expo brought together six thousand feminists, many of them students full of idealism who will shape our movement's future. This was a stunning achievement in the year 2000 and presented quite an opportunity. Imagine what might have happened if the Feminist Majority had wanted to break new ground and build a broad coalition instead of presenting a "showcase." What if the organizers had invited women from the Campaign for Economic Human Rights to talk about what it's like to be a woman on welfare in the U.S. today? What if they had flown in feminists from Belgrade or Baghdad to talk about the effects of U.S. sanctions and bombs, rather than focusing the whole discussion of foreign policy on an easy target like the Taliban? Such discussions of the impact of U.S. domestic and foreign policy would certainly have challenged the beliefs of many in the audience, made them think, and made some uncomfortable. The resulting debate would undoubtedly have flown right outside the parameters of Democratic Party politics. That's why it didn't happen. Feel-good conventions, cheerleading for feminism's past achievements, and playing on people's fears are safe; open debate and efforts to build a broader, more diverse, women's movement entail risk.

The same choice to avoid open-ended debate, the same tendency to see the women's movement as troops to be lined up and told to salute, was demonstrated in the all-out attack made by official feminist leaders on the grassroots presidential campaign of Ralph Nader and Winona LaDuke. Because these candidates gave serious attention to poverty, war, social justice, and the environment at a time when such issues were being either ignored or travestied by the two main candidates, their campaign was supported by many feminists and other activists. This could have been an opportunity to open up political discussion within the women's movement about means and ends, feminism and party politics. Instead, Nader-LaDuke supporters were reproached with a vigor normally reserved for mass murderers. A broader, stronger movement with more open debate might be more active, but it wouldn't be so easy to deliver to the Democratic Party. Corporate feminists do not need a strong movement. They need strong brand name recognition.

If this analysis is correct, mainstream feminist organizations are unlikely to initiate any broad women's coalition in the near future.

Is there anyone else who could do so? In the last ten years, some of the smartest women in the U.S. have put their energies into developing a global feminist agenda that addresses questions of poverty, violence, culture, and education as well as reproductive and legal rights. This agenda could have enormous resonance if it were taken up by American women. Its proponents, a fairly small group of lawyers and researchers and staff members of nonprofits, have helped win astonishing gains for women, particularly in the U.N. program for women's health and reproductive rights, and in redefining violence against women as a human rights abuse. And they certainly understand coalition politics, having worked in powerful international coalitions to bring about these ends. But, unfortunately, getting a message out to the women of the United States takes a different kind of organization and energy than getting it out in U.N. circles. Most American women don't even know that a global feminist agenda exists, and its creators are too busy at the U.N. to also take on the task of rebuilding the U.S. women's movement.

And what about the contemporary equivalents of the early feminist trade unionists in this book, the women active today in labor unions, the poor people's movement, community organizations, and movements for minority rights and social justice? Could the impetus for a new women's coalition come from them? The potential is there, but, unfortunately, these activists usually have so few organizational resources and are so overburdened they would find it difficult take on more work than they are doing already. They also have learned that they do not always get treated with respect when they reach out to mainstream feminists. According to Arundata Mittal, codirector of Food First, who works on poverty issues in California, "Many of those affected by welfare reform are white women in the suburbs who want to get out of abusive relationships and can't because they can't get welfare. But try to get the feminist groups who work on domestic violence to address this! In California, the mainstream groups don't even answer our calls for support."[5]

Is there any one else who could address coalition-building? What about the radical, visionary women's liberation movement of the 1960s and 1970s? For years, I have heard younger women, especially women of color, say, sure, they are feminists but they wouldn't touch the feminist movement with a ten-foot pole because it makes them feel invisible and has no concern for their issues. But when I say the big Washington organizations are not the whole women's movement, they answer, with absolute justice, "Well, where are the rest of you?" And when I relay this question over to my old friends, they respond, "But look at all we have achieved. Look at the changes in the law. Look how many of us have become doctors, lawyers, professors; look at women's studies; look at Title 9! We have changed the way people think about women, about gender, about sexuality. We have brought domestic violence, incest, and child abuse out of the closet; we have made it possible for women to live openly as lesbians. The reason we have no real movement any more is because we have won. We are everywhere!"

We may be everywhere, but to be everywhere is to be nowhere if it means nobody can find you. We did not know how to build and sustain organizations. We rejected the Washington top-down model and had no other models to go on, just dreams of nonhierarchical flow that sounded a lot like what is coming out of the environmental movement today. So, while we changed people's minds and lives, we built no enduring organizations or institutions that could keep our ideas alive. That task remains.

Of course, we were part of the left and what happened to it, happened to us. The space that had been available in the 1960s and 1970s for volunteer work drastically contracted in the political and economic climate of the 1980s and 1990s, while, at the same time, life became more expensive. Those who had planned to live on peanuts and do movement work for the rest of their lives had to figure out how to make a living. Progressive organizations that wanted to survive had to incorporate, shifting from an unstructured and spontaneous movement style of work, where free labor substituted for resources, to a staff-based style of work which not only cost more but entailed considerable interaction with the state and a corollary pressure towards hierarchical structures.

Like Maggie Hinchey, Leonora O'Reilly, and others in this book, many activists from the 1960s had trouble adapting to these changing political circumstances. And we were growing older; soon we had careers, or at least jobs, and many of us had children. Our personal options seemed to contract along with the movement. But let's not pretend this was a victory. Our goal thirty years ago was not to enable a few women to get rich working on Wall Street or to sit on their cans for the rest of their lives, talking about theory and calling it practice. We were working for the irreversible emancipation of women all over the world, not to mention the elimination of poverty, racism, and war.

Clearly, such an agenda requires more than one lifetime. That doesn't mean it is impossible, but it necessitates long-range strategic thinking, institution-building, and a means of transmitting ideas and concerns from one generation to another. My cohort of feminists had no access to the experience of earlier generations of radicals and working-class feminists. The repression of the 1950s had destroyed most of the avenues of historical transmission that normally exist between generations of radicals; that is why I had to go to the archives with my questions about coalitions and movement-building—it was very difficult to find older women activists from whom we could learn.

The answers I found in the archives are in this book. But I wouldn't have found them unless I was also engaged in political practice. Most answers to strategic questions can only be found through years of patient experimentation, using one's own life as a laboratory, trying to build unity and bring about change, failing, summing up the experience, trying again, looking for opportunities to bridge communities and issues, looking for ways to bring together the feminist movement and the women's movement so they can nourish and learn from and support one another. This book is meant for those who will take up the task.

Notes

1. I have told this story in other places and there is no need to repeat it here. See "I Had Been Hungry All the Years," in Carol Ascher, Sarah Ruddick, Louise DeSalvo, eds., *Between Women* (Boston: Beacon Press, 1984; 2d ed., 1993); reprinted in Ellen Carol DuBois and Vicki L. Ruiz, eds., *Unequal Sisters: A Multicultural Reader in U.S. Women's History* (New York: Routledge, 1990). See also "For the People Hear Us Singing, 'Bread and Roses! Bread and Roses!'" in Rachel Blau DuPlessis and Ann Snitow, eds., *The Feminist Memoir Project* (New York: Crown, 1998).

2. Ralph Nader, *The Ralph Nader Reader* (New York: Seven Stories Press, 2000), p. 7.

3. Patricia McFadden, speech at the Scholar and the Feminist Conference, Barnard College, April, 2000; author's notes.

4. Ellie Smeal, "Dear Colleague," mailed invitation to organize a delegation to the Feminist Expo.

5. Phone interview by author, July 3, 2000.

The Rising of the Women

To my friend and comrade Sarah Eisenstein, 1946–1978, who learned and knew and cared about the women in this book with as much passion as I do, and in whom political ideas burned like fire. May such fire catch and spread.

As we come marching, marching,
We bring the greater days.
The rising of the women
Means the rising of the race.
No more the drudge and idler—
Ten that toil where one reposes,
But a sharing of life's glories:
Bread and roses! Bread and roses!

—James Oppenheim, 1912

Preface

Until the development of the women's liberation movement in the late 1960s, the most diligent searcher for women in the pages of U.S. labor history could find them only sporadically. They would suddenly appear, only to disappear again like the Cheshire Cat in *Alice in Wonderland,* leaving just a smile behind. In recent years more attention has been paid to the history of working-class women. At this stage much of the work is still in survey form (necessary when the ground is so unknown) or is focused on particular organizations such as the Women's Trade Union League.[1] Not enough detailed research has yet been done to enable us to develop a solid theoretical understanding of the problems involved in connecting women's history and labor history. Still less do we have a body of elegant theory on the relationship of the working-class struggle to women's liberation. This book is an initial attempt to study that relationship at one moment in our history.

It is based on certain presumptions: the labor movement is not the same as the working-class movement as a whole, nor can the history of working-class women be restricted to the history of women in unions. Much work remains before we can develop an accurate sense of the intricate relations between workplace and home, union and community organization, socialist and feminist group, street and kitchen and school and bedroom, as these have occurred in history. The web of connections that bind all these together in the life of one woman can be like a spiderweb, preventing her from moving. Yet when a strong enough wind is blowing, the whole web and all the women in it can be seen to move together, and this is a new kind of movement, a new source of power and connectedness. For women, labor history comes attached to community history and family history and the history of reproduction. It involves not only class consciousness and the consciousness of national oppression, but also sex consciousness.

Unearthing and understanding such a complex history is a collective project, of which this book is only a tiny piece. I am confident that its limitations and omissions, as well as the errors it may contain, will be corrected by others; and if this work provokes such efforts it will have achieved its purpose. Its scope is limited, focusing mainly on organizations in two industrial cities, New York and Chicago, and dealing primarily with questions of political strategy as these were explored by socialists and feminists between the 1880s and World War I. Because black migration from the South did not really get underway on a large scale until after World War I, black women played little part in the organizing discussed here and are therefore underrepresented in this book. Nor was I able to do much more than touch on the personal and sexual concerns of the organizers I dealt with, despite the obvious ways these affect political work. In spite of these limitations, this book will make some of the political practice and strategic questions in our history accessible to those addressing similar problems today, in the hope that past concerns will enliven and broaden present ones.

I worked on this book for ten lean years, between 1969 and 1979, while holding a variety of jobs, doing political organizing, and raising a child. I could never have completed it without the help of a number of people who got me over the hard places in what seemed an endless journey. Sarah Eisenstein, to whom this book is dedicated, played a special role in the evolution of the thinking in it. She shared her own research with me, went over numerous drafts unstintingly, and was invariably precise in her criticisms, refusing to let me get away with sloppiness in thinking or formulation, and preventing me from getting so involved with the activists I was discussing that I forgot the level of consciousness and lack of organization of most women in this period. What rigor of thought there is here owes a lot to Sarah; it would be a better book if she had lived to see it finished, just as the world would be a different place if she were still in it.

Myra Rubin Murray helped me at a stage when I could not see how to move forward; she went over the manuscript in detail, encouraging me to make it true to my own ideas and intelligible to those who do not share them. She and Ann Snitow were its most enthusiastic critics from the first, steadfast in their belief in the usefulness of the project and in my ability to finish it. I could not have done so without them and their sustaining support.

Nor could I have gotten through the numerous rewrites of the book after its first publisher had rejected it without the encouragement of Kris Glen, Ginger Goldner, Ros Petchevsky, Elsa Rassback, and Ellen Ross. The final draft got a thorough going-over and minutely detailed criticisms from Elizabeth Ewen, Ann Snitow, and Sharon Thompson, each of whom spent a great deal of time helping me; their advice was invaluable. Support and practical assistance of various kinds along the way came from Hal Benenson, Temma Kaplan, and Diane Ostrofsky, as well as from my editor Susan Lowes.

In my early years of doing research and discussing women's history, a number of historians were wonderfully generous in sharing their own research and thinking. Among them were Mari Jo and Paul Buhle, Ellen DuBois, Linda Gordon, Priscilla Long Irons, Robin Jacoby, and Susan Reverby. Rosalyn Baxandall in particular was unfailingly supportive over many years, consistently giving of both her time and her source materials, helping me keep abreast of current work in women's history at moments when I was spending most of my time on other pursuits.

I used manuscript and research collections at a number of libraries, which are listed in the footnotes. Two librarians were especially helpful: Barbara Haber of the Schlesinger Library at Radcliffe College, and Dorothy Swanson of the Tamiment Library, now located at New York University.

To the women's liberation movement and to the working women of Chicago and New York, past and present, I owe more than I can describe or repay. This book contains only the shadow of what I have learned from them.

—Meredith Tax

May 1980

Part I
The United Front of Women

Earning a living away from home and often independently of the men of her family she acquired self-reliance and took a personal interest in the problem of existence. Working side by side with man and performing the same labor she came to resent his attitude of superiority. New thoughts entered her mind, a new sentiment found its way into her heart—the movement for women's freedom came to life. . . . The phenomenon became evident almost simultaneously in all countries where the change of economic conditions changed woman's position in society, where the dawn of the Industrial Revolution made possible the realization of equal rights and equal opportunities for man and woman.

Theresa Malkiel
Women and Freedom (1915)[1]

To a turn-of-the-century Marxist like Theresa Malkiel, it was a truism that the modern struggle for women's liberation was born of the same economic developments that produced the class struggle: as women began to work outside the home, they learned to resent their condition of domestic servitude and to demand the same rights as the men of their class. In the future, socialism would liberate both men and women, and if the feminist movement could only be made to see its true interests, it too would work for socialism.

Despite these certainties, it was hard for many women radicals, including Malkiel, to be content to talk about a future revolution when all around them masses of women were moving in pursuit of other, more immediate goals. A largely middle-class feminist movement was mobilizing to fight for the vote and for social equality in general; at the same time millions of immigrant women were being drawn into industry, where their exploitation was ferocious. How could they be organized—and for what? Should they be brought into the feminist movement or organized with male workers or both? Did the oppression of women cross economic lines, or was the only significant category that of class?

Then as now, there was a range of answers to these questions, for the problem of unity among women of different classes troubled women as much in the early part of the century as it does today. Those farthest to the left, especially the anarchists and the Industrial Workers of the World, tended to view the feminist movement with deep distrust. As Elizabeth Gurley Flynn, the IWW's main female leader, remarked with disgust in 1915: "The 'queen in the parlor' has no interest in common with 'the maid in the kitchen.' . . . The sisterhood of women, like the brotherhood of man, is a hollow sham to labor. Behind all its smug hypocrisy and sickly sentimentality loom the sinister outlines of the class war."[2]

Reformers like Alice Henry of the Women's Trade Union League took the opposite point of view: loving cooperation between middle-class feminists and working girls would enable the latter to organize and thus transform industry: "If the whole burden of remedying unfair industrial inequalities is left to the oppressed social group, we have the crude and primitive method of revolution. To this the only alternative is for the whole community through cooperative action to undertake the removal of industrial wrongs and the placing of industry on a basis just and fair to the worker."[3]

The problem of unity among women is more complex than it seemed to Elizabeth Gurley Flynn or Alice Henry in that alliances across class lines have sometimes worked *for* and sometimes *against* the long-term political interests of working women. In the Illinois Woman's Alliance, a coalition active in Chicago in the 1880s and 1890s, the left-wing and labor forces were strong, united, and able to take the initiative, and the middle-class women's organizations followed their lead. On this basis, the Alliance quickly won remarkable reforms. The Women's Trade Union League, founded in 1903, was organized under different historical circumstances and came under the hegemony of middle-class reformers; its politics, organizational style, and achievements were therefore different from those of the Alliance.

People concerned about organizing working women today cite

the example of the Women's Trade Union League to prove conflicting hypotheses: that the only way working women can organize is with the help of cross-class alliances, or that working with middle-class women is a terrible mistake because of the corrupting effect of their petit bourgeois ideas. Neither point of view is fully historical, for the character of any such alliance depends on a large number of factors: the strength of the labor movement; the influence of the left within it; the left's support of women's liberation; the openness of the feminist movement to influence from workers and from the left; and, of course, the political and economic character of the period in general. A strategy for women's liberation at any particular time must take such variables into account.

When I began the research for this book, I did not understand this and hoped to find a strategy that could be used to solve the problems of our own movement. I knew that there had been a strong and radical labor movement, a very substantial socialist movement, and an enormous feminist movement before World War I, and I wondered how they were related. I began to accumulate material on women in unions, on the private lives of various organizers, on their sex habits, on theories of the oppression of women, on the Industrial Workers of the World, the Socialist Party, the Women's Trade Union League, the American Federation of Labor, household technology, and any number of other things. Although the material was interesting, it had no shape; and when I tried to let the facts speak for themselves, they were as inscrutable as an oracle, open to many interpretations. As my own politics developed, I pushed the facts one way, pulled another, trying to see what they meant.

Gradually a shape—a theme—emerged from the clay. It did not really even have a name. I have called it the "united front of women," by which I mean the alliance, recurring through time in various forms, of women in the socialist movement, the labor movement, the national liberation movements, and the feminist movement. I am using the term united front not in the catchall sense of the 1930s, but as it is used currently, particularly in the Third World, to describe the coming together of different classes and their organizations (as well as different national and gender groups) for a goal of some magnitude that takes a considerable length of time to achieve. Most reform movements in the United States have been united fronts. The abolitionist movement brought together men and women from all nationalities and class backgrounds. The woman suffrage movement was a united front of men and women, blacks and whites, the wives of capitalists and professionals, farm women, self-employed professional women, trade union women, and intellectuals. It included women of every racial and national background, family arrangement, sexual preference, and political persuasion; there were bourgeois feminists, radical feminists, and socialist feminists (though none of these terms were in vogue at the time), as well as Marxists and temperance advocates.

The united front of women has been a frequent phenomenon in the history of the organization of working women in the United States: the work of Chicago women which culminated in the Illinois Woman's Alliance; the 1909 general strike of shirtwaist makers in New York City, which organized most of the trade into the International Ladies' Garment Workers' Union; and, on a much more limited scale, the Women's Trade Union League are all examples. The Lawrence strike of 1912, led by the Industrial Workers of the World, was a different sort of united front of women, one that demonstrated the strength that can come from deliberately building connections between workplace and community, between workers, housewives, and children.

A united front differs from a "coalition" which, as the word is generally used, means a coming together of various organizations for a limited end, such as a piece of legislation, an election, or a demonstration. It also differs from an "autonomous women's movement," as conceptualized during our period, although there are many points of overlap. For one thing, most of the socialist women discussed here did not see themselves as part of an autonomous movement, but as part of more than one movement—the human links between the feminist movement, the labor movement, and the socialist movement. They knew there was a dialectical relationship between the movement for women's liberation and the labor movement, and refused to give up either; while this choice often led to personal difficulties, it gave these women a historical importance that has not been sufficiently recognized. They did not think it desirable to organize women in a way that would further cut them off from other social movements; on the contrary, they felt a need to struggle against the separation and compartmentalization that already existed. Yes, they wanted to organize women to fight for their own liberation, and they wanted to do the reform work for women that other movements had neglected. But they also wanted to integrate the women they were organizing into the general struggle for socialism so that they could play an equal part in that fight.

Much Marxist history and theory has tended to treat the working class as if it included only men. When women are discussed, it is as workers, in the same terms as men only with more pity, or as "reserves" that must be mobilized on the side of the working class lest they go over to the enemy. When working men act against their own class interests, it is the result of unfortunate historical circumstances; when women do, it is their "backwardness." As history moves along and women play a more obvious, even glaring, role in it, they are given a little more space in history books. But it is never their own space, seen in terms of their own struggles and perceptions. They are always an adjunct to the main struggle.

Despite this, much Marxist history contains an accurate vision of what has happened to working-class men as they have been affected by changes in their economic and social life. Once we know as much about what has happened to working-class women as their very different lives become caught up in the same developments, we will be able to write the history of the whole class. In this history women will have a continuous, not sporadic or occasional, existence. And, as others have pointed out,[4] we should not expect that the rhythm of women's history will be that of men's any more than the character of work inside the home is identical to that outside it. The years when there were bread riots or struggles over public education—both led by women—were not necessarily the same as the years when there were mass strikes in basic industry—led by men. The early years of a depression, for instance, with rising unemployment, are seldom ones of great industrial strife, but they often show increased activism in working-class communities, expressed in food boycotts or battles against evictions. If we look only at the workplace, or only at men, when writing the history of the working class, we will find only one kind of militancy.

But when the experience of women is integrated into history, some Marxist issues become more complicated. An example is the theory of how working-class organization and consciousness develop. This theory is—very roughly and generally—as follows: with the formation of the industrial working class or proletariat, workers begin to struggle against their employers, first in the factory, then in the trade or locality. "They direct their attacks not against the bourgeois conditions of production, but against the instruments of production themselves; they smash to pieces machinery, they set factories ablaze, they seek to restore by force the vanished status of the workmen of the Middle Ages."[5] Industry develops further and the workers become concentrated in larger factories. They begin to form unions, which grow powerful enough to affect wages and working conditions and even to lead mass strikes. The workers become aware that they are not fighting their employers alone, that they are fighting the whole *class* of employers, which has at its disposal the entire state apparatus with its law courts, police forces, and armies. The struggle becomes one of the working class against the bourgeoisie; it becomes a political as well as an economic struggle.

Through the unions or through the development of a labor party, the working class will then try to influence the bourgeois political process, to get its own legislation passed, its own supporters elected. According to classical Marxist theory, at this stage the working class cannot do much more. It cannot possibly gain control over the bourgeois political process, but in order to understand this, the working class needs Marxism—scientific socialist theory which sums up the international experience of the struggle between classes. When the workers grasp socialist theory, they transform it into a living force; only then can they organize a party capable of leading a revolution and overthrowing bourgeois rule.

In the period between 1880 and World War I, parts of this process seemed to have begun in the United States. Workers had formed unions and Marxists were active in them, trying to link the workers' economic needs with their political ones. But the process was different for women than for men. Even though some of the earliest concentrations of industrial workers were among women employed in the New England textile mills, substantial numbers of women did not enter industry until after the Civil War. It takes time for new workers to see themselves as members of a class, and by the time women were ready to do so, men were already organized into craft unions in most of the industries where women worked.

Thus the history of worker organization and of the development of class consciousness was different for women. Rather than entering industry side by side with men, women entered a situation in which male workers had an organization but seldom extended its benefits to their sisters. In fact, because they viewed women as competitors who undercut their wages, many trade unionists preferred to leave them unorganized, hoping this would drive them back into the home where they belonged.

Women had to approach the established unions as suppliants, knocking on the door and asking to be let in. Working men did not accept them as equal partners in the class struggle, because the socially caused differences in their situations made them unequal. Women were hired because their need was so desperate that they would work for less than men: their wages were depressed; their working conditions were horrible; their jobs were increasingly sex-segregated. They did not earn enough to pay high union dues. Many of them were young girls working only until they got married. Those who were married had to rush home to their "other" job and seldom had the time to attend union meetings, which were in any case held in saloons where "nice girls" didn't go. The differences in the lives of men and women outside the workplace reinforced and were used to justify unequal treatment within it.

But if the men who guarded the doors to the labor movement did not always ask them in, working women found support from other sources. From the 1880s until after World War I efforts to organize women came less from the mainstream of the labor movement than from a series of united front efforts by socialists and feminists. The first comprehensive history of women in U.S.

trade unions, written in 1911 by John B. Andrews and W. D. P.
Bliss as part of a government survey of the working conditions of
women and children, noted with some uneasiness that the organizational history of working women was strikingly different from
that of working men because of such united fronts:

> The women's unions, moreover, to a much greater degree than
> those of the men, have been developed and influenced by leader-
> ship from without the ranks of the wage-earner. This external
> leadership has often furnished elements of weakness to the pure
> trade-union movement among women, but it has also furnished
> necessary support as unselfish and inspiring as can be found any-
> where in the annals of the development of our industrial or political
> democracy.
>
> External leadership has often been necessary in furnishing initial
> direction and financial support. It has frequently induced and
> sustained the movement until a growing sense of independence
> and an understanding of personal rights enabled the women wage-
> earners to act together on their own account. On the other hand,
> external leadership has often worked injury to the trade-union
> women by drawing them away from plans for immediate advan-
> tages, to the consideration of more remote and less tangible schemes
> for universal reform.[6]

In other words, socialism. To a pronounced extent the history of
the organizing efforts in this book is a history of the work of
socialists of one kind or another.

There were three basic types of socialist in this period, and
from 1901 on all of them coexisted inside the same organization,
the Socialist Party. The first type often called themselves "Christian
socialists"; they would be called utopian socialists today. They believed the cooperative commonwealth would come to pass through
peaceful efforts to build class harmony and human brotherhood.
They were fond of communal experiments and producer or
consumer cooperatives, and saw class conflict as something to be
avoided if possible. Leonora O'Reilly of the Women's Trade
Union League was a socialist of this type, preaching that the world
should be run by labor because "labor is the law of life"—sooner
or later, everyone would work and be as brothers and sisters to
one another.

The second type were reform socialists or social-democrats, as
they would be termed now. They called themselves "constructive

socialists," to distinguish themselves from those on their left whom they called "impossibilists." While they saw the world in terms of fundamental class conflict rather than the brotherhood of man, they believed this conflict could be peacefully resolved by building a working-class political party that would gain in electoral strength until it finally swept the country. At that point the victorious working-class movement would vote in socialism and nationalize industry, thus eliminating the power of the bourgeoisie. Most reform socialists saw trade unions as an important step in this process: unions would help develop a class-conscious proletariat capable of voting in its own interests. Even more than unions, however, they emphasized educational and electoral work, particularly at a municipal level, where their policies became known as "sewer socialism" because of their emphasis on sanitation and city services. Many of the labor members of the Women's Trade Union League were reform socialists.

The third type called themselves "revolutionary socialists" or "red socialists," as opposed to those on their right, whom they called "yellow socialists." They believed that class conflict could not be resolved through elections, and that the revolution would be brought about through militant industrial unionism and the use of the general strike—though this might be combined with socialist political action as a minor theme. Many revolutionary socialists belonged to the Socialist Party but looked to the Industrial Workers of the World for leadership. They were more associated with sex experimentation, birth control propaganda, and cultural radicalism than were the other socialists.

A small but significant percentage of all three types was female. An estimate made in 1912 by the editor of *Progressive Woman,* a socialist woman's magazine, put the female membership of the Socialist Party at 10 percent.[7] Considering the limited participation of women in the work force at the time, most of these were probably housewives rather than industrial workers. This was equally true of earlier socialist organizations and is hardly surprising: the only working-class women with the time for political activity were unmarried working women who lived at home (where their mothers took care of their cooking, cleaning, and laundry) or married women whose children were grown and whose husbands supported their political work.

The participation of housewives in the socialist movement is worth stressing because of the persistent idea that housewives are "backward," possibly the most backward sector of the working class, and that socialist organizers should therefore concentrate on wage-earning women. In fact most activist housewives had at one time worked for wages, and they were particularly able to sense the needs of the working class as a whole, rather than the narrower needs of workers in one industry. The largely untold history of women's auxiliaries in the mines and other basic industries, and of the numerous militant working-class consumer revolts, bears witness to the fact that housewives can be anything but "backward."[8]

Socialist housewives, settlement workers, and the left wing of the feminist movement were the main allies of working women in the period between the 1880s and World War I. Their support could not make up for the general lack of help from the labor movement, however; there were so many obstacles to the organization of working women that it took the combined forces of the united front of women and organized labor to make it possible. In the exceptional cases where such help was forthcoming—Chicago in the 1880s, the 1909 shirtwaist makers' strike in New York—working women got up enough steam to crash through the barriers to union organization, at least for a time. It is no coincidence that these were also situations in which the local labor movement had left-wing leadership.

The united front of women—the alliance of socialists, feminists, and trade unionists—was therefore a major factor in giving working women the social muscle necessary to organize into trade unions in this period. But its success depended on the strength of the labor movement as a whole, the strength of socialists within it, and how progressive the feminist movement was. Above all, the united front's ability to organize working women depended on who led it—what class and with what kind of politics. When the working-class and left forces were strong, when they had deep enough roots among the people to be able to organize women without the help of the middle class, and when they were clear about what they were trying to achieve, they were able to lead the whole united front of women and build vital links between women's struggles at work and in the community. This was the case in the

Illinois Woman's Alliance. But when the working-class and left forces were weak, they lost leadership to those who dissolved the class contradiction in a middle-class version of sisterhood or who elevated certain individual working-class women into a miniature version of the labor aristocracy. This is what happened in the Women's Trade Union League. In neither case was the question one of working-class "purity" versus cross-class "sisterhood." The important question was which class was dominant in ideas, organization, and energy, and could therefore lead the rest.

The Illinois Woman's Alliance was formed at a time when the labor movement in Chicago was strong; it was led by a handful of women from the Socialist Labor Party, with ten and twenty years of industrial and political experience behind them. They were able to unite every significant women's organization in Chicago with the city federation of trade unions, and to bring about enormous political changes—a child labor law, a compulsory education bill, a factory inspection act, the construction of new school buildings and public baths. They even campaigned against police victimization of prostitutes.

By the time the Women's Trade Union League was underway, however, conditions were very different. The labor movement was deeply divided: the IWW, its left wing, had split off from the craft unions in the American Federation of Labor, and the AFL was led by men who had little interest in organizing women. The working-class and left-wing women in the League were not seasoned organizers—some were only teenage girls. They did not see the problems inherent in their situation clearly and were unable to give overall ideological or programmatic leadership in such complex circumstances. Middle-class members were thus able to implement their own ideas of how a women's labor movement should be led and by whom. They had great influence, not only in their emphasis on legislation as opposed to organizing, but in fostering a small but significant female leadership elite comparable in politics if not in power to the men who led the AFL.

Of course by World War I the stakes were higher than they had been in the 1880s and 1890s. Significant numbers of women were working outside the home. The U.S. working class as a whole was larger, better organized, and more powerful. The economy had been transformed: U.S. capitalism had entered the stage of monopoly concentration and would soon embark on its second imperialist war. From the point of view of the bourgeoisie, it began to make more sense to find ways to control and assimilate the labor movement developing among women than to drive it to insurgency by trying to stifle it. Far better that the AFL, which worked docilely with the government throughout the war, be the source of leadership for working women–not the socialists or feminists. But if working women were to be assimilated to the "pure-and-simple" antipolitical unionism of the AFL, the left-wing components of the united front of women had to be isolated and eliminated. This happened during the war. While the leaders of the mainstream suffrage movement and the Women's Trade Union League became part of the government to help the war effort, radical feminists chained themselves to the White House fence and were jailed; pacifist women protested the war and were ostracized; and IWW members and socialists who actively opposed the war were persecuted, jailed, and even killed. A postwar government campaign of arrests and deportations further isolated the left. At the same time, the issues of protective legislation and the Equal Rights Amendment divided socialists and radical feminists from one another. The united front of women lay in fragments with a split between its left and its feminist parts, and both divided from labor.

The development of the united front of women in the 1880s, the contradictions that emerged inside it, and its eventual fragmentation are of interest to anyone who wants to develop a strategy for organizing women today. The particulars of our situation differ from the earlier history in many respects—including the recent development of the national liberation struggles in the Third World and the United States; the splits in the international socialist movement; and the far-reaching changes in women's lives, such as the development of scientific birth control and the enormous increase in the number of working women. Still, while it would be folly to overlook the momentous differences between 1880 and 1980, understanding the complexities of organizing women in another period in the United States should enable us to better grasp the many-sided nature of our own task.

Part II
"Chicago Will Be Ours"

1
"There Must Be Something Wrong"

When earth produces free and fair
  The golden waving corn;
When fragrant fruits perfume the air,
  And fleecy flocks are shorn;
Whilst thousands move with aching head,
  And sing the ceaseless song—
"We starve, we die; oh, give us bread,"
  There must be something wrong.

When wealth is wrought as seasons roll,
  From off the fruitful soil,
When luxury, from pole to pole,
  Reaps fruits of human toil;
When, for a thousand, one alone
  In plenty rolls along,
And others only gnaw the bone,
  There must be something wrong.

Then let the law give equal rights
  To wealthy and to poor;
Let freedom crush the arm of might
  We ask for nothing more.
Until this system is begun,
  The burden of our song
Must be, and can be, only one—
  There must be something wrong.

"Factory Girls' Album" (1847)[1]

The entrance of large numbers of women into industry and their subsequent efforts to organize were part of the vast social upheaval of the period of massive industrialization that followed the Civil War. As the century progressed, more and more workers began to echo this refrain from the New England mills: "There must be something wrong!" The fabric of traditional American society was being wrenched apart. Families were being driven off the land into the cities. Women were going to work for wages. All political life seemed touched with corruption, and the vast wealth that was being produced in the new factories was accumulating in a few hands.

This was the period of the concentration of economic and political power in the hands of the monopoly capitalist class. While the economy boomed and periodically crashed—there were depressions in 1873, 1877, 1903, and 1914—the power of a small group of capitalists expanded wildly and in every direction. Cross-country railroads were built in the 1880s: the Canadian Pacific, Southern Pacific, Great Northern, and the Atchison, Topeka & Santa Fe. By 1906 Edward H. Harriman controlled a third of the total railway mileage in the United States, while James Hill controlled the Great Northern and the Northern Pacific, and the J. P. Morgan group controlled most of the rest. Fierce competition resulted in collusion: the railway magnates created a trust that put all the railroads in the country under the control of three or four men who were already immensely rich and became more so. As Leo Huberman put it, "Up to the 1880s most businessmen competed with one another. After the 1880s smart businessmen combined with one another."[2]

With the building of the railroads new industries opened up, to become monopolized in their turn. The invention of the refrigerator car revolutionized meat packing and made Chicago "hog butcher to the world." The forests of the Great Lakes and Pacific Northwest, and the iron and copper mines of the Midwest and West, became accessible by rail and therefore profitable. Under Rockefeller's leadership, the oil industry was developed until the Standard Oil Trust was worth $70 million and controlled virtually all oil production in the United States from start to finish. Frick and Carnegie established a similar monopoly in steel. J. P. Morgan was one of the handful of men who really ran the country regardless of who was president. In 1901 he united Rockefeller's Standard Oil with Carnegie's steel trust to form U.S. Steel, worth $1.4 billion. His financial group dominated the railways, electricity, steel, shipping, farm machinery, anthracite, telephones, telegraph, and insurance. Morgan was also closely allied with the First National Bank of New York.

While a few became fabulously wealthy, most people owned little or nothing. In 1896, according to a survey by Charles B. Spahr, the top 1 percent of U.S. families had more wealth than the bottom 50 percent.[3] The profits of those at the top grew so rapidly that they constantly had to seek new investment markets in order to maintain the same high rate of return. Between 1889 and 1917 the United States took over Samoa, Hawaii, Puerto Rico, Guam, Cuba, the Philippines, the Dominican Republic, Panama, Haiti, Nicaragua, and part of the Virgin Islands. Meanwhile, U.S. workers were paid as little as possible, worked as long as human bodies could tolerate, and were crushed by blacklists, "ironclad oaths" not to join unions, and, if necessary, the courts and federal troops.

Many of the most exploited of these workers were new immigrants. Between 1901 and 1920 over 14.5 million immigrants came to the United States, and they and their children made up the majority of the industrial working class. In 1900 44 percent of U.S. miners were foreign-born and 61 percent had immigrant parents; 36 percent of iron and steel workers were immigrants and 63 percent had immigrant parents.[4] An 1887 government survey found that 75 percent of women factory workers in the large cities were either immigrants or the daughters of immigrants.[5] Immigrants—especially those who could not speak English—filled the lower rungs of the industrial ladder; they were segregated into the worst jobs, usually paid less than their native-born counterparts, and ghettoized in their own slums.

The differences between native-born and immigrant workers were used to split the working class and prevent its organization. Employers and politicians cultivated antagonisms by using immigrants to break strikes or undercut wages. If a big manufacturer like Carnegie had a strike on his hands, he would send down to the docks for immigrants to use as scabs. He would take them into his mills under guard—so that the strikers could not explain the situation to them—and even lock them into the factory at night, supposedly to protect them. Sometimes immigrants just off the boat were sent clear across the country in locked trains on the promise of a job and, once there, were used as scabs and forced to work under appalling conditions, even at gunpoint. The steel trust broke a number of strikes in both its mills and mines this way. In addition, one immigrant group would be used to undercut another. For instance, an employer would deliberately split his workforce among two or more nationalities, each speaking a different language, thus making it more difficult for them to organize. The boss might further complicate things by favoring one nationality over another or by persuading each that he favored the other.

Despite these hardships, life in the U.S. had much to offer the new immigrants, particularly the women. Most of them came from countries that were largely agrarian, where women were servants or farm wives. Factory work had liberating aspects for them, despite appalling working conditions, discrimination, and disorientation. Middle and southern European peasants stepped over centuries of historical development when they crossed the Atlantic. Customs such as matchmaking and arranged marriages, chaperons, shaved heads and veils, black floor-length dresses, and enforced female illiteracy broke down before the needs of U.S. capitalism. Escaping from these feudal forms of patriarchal control, earning their own money and the right to an independent voice, seemed a great step forward to these women. Abraham Bisno, a Jewish socialist and leader of the cloakmakers in Chicago, described the way work changed their lives:

> I found that immigrants who were farmers in the old country considered opportunities to work in factories as a great boon. Women who earned very little on the farm and who earned livings mostly by housework, either in their own homes or as servants, appreciated the opportunity of working a limited number of hours and earning money. Though their wage was small, they considered it large; while the majority of them turned their money over to the family chest, there were quite a significant number who would themselves be holders of their earnings, pay regular board to their families, and either spend or save money for themselves.
>
> This change in their lives which gave them a right to do whatsoever they pleased with their own money, and gave them standing and authority in their families because of their earnings and contributions, was for them a very significant item in their lives. They acquired the right to a personality which they had not ever before possessed in the old country, even married women who worked in

shops and were obliged to maintain a household at the same time. These latter felt they were much better off because they had a money-earning capacity, though they had to work very hard. So the factory and even the sweatshop were very much appreciated by these women. It was a historic revolution in their lives and in the lives of their entire people.[6]

Native-born farm girls were affected similarly by the changes in the national economy; as the U.S. became a great industrial power, millions of women poured into the paid labor force from rural farms and kitchens, as well as from overseas. In 1880 about two and a half million women worked for wages; ten years later, this number had nearly doubled; by 1910, there were over eight million women in the work force, making up 23.4 percent of all women in the U.S.[7] Nearly one-third of these women (31.3 percent) went into domestic service as maids, cooks, or laundresses. Another large group went to work in factories—1,820,570 women, or 22.3 percent of all women wage earners. They worked in clothing, textiles, cigar and tobacco processing, shoes, food production, and metalworking. Over a million worked on farms for wages, while more than one hundred thousand worked in white-collar jobs as salesclerks, schoolteachers, and nurses.[8]

The worst conditions for women workers occurred in industries where work was done on a small scale at home: the garment industry, cigar manufacturing, nutpicking, and various luxury trades. This was the era of the sweatshop, or home workshop, staffed mainly by immigrants from Eastern Europe and Italy. In the sweatshop everybody worked—young children, invalids, the aged—on jobs like stringing beads, sewing buttons, or plucking feathers to make feather boas. Such work got minimal pay—five or six cents an hour was the average wage—and the health hazards were immense; filth, disease, and death were the inescapable consequences.[9] The workroom spread into the kitchen and bedroom. Many people were crammed together in rooms where they both lived and worked, with no heat, no windows, no hot water. There was never enough space or air. Lint, dust, bits of cloth, and dirt permeated the air, the food, the water, and the bed. Such places were breeding grounds for tuberculosis (the "sweaters' disease"), smallpox, glaucoma, diptheria, and other diseases of the very poor. Public health authorities pointed to the danger of epidemics caused by germs carried on sweatshop-made clothing, and campaigns to eliminate sweatshops began to get widespread middle-class support.

Although a wage envelope sometimes gave a woman more power within the patriarchal family, it did not completely transform her social situation. Rather, her subordinate position in the home and in society at large was reinforced in the workplace, where employers were able to grossly underpay her and thus derive huge profits from her labor. A Senate commission that carried out a monumental survey of the working conditions of women and children in the United States found that in 1910, as today, there was a division of labor by sex: "Ordinarily the occupations involving skill, training, and responsibility were in the hands of men, while the work of women was apt to be at best only semiskilled and in many cases purely mechanical. Under these circumstances the difference in earnings of the sexes was very marked."[10] Forty percent of women workers earned under six dollars a week.[11] Their work tended to be segregated from that of men. They did work men were not trained to do, such as needlework; work that was considered women's work, such as laundry and food processing; and work that was so labor-intensive that it did not pay to get men to do it, such as garment work. They did their work for less than men, and they were used to undercut the wages of organized men, like the cigarworkers, when an industry mechanized. These women did not work for self-fulfillment; they worked because they had to. The majority were unmarried girls in their mid- to late-teens and early twenties, whose earnings were essential to their families' survival. Most of the girl clothing workers under sixteen gave their entire wage envelope to the family budget. Those married women who worked did so either because they were the only support of their children (being widowed, divorced, or deserted) or because their husbands could not earn enough to feed the family.

The high profits derived from their labor were justified by the general belief that women were not really meant to work for wages, that it was "unnatural" for them to do so, that they didn't really need to work but only wanted "pin money," and that they deserved less money than men because they were less valuable people. Women were kept both underpaid and unorganized partly by arguments such as these:

1. Women work only to supplement the earnings of their fathers or husbands, therefore they don't need to earn much, and certainly don't need equal pay.
2. Women should not be working anyway: it is not their "sphere," it makes them unfeminine, and they should be home caring for their families. Therefore they do not deserve much money and should be punished for their violation of decency by earning as little as possible.
3. Women are unskilled workers. Naturally unskilled workers earn less than skilled workers. (For some reason construction work has always been considered skilled, but needlework has not, even though aspects of one take no less skill than the other.)
4. Women are only working until they catch a husband. Getting married is their job in life: they are in the workforce too briefly to want to join unions, and they are in any case unorganizable, since all they think about is men. Further, they have neither the staying power nor the fighting ability to succeed even if they want to unionize, because they are women and therefore weak. Consequently there is no point in even trying to organize them.

It is clear that these were not rational arguments based on an objective interpretation of facts, but ideas that grew out of a traditional way of life that was becoming obsolete. On the farm there was so much work reserved for women that there was an economic rationale behind the "separate sphere." In the city working-class women took jobs because they had to if their families were to eat, and a separate sphere for women was a luxury they could not afford. Still, traditional ideas about woman's place had considerable strength in the minds of both men and women workers. They were, after all, the ruling ideology, broadcast in every paper, from every pulpit, by every politician. And as time went on they were used increasingly by the labor leaders of the AFL who wished to justify their neglect of working women: "Nice girls don't work."

These ideas clashed with reality. Of course most factory girls wanted to get married, and of course they quit work when they did: this was their only possible escape, on an individual level, from the miseries of the workplace. But for increasing numbers of women this escape was an illusion, particularly in the single-industry textile towns of New England.[12] Black women had almost never been able to entertain such illusions. No matter how often women were told their place was in the home, the fact was inescapable that they were being driven out of it in ways that brought both greater suffering and greater freedom. The argument that most women stopped working when they got married, and hence could not be organized, was proved totally untrue by the young girls in the New York and Chicago garment industries. Nevertheless, even researchers who were sympathetic to organizing women tended to believe in their docility and flightiness.

> The employer invited [the women's] entrance *en masse* because they were cheap and above all because they were docile and easily managed. They were cheap and easily managed because they were in the main young, partly because they were unorganized, and partly because, as they expected to stay in the industrial world only a short time, they considered it better to accept conditions as they found them than to fight for improvements.[13]

So women were unorganized because they were docile, easily managed, and cheap; and they were docile, easily managed, and cheap because they were unorganized. In fact they were unorganized because they had just become workers; because they had so much work to do at home that they could hardly move; because their husbands, boyfriends, and fathers did not let them go to meetings; because they earned so little that they could not afford to take extra risks; and because no one would organize them. And when anyone tried, women often showed that, despite all these barriers, they were raring to go.

The late nineteenth century was a period of great activity among women of all classes. Throughout the country there was a groundswell of discontent that found expression in the People's Party, the Knights of Labor, the AFL, the settlement movement, the anarchist movement, the Socialist Labor Party, and, among women in particular, in the Women's Christian Temperance Union, the suffrage movement, and the women's clubs. Membership in these groups overlapped; many trade unionists and Knights of Labor were also socialists or "Nationalists"—single-taxers, who believed in the universal panacea of a single property tax, as advocated by the prophet Henry George in his best-selling *Progress and Poverty*. WCTU members were also suffragists, settlement workers, members of women's clubs, Knights of Labor, Nationalists, and sometimes even socialists. All this overlap was a sign of the ferment of the period, the radicalism of the laboring classes in the 1880s and 1890s. The actions of the monopolies and the state, the frequent industrial depressions, the blatant alliances of the corporations, courts, and federal government against the unions—all these fed radical sentiments. Such grassroots feelings were summed up at the People's Party convention in 1892:

> We meet in the midst of a nation brought to the verge of moral, political and material ruin. Corruption dominates the ballot-box, the legislatures, the Congress, and touches even the ermine of the bench. . . . The newspapers are largely subsidized or muzzled; public opinion is silenced and business prostrated; our homes covered with mortgages; labor impoverished; and the land concentrating in the hands of the capitalists.
>
> The urban workers are denied the right of organizing for self-protection . . . a hireling standing army [Pinkertons], unrecognized by our laws, is established to shoot them down, and they are rapidly degenerating into European conditions. The fruits of the toil of millions are boldly stolen to build up colossal fortunes for a few, unprecedented in the history of mankind; and the possessors of these in turn despise the republic and endanger liberty.[14]

The newly formed American Federation of Labor was part of this upsurge of popular militance. This may seem odd to those who think of the AFL as a collection of narrow-minded labor aristocrats who kept women and blacks out of the labor movement and cared only about protecting the privileged position of its skilled membership at the expense of the rest of the working class.[15] While this was certainly true after the turn of the century, two things must be remembered: first, the AFL was a federation that left room for local variations in the direction of either progress or reaction, and the politics of the top leadership did not necessarily reflect the sentiments of the membership; and second, like any other mass organization the AFL responded to the political climate of the times. Even AFL leader Samuel Gompers, later known for his conservatism, was a socialist in the 1870s.[16]

The AFL was founded in 1886, when existing trade unions— carpenters, cigarmakers, ironmolders, and other skilled workmen— joined together to defend themselves against raiding and scabbing by certain factions in the Knights of Labor, a rival organization (see chapter 2). The AFL reacted against anti-union aspects of the Knights and felt its cross-class membership made the Knights prone to turn away from union organizing and strikes to such middle-class panaceas as cooperatives and electoral campaigns. In contrast, the AFL elaborated the concept of "pure-and-simple" trade unionism; the union would avoid politics so as not to get dragged into electioneering and forget its economic interests. It would be a purely working-class organization, excluding middle-class people with abstract revolutionary or reformist schemes on behalf of the workers. It would be a federation of separate craft unions with little central control. In practice, the AFL's pure-and-simple unionism degenerated over the years into protecting the interests of the organized against the unorganized, and jockeying between jurisdictional disputes, but this was not envisioned at the time.

It was early days in the labor movement and there was little to distinguish trade unionists from revolutionaries. Both were lepers as far as the molders of public opinion were concerned. Many of the early leaders of the AFL were Marxists in the loose sense in which this term was understood at the time. Marxism was in its infancy and few of the works of Marx and Engels had as yet been translated into English. Samuel Gompers, the AFL's founder and first president, had to learn German in order to read *Capital*. He looked forward to the "first emancipation of the working class" through trade unions.[17] Gompers believed that he and the others who built the AFL were the heirs of Marx and Engels, who themselves had believed in building unions, and, like Marx, Gompers opposed the Lassallean socialists who insisted that there was no point in building unions because nothing could be won under capitalism.

In fact the constitution of the infant AFL was a clear class struggle document: "A struggle is going on . . . between the oppressors and the oppressed . . . a struggle between capital and labor, which must grow in intensity year by year, and work disastrous results to the toiling millions . . . if not combined for mutual protection."[18]

Despite this militant statement, the AFL avoided taking a position on most general political questions and did not endorse political candidates. Gompers responded to the Lassallean socialists, who were prominent in New York, by insisting on a complete separation between economics and politics; politics, he said, had no place in the labor movement. This was, ultimately, to become the general rule in the AFL unions. But in Chicago the lineup of forces in the craft unions was quite different from that in New York: instead of Lassallean socialists versus pure-and-simple unionists, the antagonists were socialist unionists and labor racketeers.

In the 1870s the Chicago labor movement had been heavily infiltrated by the city political machine and by gangster elements. The head labor politician, also a leader in the Chicago Trades and Labor Federation, was Billy Pomeroy. His associate, Skinny Madden of the steamfitters, charged $1,000 and up for not striking on construction jobs; his motto was "Show me an honest man and I'll show you a damn fool."[19] Abraham Bisno describes the kind of unionism represented by these men:

> There developed a sort of irresponsible and gang affiliation between the respective business agents of the respective trades in the building industry, and those leaders would protect the wages of their members loyally but would at the same time use the club of strike over the employers, contractors, and builders for the purposes of getting personal graft. That put the building industry almost constantly in chaos and turmoil; very seldom did a job go through without strikes and violence and slugging and injunctions, with police violence and graft added to it all, and the leaders of the strikers forming a gang with the politicians and crooked policemen forming a fellowship for dishonest purposes.
>
> The initiation fee in all these unions was very high, and grew higher from year to year. To get into any of these unions became very difficult, and each separate union formed a sort of monopoly in its own small group. Most members were continually bent on the

idea of allowing fewer and fewer people to enter, making a scarcity of labor in their own calling and therefore making for the maintaining of their standard of wages—but these ideas militated for a selfish group idealism, and were against the sense of solidarity of labor. They made for a sort of aristocracy in each special group.[20]

In the 1880s and 1890s the leadership of the Chicago labor movement went back and forth between the "labor skates," led by Billy Pomeroy, and the socialists, led by Albert Parsons, George Spies, and Tommy Morgan. The socialists looked like apostles of purity next to these gangsters. They stood for absolute fiscal honesty, class struggle, and morality—they even opposed free tram passes for factory inspectors as possible graft. They were strong enough to fight the crooks, and workers followed them as much because of their honesty and their class struggle attitudes as because of their theories about revolution.

The issue of who was to lead the labor movements in Chicago and New York was important to women workers because to a substantial degree it determined whether or not they would be organized. In Chicago the socialists actively supported the organization of women, while the racketeers busted up their unions.[21] The basic socialist approach to the oppression of women, as developed by Engels and Bebel, saw the integration of women into production as the major way to end their inequality. Though a few backward socialists held onto the idea that women's place was in the home and that men should protect them, most saw that women were in industry to stay, that this was progressive, and that they should be organized on an equal basis with men.

Gompers, in this period, reiterated the prevailing belief that women belonged at home, and that it was unnecessary for the wife to contribute to the support of the family by working.[22] There was therefore no need to organize women, and the priority should be to raise the wage of the working man. Though not all unionists agreed with Gompers' views, the influx of women into the work force during this period met with a variety of proposals: they should be driven out of the factories; they should be treated with benign neglect; they should be organized as equals into unions or segregated into separate locals or integrated as subordinate members of mixed locals. Many trade unionists undoubtedly hoped the problem would disappear once men had won wage increases that would allow their wives and children to stay home.

Only the socialists worked out a consistent and scientific understanding of the changes in women's conditions, one that led, in theory, and in Chicago in practice, to the idea that women had to be organized for the good of the entire working class. This approach was developed by the German socialist, August Bebel, whose book *Women and Socialism* was translated into English in 1903 by Daniel De Leon, leader of the Socialist Labor Party. It immediately became the most popular book on the subject for generations of women activists. After outlining the appalling exploitation and suffering of women and child laborers, and discussing the fact that this suffering often led people to want to turn back the clock and send women out of the factories, Bebel went on:

> The trend . . . of our social life is not to banish woman back to the house and the hearth, as our "domestic life" fanatics prescribe. . . . *On the contrary, the whole trend of society is to lead women out of the narrow sphere of strictly domestic life to a full participation in the public life of the people*—a designation that will not then cover the male sex only— and in the task of *human civilization*. . . . The dark sides that accompany also this form of development, are not necessarily connected with it; they lie in the social conditions of our times.[23]

Most U.S. socialists concluded from this that women should be organized alongside men, into both unions and socialist organizations. Nowhere was this idea tested in practice more ardently than in Chicago where, under the leadership of female socialists, the task of organizing working women was taken up more successfully than anywhere else in the country. The trade unions that developed there were supported by a powerful united front of women which combined both the labor movement and the feminist movement.

2
"Shouting Amazons"

We shall have the sham reformers self-stultified and self-convicted; we shall have the radical Democracy left without a lie with which to cover its nakedness! And then will begin the rush that never will be checked, the tide that will never turn until it has reached its flood—that will be irresistable, overwhelming—the rallying of the outraged workingmen of Chicago to our standard! And we shall organize them, we shall drill them, we shall marshal them for victory! We shall bear down the opposition, we shall sweep it before us—and Chicago will be ours! *Chicago will be ours!* CHICAGO WILL BE OURS!

Upton Sinclair
The Jungle (1905)

"Vat is the matter mit the vimmins?" shouted an enthusiastic German-American socialist as he watched the parade go by. "They're all right!" Thirty-five thousand women—a number matched by few U.S. labor demonstrations since—marched down Michigan Avenue in the 1903 Chicago Labor Day parade; among them were garment workers, sausage girls, cracker packers, waitresses, schoolteachers, candy dippers, and scrubwomen. The scrubwomen sang as they marched, "Shall idle drones still live like queens on labor not their own?" and the candy dippers, dressed in white and perched on a muslin-draped float, made marshmallows and tossed them out to the watching crowd. The unprecedented turnout was discussed by the labor press around the country: how did it happen that Chicago had so many working women organized when New York, a far bigger city, had only 5,000 female union members?[1]

The answer to this question lay in the previous twenty years of efforts to organize working women in Chicago. In the early days of the local labor movement, 1876–1886, trade union and revolutionary activity were virtually merged and only a few women became active. Their political development, however, and the practical experience they gained made their leadership crucial to the next stage, when it became possible to build more stable women's unions and coalitions.

Flattened by the Chicago fire in 1871, the city became an industrial boom town in the 1880s, rebuilt in high style. Its front office area, the Loop with its gorgeous lakefront views, gleamed with the new architecture of Louis Sullivan and his followers; the splendid Palmer House Hotel, built in 1875 with ninety thousand square feet of Italian marble tile, became the symbol of the new Chicago bourgeoisie. North and west of the Loop lay its economic foundations—the working-class slums made up of miles of wooden tenements and jerry-built flats housing wave upon wave of displaced farmers and immigrants: Irish, English, German, Polish, Russian, Jewish, Bohemian, and French Canadian. Each ethnic group had its own turf, and, as settlement worker Jane Addams described her own Halstead Street neighborhood, conditions were deplorable:

> The streets are inexpressibly dirty, the number of schools inadequate, sanitary legislation unenforced, the street lighting bad, the paving miserable and altogether lacking in the alleys and smaller streets, and the stables foul beyond description. Hundreds of houses are unconnected with the street sewer. . . . Rear tenements flourish; many houses have no water supply save the faucet in the back yards, there are no fire escapes, the garbage and ashes are placed in wooden boxes which are fastened to the street pavements.[2]

In such tenements lived the factory workers of Chicago, many of them American-born women from the countryside, with an increasing leavening of immigrants. Both groups were "just off the farm," bewildered by their new industrial condition and deprived of their traditional support systems, but the native-born women had one advantage most immigrants lacked—they spoke English. As one of them, Lizzie Swank, recalled:

> These women, most of them, were Americans who had been carefully looked after and protected in their own comfortable homes, and whose mothers and grandmothers before them had been similarly treated. Perhaps they had worked as hard in the home and as thoroughly earned their living as now, but it had been in a manner that the world knew nothing about.

> With these traditional ideas, they still considered that their affairs were their own, and if they worked hard and got little for it, it was nobody's business. They preferred to bear their privations alone, and allow others to think that they were comfortably situated, quite well off, and needed no one's sympathy.[3]

The new women workers were ashamed of their poverty; they took it personally, and such things were not to be discussed with strangers. They had not been workers long enough to have developed the consciousness of workers; for this they needed years of industrial experience as part of a group, with the consequent realization that it was not their fault as individuals if they were poor. Lizzie Swank had resolved to help them come to such an understanding.

An Ohio farm girl herself, Lizzie Swank began working when she was fifteen, teaching in a one-room schoolhouse like the one she had attended. In two years she was married, and when her husband died five years later, she supported herself and her two children by teaching music. She might have stayed in the Ohio countryside forever had it not been for the great railroad strike of 1877. It awakened something in her that made her long for change.

It was an epic battle, a nationwide strike of over one hundred thousand men, with active support from the labor movement, socialists, masses of working-class women, and farmers. The strike was particularly bitter in Chicago, where the police organized a special militia to subdue the workers; that being insufficient, federal troops were sent in fresh from the Indian wars. When the workers were attacked, they fought back, and bloody battles took place at the Halstead Street viaduct and at the German workers' Turner Hall. The role of women in these struggles was particularly remarked upon by the press: "Enraged female rioters . . . the unsexed mob of female incendiaries . . . the Amazonian army."[4] When the strike was broken, the bitterness of Chicago workers knew no bounds; they formed armed self-defense bands, *lehr und wehr verein,* which repeatedly marched down Ashland Avenue during the 1880s.[5]

Such activity was unheard of in the farmlands of Ohio, and in 1879, her children grown, Lizzie Swank came to Chicago with her sister to learn more about the labor movement:

"The working classes" was a term that was just beginning to be heard and I longed to know more of the people set off as belonging to a caste.... With my sister I went to work at a cloak factory and during the next two years passed through every phase of a struggling sewing woman's existence. I have worked in the largest factories of the city, during the busiest season, and earned $1.50 a day. I have sewed in sweat shops in dull seasons and earned $3 a week. I have made children's trimmed dresses at $1 per day, linen ulsters at $1.75 a dozen, worked button holes on shirts at 50 cents per dozen shirts and furnished my own thread. I know of all the struggles, the efforts of genteel poverty, the pitiful pride with which working girls hide their destitution and drudgery from the world.[6]

She looked around for a union to join. It took her a year to track down the Working Women's Union, the only woman's union in Chicago. It had been organized in 1878 by "a few energetic women who had become interested in economics"—in other words, by socialists, among whom were Alzina Stevens, Lucy Parsons, and Elizabeth Rodgers.[7] Most of its members were housewives, but the organization had about a thousand members, including women from a variety of trades. Lizzie Swank saw an advertisement for one of their meetings, and brought four of her fellow workers.

She organized with so much enthusiasm that within a year she was made secretary of the Working Women's Union, and she was soon writing stirring exposures of conditions in the garment industry. There were punitive fines for everything from tardiness to talking. Stacks of unfinished cloaks lay everywhere amid piles of lint and dust, posing a constant danger of fire and lung damage to workers. Cloaks that sold for $12.00 or $15.00 retail were made for only $.75 or $1.00; somebody was getting rich, but it certainly wasn't the women workers. While Lizzie Swank agitated about these things inside the shop, other members of the Working Women's Union visited workplaces to talk to the women and encourage them to organize. They handed out leaflets and spoke outside the factory gates. It was slow work: most of the women were either uninterested or shocked and "we could see but little accomplished in comparison with our ardent hopes."[8]

Chicago Will Be Ours

It took considerable dedication to go on organizing with so little success:

> Women looked askance at gatherings where "women spoke in meetin'," and "no nice girl would belong to one." The idea that working women had "a cause" was new and unconventional and scarcely to be entertained by these women so recently from the retirement of the fireside. They might be induced to attend a meeting or two, and even be delighted there, but joining a union— that was a different thing, and too bold and decided a step for women in those days.
>
> Besides, most of the young and good-looking girls looked upon their employment as only temporary; they would marry sooner or later, and thus escape from the shop. What became of sewing women as a class they did not care.[9]

The members of the Working Women's Union were distinguished from those they sought to organize mainly by their politics. Most were decidedly radical in their views; some—Elizabeth Rodgers and Lucy Parsons, for instance—had spent years in the socialist movement, others—Alzina Stevens and Lizzie Swank— became converts through their union work. Lizzie Swank was soon going to meetings of the Socialist Labor Party. At the first one, she reported, "it took but four hours of earnest discussion with an old-time Socialist to convert and make me a pledged worker for the great cause for life."[10] Their political radicalism is important, for only a larger and more consistent vision of social change than that of simple trade unionism could sustain them in such difficult work and explain the risks they took and the isolation from other women that was sometimes their lot.

In these early days of the labor movement, trade union activism was equated by the press, police, and much of the public with being a "Commune-ist"—advocating something like the Paris Commune. Anyone with such views left respectability far behind; if this was hard for men, it was much harder for women, who were under consistently greater social pressure to conform or be cast out into the terrors of life as fallen women, beyond the protecting arm of any father or husband. Any woman who was an active trade unionist in 1880 had to be willing to risk being jailed, being called an "unsexed female incendiary" or prostitute, and being an outcast in much of society. Women organizers in the 1880s thus tended to be very highly motivated and strong individuals who were often both social and sexual radicals as well.

Lucy Parsons is the best known of the Chicago group, because of her later career as an anarchist speaker and because she was the widow of the Haymarket martyr, Albert Parsons. The Parsons were Southerners who came north to escape the Ku Klux Klan backlash against blacks and Radical Republicans that followed Reconstruction. It was easier for them to live together in the North, since they were forbidden to do so under the South's miscegenation laws—Lucy Parsons was black. They moved into a German neighborhood on the near north side of Chicago, where they came in contact with socialist refugees and soon became Marxists. When Parsons, a printer by trade, was blacklisted because of their activism in the 1877 railroad strike, Lucy Parsons opened a dressmaking shop and her husband further supplemented their income with an unsteady salary as a socialist journalist. With other socialists he helped found the Chicago Trades and Labor Assembly in 1878 and was elected its president; Lucy Parsons was a frequent speaker at both the Working Women's Union and socialist meetings.[11]

Another leader in the Working Women's Union, Elizabeth Rodgers, was active as a socialist in the West before she and her husband moved to Chicago. According to an 1887 interview, "I also organized the Rocky Mountain social clubs, but our red badges are now folded and laid away. I also organized socialistic groups all through the western country."[12]

Unlike Lucy Parsons, Lizzie Swank, and Elizabeth Rodgers, Alzina Stevens, the founder and president of the Working Women's Union, came from a wealthy background; she was the declassed daughter of a once-proud New England family, the Parsons of Parsonsfield, Maine. Her father was a rich farmer and small manufacturer, but when he was killed in the Civil War, the family lost everything, and in 1862 Alzina Stevens went to work in the textile mills of Lowell, Massachusetts, a child laborer like any other.[13] On her thirteenth birthday her right index finger got caught in a machine. The company doctor cut the mangled digit off without bothering with anesthetic—nor did he trouble to inform her mother. Alzina Stevens later remarked: "If my interest in the cause of organized labor had ever flagged, if I had ever been in danger of growing discouraged, the sight of that poor finger and the memory of the horror of that day would have been spur enough."[14]

In the 1830s Lowell was known as a new kind of model factory town where the female work force was so cultured that they even put out literary magazines. But due to monopolization and speed-up, conditions in the famous "City of Spindles" began to decline soon afterward. The first union of female factory workers in the United States, the Lowell Female Labor Reform Association, was formed in the 1840s to fight declining conditions in the mills, and though it was long dead by the time Alzina Stevens arrived, she was bound to hear tales of its "turn-outs," or strikes, its petitions to the legislature, and its campaign for the ten-hour day. She was uniquely in touch with this first stirring of a women's labor movement and she took the example of Lowell westward to Chicago to the next generation of activists.

In 1866 she left the Lowell mills, no longer able to tolerate the wage reductions which were "so frequent and excessive that self-respecting American girls, who wished to live the rational life of human beings, were finally forced out of the mills entirely and compelled to seek new fields of industry."[15] At some point between then and 1872, when she appeared in Chicago, she married a man named Stevens. We know no more than that; the marriage ended in divorce and she never spoke about it to even her most intimate friends.[16] In Chicago, she determined to learn the printing trade, and got a job as a "copy-holder" with "the privilege of filling in odd times working at the case." After she had taught herself typesetting and the other "mysteries of the craft," she applied to Typographical Union No. 16 for membership— she thought it likely that she was the first woman ever admitted.[17] She then felt that she must spread the message of unionization to other women workers:

> I have always deplored the unorganized condition of women wage workers. To it may be principally attributed, I believe, the low wages which most of them receive and the numerous petty exactions and tyrannies of which they are made the victims. Therefore I have constantly maintained the necessity for their industrial or-

ganization on the same lines as men. I have been a firm believer
and a persistent advocate of thorough industrial organization for
both sexes and have never ceased to urge the paramount importance of independent political action on the part of wage workers,
realizing that it is the only complete and ultimate solution of the
labor problem.[18]

She did not at first consider herself a radical, however, and did
not announce her conversion to socialism until 1879, a year after
the Working Women's Union was founded.[19]

With women leaders like Alzina Stevens, Lizzie Swank, Elizabeth Rodgers, and Lucy Parsons, the Working Women's Union
naturally took a broad view of its tasks. It not only tried to
organize women into unions, but also played an active role in
larger labor struggles, particularly the long and militant campaign for the eight-hour day which was just beginning. In 1879
the Chicago Eight-Hour League held a three-day festival, culminating in a Fourth of July parade. The Working Women's
Union had a pink float, bearing banners with slogans that showed
both its labor and feminist aspects: "IN A UNION OF STRENGTH WE
SEEK THE STRENGTH OF UNION," and "WHEN WOMAN IS ADMITTED
INTO THE COUNCIL OF NATIONS, WAR WILL COME TO AN END, FOR
WOMAN MORE THAN MAN, KNOWS THE VALUE OF LIFE."[20]

The few members of the Working Women's Union who were
wage earners rather than housewives tried to do workplace organizing. Most women workers were not yet interested in joining
an organization, however, and it was all too easy for a militant
spirit like Lizzie Swank to go out on a limb and become isolated.
She was working at S—— & Co.'s cloak and suit factory when Mr.
S. cut prices during the busy season, at the same time making a
new rule that no worker could be paid for her share of work on a
cloak until work on the whole cloak had been finished. He made
no provision for paying interim wages during the changeover
from one system to another, and many women went without
income for several weeks and could not pay their boardinghouse
keepers. They complained, and Lizzie Swank suggested they
write up their grievances, sign them, and give them to the boss.
All but 4 out of 150 workers signed. They then stopped work and
the forelady could do nothing with them. Soon Mr. S. stormed in,

screaming, "What do you silly hussies mean by sending me such a paper as dis? Dis is not ladylike!" He advised them to stop listening to agitators and to talk to his wife if they had any problems. "I know who wrote dis paper," he continued. "Nobody here could or would do it but Mrs. Swank. She has been going to some of dem bad labor meetings and dere is where she got dis idea. She and her sister, Miss Hunt, may get deir books made out and go home. . . . De rest of you go back to work and see dat you behafes yourselfs."[21]

The other workers backed down and only Lizzie Swank and her sister were fired. She later heard that Mr. S. had changed the offending rules. "They reaped the benefit of the protest and we the disgrace." The strike—which she believed to have been the first women's strike in Chicago's history—had lasted all of three hours. "Ten years later," she said, "such a strike would have had a different ending."[22]

Lizzie Swank did factory work for two years, after which her health declined and she returned to teaching music. By then, however, the Working Women's Union had been transformed into a female local of a new national labor organization, the Noble Order of the Knights of Labor. This was a combination of union, reform organization, and fraternal society. Founded in secret in 1869, it became successful only after 1881, when it began to organize openly. It was at this point that it began to charter women's assemblies and admit women to its mixed assemblies.

The Knights of Labor was not a strictly working-class organization. Unlike later labor unions, it allowed middle-class people to be members; it admitted anyone, in fact, except lawyers, saloonkeepers, bankers, stockbrokers, and professional gamblers, all of whom the Order felt to be parasites. It stood for equal pay for equal work, an end to child labor, and no discrimination against women or blacks. It led massive boycotts and militant strikes, especially on the railroads. It identified with the eight-hour movement, and its principal motto was "An injury to one is the concern of all."

The Working Women's Union was given a charter as Knights of Labor Local Assembly No. 1789 in 1881. There were several other female assemblies in Chicago, each organized by trade, and 120 in the country as a whole. There were also many women in mixed assemblies. In such favorable conditions, strong women leaders quickly began to develop and achieve recognition within the Order, and in fact the development of such women was one of the chief contributions of the Knights to later stages of organization. Among them were Elizabeth Rodgers and Elizabeth Morgan, both active in Local Assembly No. 1789, as well as Alzina Stevens, who continued active in the labor movement after she moved to Ohio and became leader of the Joan of Arc Assembly in Toledo.

In 1886 Elizabeth Rodgers became the head of the Chicago district organization of the Knights of Labor, the first woman to achieve such high office. That year she brought her youngest child, a two-week-old infant, to the national convention in Richmond rather than stay home. Her husband George was a union man himself and at first supported her endeavors, as she explained to Emma Willard, a fellow member of the Knights of Labor and the leader of the Women's Christian Temperance Union:

> My husband always believed that women should do anything they liked that was good and which they could do well. . . . But for him I would never have got on so well as a Master Workman. I was the first woman in Chicago to join the Knights. They offered us the chance, and I said to myself, "There must be a first one, and so I'll go forward."[23]

But in 1886 George Rodgers changed his mind. She continued anyway: "My husband tried hard to persuade me to resign, on account of so much turmoil and trouble in labor circles at that time. Feeling the responsibility, but knowing my duty to my sex, I thought it was an opportunity to show our brothers how false the theory is that women are not good for anything."[24]

Like Elizabeth Rodgers, Elizabeth Morgan was married to an activist, Tommy Morgan. One of the founders of the Chicago Trades and Labor Assembly, he was known as "Resolution Morgan," because of the large numbers of progressive resolutions he introduced. Among them was one that led to the passage of the first compulsory education bill in Illinois in 1879, an unenforced city ordinance; he was also responsible for the AFL's passage of a resolution supporting woman suffrage in 1890.

Both Morgans were English immigrants who had grown up as

child laborers in Birmingham, and neither had much formal education. Tommy Morgan, a machinist and engraver, managed to educate himself thoroughly while working at his trade; his wife had less intellectual self-confidence, as she wrote Samuel Gompers: "My education is but poor but I will do the best I can as I, like many children, had to work when but eleven years old . . . and for that reason I am not very good to write."[25] Her strengths were strategic and organizational, and she showed them in both her political life and her private business.

Tommy Morgan came to Chicago in 1869 and sent for his wife a year later, saving the money for her passage by walking the eight miles back and forth to his job at the Illinois Central Railway. The family did well enough until the panic of 1873, when he was out of work for fifteen weeks. They had no credit. Elizabeth Morgan waited in the house without food, heat, or rent money, with two babies, while her husband tramped around looking for work. It was a time of great suffering and fear and one which changed the course of their lives. They realized that immigrating to the United States had not solved their economic problems; "in this land flowing with milk and honey thousands were starving."[26]

Both became socialists as a result of this experience. Elizabeth Morgan, busy with housekeeping and childcare, at first did not have as much time for the movement as her husband did, although she did become a charter member of the Sovereigns of Industry, a cooperative society, in 1874.[27] She kept a large garden from which she fed her family, selling the surplus, and was determined to accumulate enough real estate so they would never again have to worry about the rent. By 1894, despite the enormous amount of time she spent on political work, she had saved enough to buy three houses, one of which she ran as "Morgan's Hotel" for tourists to the 1893 World's Fair. "Yes," she told a reporter, "I am a practical woman. Idealists are all very well, but they would find it hard to get along without us, after all."[28]

Her practical sense and ability to get things done were to prove of enormous value to the working women and children of Chicago. A founding member of Local Assembly No. 1789, she was elected its delegate to the Chicago Trades and Labor Assembly. The experience she gained there in the intricacies of the labor movement was to make her a vital link in the chain of continuity between the early women's organizations and those that developed after the demise of the Knights of Labor.

Like her, Lizzie Swank and Lucy Parsons were active in Local Assembly No. 1789, but they became increasingly dissatisfied with its socialist vision of revolution through "independent political action" and, with Albert Parsons, moved rapidly toward anarchism as they became convinced that the powers-that-be would never let them win an election. They began to concentrate on labor organizing as an alternative to electoral work, initiating a campaign for the eight-hour day. Although they accompanied their organizing with considerable eloquence on the subjects of "FORCE!" (in Parsons' typography) and "DYNAMITE!" in their paper the *Alarm,* which Albert Parsons edited with Lizzie Swank, only their words were incendiary. In practice they were more interested in demonstrations than bombs. Their successes in mass organizing were unquestionably the reason that the Chicago bourgeoisie made them a target of a campaign of repression culminating in the Haymarket riot.

The story of the great eight-hour movement, its culmination in the police-staged riot at Haymarket Square, and its tragic denouement in the judicial murder of Parsons and four of his fellow anarchists has been too often told to need extensive repetition here.[29] What has not been sufficiently noted is the participation of Chicago working women in the movement that led up to Haymarket.

The eight-hour agitation climaxed with a march of eighty thousand workers down Chicago's Michigan Avenue on May Day, 1886. Most of those who marched were men, but the women who watched were inspired by their example. That night two new assemblies of the Knights of Labor, one of mixed trades and the other of tailors and seamstresses, were formed to build the general strike for the eight-hour day. A woman at one saloon meeting told the *Chicago Tribune:* "No, we'll never give in. . . . we want eight hours' work with ten hours' pay, which means a fair advance. Why, all the tailor girls on the North, West, and South sides are in this thing with us."[30] The sewing women whom Lizzie Swank had been powerless to organize six years before had begun to move at last.

The next morning Lizzie Swank led a delegation of hundreds of working women on their own eight-hour march. She began in the garment district, where a number of women formed a procession and visited all the shops, calling on the women to come out. As the parade moved along, it left "garrisons of women" on each corner to "buttonhole others and induce them to join the movement," according to the *Chicago Tribune*. The paper described the hated "shouting Amazons" with a touch of admiration:

> The ranks were composed of women whose exterior denoted incessant toil, their in many instances worn faces and threadbare clothing bearing evidence of a struggle for an uncomfortable existence. As the procession moved along the girls shouted and sang and laughed in a whirlwind of exuberance that did not lessen with the distance traveled.[31]

The next day, May 3, the police marched on a peaceful rally in Haymarket Square and ordered it to disperse. As if by signal, a bomb was thrown at them and they opened fire on the crowd, injuring over two hundred workers and killing an unknown number. The next morning a dragnet swept up most of the activists in the Chicago labor movement, eight of whom were eventually selected for prosecution on charges of murdering the policemen killed during the riot, although they probably died as a result of crossfire from their own forces. Only one of the men arrested was even present in Haymarket Square at the time and he was on the stage in full view. But alibis made no difference; the goal of the prosecution was clearly to kill off the most militant sector of the labor leadership in Chicago and thus destroy the movement. As one clothing manufacturer explained, "I'm not afraid of anarchy; oh no; it's the utopian scheme of a few, a *very* few, philosophizing cranks, who are amiable withal, but I do consider that the *labor movement should be crushed!* The Knights of Labor will never dare to create discontent again if these men are hanged!"[32]

Five of the eight were executed on November 11, 1887, despite an international protest of unprecedented size. One of them, August Spies, stated confidently in his final defense speech: "If you think that by hanging us you can stamp out the labor movement . . . the movement from which the downtrodden millions, the millions who toil in want and misery—expect salvation—if this is your opinion, then hang us! Here you will tread upon a spark, but there and there, behind you and in front of you, and everywhere, flames blaze up. It is a subterranean fire. You cannot put it out."[33]

But although Spies was right, and the Haymarket tragedy did not put an end to the labor movement, it did split it. The Master Workman of the Knights of Labor, Terence Powderly, and certain other of its leaders had been lukewarm in their support of the militant eight-hour movement to begin with. After Haymarket, Powderly grew extremely distrustful of any industrial action, favoring instead a strategy of building "a system of cooperatives, which will make every man his own master, and every man his own employer."[34] Powderly broke strikes called by his own members and encouraged them to scab on strikes called by craft unions outside the Order. Under such circumstances the organization began to decline, and by 1890 it was no more than a hollow shell.

Local Assembly No. 1789 had dissolved some time before. As Lizzie Swank noted, the "useful career" of the female assembly came to an end after Haymarket, when "a difference of opinion grew up among the members, some going on to extreme radical views, others turning back to absolute conservatism."[35]

Elizabeth Rodgers appears to have been one of the latter. She was accused in the labor press of saying, in reference to the Haymarket martyrs, "The bone and sinew of honest labor has no sympathy with the condemned men in the county jail. They are not of us. They are men whose capital was the credulity of misled workingmen. If the fate of the prisoners was submitted to a vote in my district they would be hung tomorrow." When her lack of solidarity was criticized, she responded only by saying, "I am not in favor of capital punishment, and think it barbarous and a relic of past ages. Not being in favor of the above, I never could have said to anyone that the condemned men should be hanged."[36] She dropped out of the labor movement entirely and in 1888 nearly sued the Chicago Trades and Labor Assembly, swearing out a writ for the return of her sewing machine.[37] She went into the insurance business, organizing a mutual fund under the auspices of the Women's Catholic Order of Foresters, whose members paid ten cents a week in return for being able to turn to the society when ill, thus avoiding an appeal to charity.[38]

Of the women who had been leaders in the women's labor organizing of the 1880s, only Lizzie Swank and Elizabeth Morgan remained involved. Lucy Parsons continued as a spokeswoman for a variety of anarchist causes, but did not concentrate on work with women. Lizzie Swank also confined much of her activity to the anarchist movement, marrying a fellow radical, William Holmes, changing her name to Lizzie Swank Holmes and continuing to work on the *Alarm*. She did, however, help Elizabeth Morgan spearhead the formation of the Ladies' Federal Labor Union and the Illinois Woman's Alliance, the organizations that were to lead the next wave of radical work with women.

Some years after the demise of Local Assembly No. 1789, Lizzie Swank Holmes summed up her early organizing efforts for the AFL magazine, the *American Federationist,* pointing to the enormous problems the organizers of her generation had faced:

> They had really done more than they knew. They had blazed the way for future organizations to follow. They had familiarized timid, ignorant women with the idea of organization for mutual benefit. They had taught these women that the conditions of labor were not the same as in the old days of home work, and that it was necessary to meet new conditions with new methods.
>
> The logic of events also helped, and when other organizers who were more clearly trade unionists and not amateur economists came on the scene, they found the field partly ripe for harvesting. . . .
>
> The work of the pioneers can not be defined, counted, and set down in statistical figures. At first glance, it may look as though there were little to show for their efforts. But it is true, nevertheless, that the latter workers could not have accomplished what they have had it not been for the devoted, earnest, often disheartening toil that the pioneers in trade unionism performed.[39]

In 1878 Lizzie Swank Holmes could find very few working women who would even dare come to a meeting. By 1886 she could lead a march of hundreds of working women for the eight-hour day. By 1903 thirty-five thousand were ready to march on Labor Day. This change is a measure of her achievement as well as of the maturation of the female part of the industrial working class. While her work and that of other early organizers like Lucy Parsons, Alzina Stevens, Elizabeth Rodgers, and Elizabeth Morgan resulted in no permanent organizational gains for women, these pioneers set an example of militance and involvement, making it possible for working women to imagine new ways of being, and changing the climate for organizing women in Chicago.

3
Mary Kenney and the Ladies' Federal Labor Union

No, I wouldn't like to die, sir, for I think the good Lord's hard
On us common working women, an' the likes of me's debarred
From his high, uncertain heaven, where fine ladies all go to,
So I try to keep on livin', though the Lord knows how I do.
I wonder, an' I wonder, as I sometimes sit and sew,
If lady callers take us for a sort o' wax-work show;
An' what they'd say about us if one half the truth they knew,
An' whether they would manage any better than we do.

Elizabeth Morgan
"I Am Only a Working Woman" (1897)[1]

Although Local Assembly No. 1789 disintegrated in the wake of the repression following the Haymarket Square riot, its members were far from abandoning their organizational goals. In 1888 Elizabeth Morgan succeeded in getting Samuel Gompers of the AFL to grant them a charter as a federal, or occupationally mixed, women's union: the Ladies' Federal Labor Union Local No. 2703. Its other founders included Lizzie Swank Holmes, Elizabeth Korth, and Corinne Brown. None were wage earners. Corinne Brown had been at one time a teacher and a principal in the Chicago public school system, but she stopped working when she married Frank Brown, a banker. Lizzie Swank Holmes was a radical journalist, and Elizabeth Morgan and Elizabeth Korth were both housewives. Nevertheless, the women had no difficulty in getting an AFL charter as a federal union, a catchall form designed for precisely such ambiguous situations.

The AFL used the form of the federal union not only when there were not enough men in any one trade to start regular craft unions, but also in order to organize women (or blacks) separately. Sex-segregated unions short-circuited local male opposition to organizing females since the women could organize a federal local and appeal directly to Gompers for a charter. By organizing on a gender rather than an occupational basis, they could thus escape the jurisdiction of the men who ran the craft locals in their city. There were other advantages to the form: it enabled working women to meet in a large group even though there might be only a few of them active from any single trade; it allowed them to work together with progressive housewives, who often had more time and energy than they did; and it made the union into a social center for women, who usually felt ill-at-ease in the saloons where the men's unions met. Of course, sex-segregated unionism also had disadvantages for women. Often male and female locals in the same shop would bargain separately, with the women getting the worst of it; or the men would bargain for the women, but would not fight for their raises as hard as they did for their own.[2]

Like most early women's labor organizations, the Ladies' Federal Labor Union combined organizing goals with intellectual ones, and stressed the need for reliable statistical information on the number and conditions of women workers, at a time when such information was hard to come by. The LFLU's announcements of its existence laid out these purposes:

> Without organization for self-protection, with the many disadvantages of sex, and the help[less]ness of childhood, the female and child workers are the victims of every avaricious, unscrupulous, and immoral employer. The Ladies' Federal Labor Union has been organized to prevent, to some extent, the moral, physical, and mental degradation of women and children employed as wage-workers in this city.
>
> First, by the organization of all women who realize the necessity for a protective society.
>
> Second, to receive reports from and inquire into the complaints of women and children, made against unjust and inhuman employers, and by every honorable means attempt to remove the wrongs complained of.
>
> Third, to secure the enforcement of such local and state laws as will tend to improve the conditions of employment of women and children, and to agitate for the enactment of such further legislation as may be required.
>
> Fourth, to secure the aid and cooperation of the great labor organizations of this city and country, and the active assistance of the many women's organizations.
>
> Fifth, the discussion of the labor question for intellectual improvement.
>
> Sixth, social enjoyment.[3]

Initially, the LFLU's members included typists, seamstresses, dressmakers, clerks, music teachers, candy makers, and gum makers, with only one or two of each. In the next four years, however, LFLU Local No. 2703 gave birth to women's locals in twenty-three trades, including bookbinding, shirtmaking, cloakmaking, watchmaking, and shoe making.[4]

Within a few months its founders realized that a union was not the most appropriate form of organization for achieving such diverse ends. They turned their attention to their fourth purpose, "to secure ... the active assistance of the many women's organizations," and formed the Illinois Woman's Alliance. From that point on, the LFLU and the Alliance worked hand in hand, one concentrating on labor organization, the other on those community issues (education, child labor, police brutality, public institutions) that most affected working-class women and children. Elizabeth Morgan, Elizabeth Korth, and Corinne Brown soon made the Alliance's work their major concern, since they were not themselves factory workers; and a new generation of wage-earning women began to organize a women's labor movement in Chicago through the LFLU.

Pre-eminent among these was Mary Kenney, a young bookbinder who grew up in the pioneer community of Hannibal, Missouri, Mark Twain's hometown. As a child she learned how to work: scrubbing, scouring, splitting wood, carrying water, making candles and soap, milking cows, and doing the other back-breaking household chores of rural life. When she was fourteen her father died and she went to work for wages, first as a dressmaker's apprentice, then at a printing press at $2 a week. She learned "every branch of the trade done by women"[5] and in four years worked her way up to forewoman. Every day after work she went home to nurse her invalid mother, do the washing and ironing, carry the wood and water, and prepare meals. Though she didn't get a lot of sleep, she later remembered this as the happiest period of her life because of the fellowship with the other girls from work. When the factory she worked in moved to Keokuk, Iowa, Mary Kenney followed, but after the business failed in 1886 she resolved to go to Chicago where she could make more money.

Her first Chicago job was at J. M. W. Jones, a large printing press that did work for the city. Mary Kenney was a good worker and she knew it, so even in these new surroundings she did not hesitate to push for her rights—in fact, the foreman soon nick-named her "Woman's Rights." When the man in charge of per-forating bank supplies went on sick leave, she was asked to fill in for him, and she kept the job after he came back. She said she would only do the job if she got the pay he had been getting, but the foreman replied that she was already getting more than workers who had been there ten years. "I refuse to do a man's job without a man's pay," she said.[6] She won. She even took work breaks, which were unheard of at the time, stopping work for fifteen minutes at ten and at three o'clock. She insisted that to do otherwise would impair her efficiency.[7] She also refused to have her pay docked or to be subjected to other of the routine harass-ments common in factories of the period:

> The bindery was on the top floor, the seventh. One morning the elevator was stopped for about ten minutes and, for the first time, I was late. When my week's pay came, they had deducted ten cents. I went to the foreman and asked him if he would go to the man who had my ten cents and say that if I was worth ten cents for ten minutes when I was not at work, I was worth at least ten cents for ten minutes when I was. He agreed and brought back the money.[8]

From her relatively privileged position, Mary Kenney could see and identify with the misery of less fortunate workers. She realized that most workers could not win fifteen-minute breaks for themselves as individuals, and that they would have to win them collectively.

> After my experience with J. M. W. Jones Co., I was convinced that the workers must organize. I felt I could depend on many of the employees in this shop. If I invited Mary Grace and Mary Costigan to attend a meeting, they would do their best to get others. Some-one must go from shop to shop and find out who the workers were that were willing to work for better working conditions. I must be that someone. So I decided to find another job. I searched through the advertisements and went out during the noon hour for in-terviews. In this way I didn't lose time. My recommendation as a general skilled worker and my connection with J. M. W. Jones Co. gave me good standing.[9]

Almost without thinking, Mary Kenney sacrificed the benefits of staying in one job and earning a steady wage so that she could organize other women workers. Her extreme independence and her willingness to take up such a task singlehanded were characteristic of women labor leaders of this period. To Mary Kenney such initiative was a principle of women's organization.

> There are several reasons which prevent women from wishing to organize. In the first place they are reared from childhood with one sole object in view—an object I do not wish to discourage but to elevate from present conditions—that is looking forward to marriage. If our mothers would teach us self-reliance and independence, that it is our duty to wholly depend upon ourselves, we would then feel the necessity of organization and especially of the new form of organization which is voluntary co-operation. . . . [But women workers feel] that an institution which has for its platform protection, is for men only and the only protection they expect is the protection given them by men, not realizing that it is their duty to protect themselves. So that the only hope in the organization of women is in getting them to feel that [they] are, or should learn to be, independent.[10]

As she went about her organizing, Mary Kenney became interested in the question of sanitation.

> I became a tramp bookbinder, going from shop to shop to organize the trade. I found the toilets in three out of four shops so unsanitary as to be dangerous. The Chicago Board of Health was the only organizer with the power to make employers keep the toilets clean, but they didn't have inspectors enough. Whenever I found unsanitary conditions, I would send a post card with the name and the number of the street, but with no signature.[11]

The Illinois Woman's Alliance was at this time conducting a ferocious campaign against bad working conditions for women, so the board of health was unusually sensitive to such charges. If she had known the right people, Mary Kenney's agitation for clean toilets could have gotten her a job with the Democratic machine that ran Chicago, which was under pressure from the Illinois Woman's Alliance to appoint women:

> A woman inspector came to a shop where I was working and said the Chairman of the Board of Health wanted to see me. "He's been

trying to find you for some time," she said. "He asked me if I knew a woman working in a bindery that went from one shop to another. I told him that I thought it was Miss Kenney. . . . I said you had asked me if there was a law to compel employers to keep toilets clean."

I asked what the Chairman of the Board of Health wanted and she said that she didn't know.

When I went to his office, he said, "Miss Kenney, you have sent in more complaints about unsanitary conditions than all the people in Chicago together. There's a vacancy here and I want you to apply for the position."

I said, "Fine. When do I get it?"

"Who do you know?"

"Nobody."[12]

She did not get the job. Instead she continued to go from shop to shop, getting to know the women in her industry, making propaganda about unions, trying never to stay more than two weeks in the same place. The eight-hour movement, strong even after Haymarket, gave her many examples of the benefits unionization could bring women workers. Construction workers building a factory across the street from one shop where she worked had a union and the eight-hour day, while the bookbinders began work an hour before them and stopped an hour later. Whenever the whistle blew across the street, Mary Kenney would ask her fellow workers if they were doing their "share in the fight for a shorter workday." In that shop, she noted, "not only the women, but the men were willing to organize."[13]

Once she had established herself in Chicago, Mary Kenney sent for her mother and installed them both in a "home for working girls," a new kind of institution being developed by philanthropists to allow single women to live on their meager salaries. While some protested that such homes made it even harder to get decent pay for women,[14] working girls who could get into them usually did, not only for economic reasons, but also for the social life, the collective living, they provided.

These homes were often linked to the Working Girls Clubs, which were first formed in 1884 by Grace Dodge, a New York society woman, in order to give young women factory workers an opportunity to hear "practical talks" on moral and religious questions. In 1885, these clubs were united in a national association with its own magazine, *Far and Near*. Soon the women at the residence where Mary Kenney lived formed a Working Girls Club and she was elected president.

It was not long before she became aware of the limitations of this form of organization, however: "I was much disgusted with the talk of the group. It was always about outings. I thought that helping to get better wages was much more important. If you had good wages you could have your own outings."[15] As soon as she heard about the Ladies' Federal Labor Union, which some club members belonged to, she hastened to join. Before long she was one of its delegates to the Chicago Trades and Labor Assembly.

Through the Ladies' Federal Labor Union and the Chicago Trades and Labor Assembly, Mary Kenney began to make the kind of union contacts that enabled her to organize her trade successfully. She also found allies and resources among middle-class feminists and reformers, particularly those at Hull House.

Jane Addams, the founder of modern American social settlement work, established herself at Hull House on the west side of Chicago in 1888. She heard about Mary Kenney and sent her an invitation to dinner. Since Mary Kenney had not found the "ladies" she met in the Working Girls Club particularly appealing, she decided not to go. As she noted, "Small wages and the meagre way Mother and I had been living had made me grow more and more class conscious."[16] Her mother, however, insisted that she give Jane Addams a hearing: "You can't judge without knowing her and she might be different from the other club women. It's condemning you are." So Mary Kenney went to the dinner. Her first thought upon seeing Hull House's large and beautiful rooms was: "If the Union could only meet here!"[17] When Jane Addams asked how she could help organize the bookbinders, Mary Kenney replied, "We haven't a good meeting place, we are meeting over a saloon on Clark Street and it is a dirty and noisy place, but we can't afford anything better." Jane Addams not only said the bookbinders could meet at Hull House, but she volunteered to go through the factory district and help leaflet for their meetings herself. Mary Kenney was won over: "When I saw there was someone who cared enough to help us and to help us in our way, it was like having a new world opened up."[18]

After organizing the bookbinders, Mary Kenney went on to other trades, continuing to use Hull House as a base. Jane Addams asked her if she wanted to live there, and soon she was attending classes to improve her reading and writing. In 1891, knowing of Mary Kenney's interest in communal living, Jane Addams told her that if she could find enough people to form a cooperative boardinghouse, Hull House would put up the first month's rent and supply the furniture. She suggested a vacant apartment building on nearby Ewing Street. By the end of the following week Mary Kenney had six members; within a year the "Jane Club" had taken over the entire apartment building. They had weekly meetings and each member paid $3 a week for food, service, and living expenses. Life at the Jane Club had a spirit as different from the ordinary boarding house as wine is from water.

> The social spirit was just as cooperative as the financial relationships. We enjoyed doing things together. While I was doing social and organization work, I had the opportunity of meeting a good many men, and if there was a dance or a ball we wanted to attend, I would tell an acquaintance that about twenty "Janes" would like to attend a certain ball and ask him to bring each an escort. Such fun in the introductions! And no choosing of a special girl, except for height. . . . Some of us were advocates of the union label and, as the young men entered and we took their hats, we looked to see if there was a union label inside. And we looked for the union label on their cigars.[19]

It was through Hull House that Mary Kenney met Samuel Gompers, who had come there collecting signatures for a petition for woman suffrage that the AFL was to present to Congress. Tommy Morgan had raised this issue in the AFL, and by 1891 Gompers was able to give Congress 229,000 signatures in support of the Susan B. Anthony amendment.[20] Gompers was struck by Mary Kenney's organizing ability and remembered her at the AFL convention in that same year. The only two women delegates to the convention—Ida Van Etten of the Working Women's Society of New York and Eva McDonald Valesh, a journalist from Minnesota—recommended that the AFL create the post of national organizer for women at a salary of $1,200 a year plus expenses; that it appoint a woman to fill this post; and that it make her a member of the executive council. They argued that unless women workers were organized, they would undercut wages and the whole working class would suffer. Gompers agreed to the first two proposals and in 1892 appointed Mary Kenney general organizer for women, though he did not give her executive board status. She was twenty-eight years old at the time.

Mary Kenney served in this post for six months, during which she accomplished a great deal: she organized unions of boot and shoe workers, shirt workers, male bookbinders, garment workers, hackmen, and retail clerks in Chicago; she went to New York and organized locals of bookbinders and shirtmakers; and then she helped with the Homestead strike in Pennsylvania.[21] When the garment workers struck in Chicago in 1893, she creatively combined labor union activity with support work by the women's movement—a pattern that was to become the rule in garment strikes led by the Women's Trade Union League which she later founded: "At Hull House we formed committees of well-known women to visit the [strikers'] homes. They carried relief, food, clothing, and money. Newspaper reporters came daily to Hull House to hear the reports of these committees. Day after day their reports went before the public. . . . With three thousand people out of work and the days passing, our responsibilities were great."[22]

At the same time, Mary Kenney learned what she and other working-class women were to find again and again through the years: they had to keep an eye on their middle-class allies. One of the newspapers ran a feature on the garment employer who paid the lowest wages and who had refused to arbitrate; he then came to Hull House, said he was sorry for the hungry children, and offered Mary Kenney a check for $200.

> When I realized whose name was on the check, I said, "But you have had two opportunities to settle this strike."
> He said, "I won't give into those agitators."
> I said, "We are out for justice, not charity. Here is your check."
> Miss Gertrude Barnum, who at that time belonged to the "Perfect Lady" class, and who was assisting us for the first time, was indignant. She said to me, "How dare you refuse that check and insult a gentleman?"

"Pardon me, Miss Barnum, you are mistaken; I have never insulted a Gentleman."[23]

Despite all Mary Kenney's organizational successes, her job lasted only six months before members of the AFL executive board charged that her work had been futile, and that the AFL "is not in a condition financially to keep a woman organizer in the field without better hope of success than at present indicated."[24] Mary Kenney returned to Chicago, taking the job of factory inspector that she had been denied a few years before. The tireless agitation of the LFLU and the Illinois Woman's Alliance and the recent election of the reform Governor John Altgeld, had resulted in the appointment of Florence Kelley of Hull House as chief factory inspector. She appointed all labor people to her staff, including not only Mary Kenney but also Alzina Stevens and Abraham Bisno.

Mary Kenney did not stay long in this job, however. While organizing in Boston she had met Jack O'Sullivan, an active trade unionist and the labor editor of the *Boston Globe*. In 1894 they were married and she moved to Boston, where she continued her union organizing despite four pregnancies, and also did further settlement work. Her enduring concern about the conditions of working women led her to become one of the founders in 1903 of the National Women's Trade Union League.

Meanwhile in Chicago the trend towards separate women's unions which she exemplified became increasingly strong, and the AFL executive board's gloomy predictions of the impossibility of organizing women were belied by the successes of the women's labor movement. In 1903, ten years after Mary Kenney O'Sullivan was fired by the AFL, a reporter for *Leslie's Monthly Magazine* was sent to Chicago to investigate the remarkable record of working women there. She found that, building on the early work of such organizers as Lizzie Swank Holmes and Mary Kenney O'Sullivan, "the Woman's Labor Movement developed in Chicago as nowhere else in the country,—developed into a complete and powerful system, comprising an overwhelming majority of the workers in twenty-six different trades, and embracing an aggregate membership of thirty-five thousand women." There were unions in almost every trade in which women worked. Further, the gains made by these locals were enormous; women's wages in Chicago had gone up between 10 and 40 percent with unionization, while their work week had dropped from sixty to fifty-three hours with extra pay for overtime. Child labor had been nearly eradicated. Each union had its shop stewards—"walking delegates"—who helped union members struggle with their foremen over arbitrary dismissals and unjust fines. In short, "the working women of Chicago . . . [had] evolved step by step, to the cool sanity of a complex, splendidly organized system of individual trade-unions, recruited exclusively by feminine wage-earners, and controlled by 'lady' bosses and 'lady' walking delegates."[25]

No longer were women organizers isolated mavericks, so highly motivated they seemed superhuman. Their example had taken root and a high degree of organization had produced large numbers of women who were willing to become leaders in their local unions. The female part of the labor movement was beginning to mature.

4
The Illinois Woman's Alliance

Who bids for the little children—
    Body and soul and brain?
Who bids for the little children—
    Young and without a stain?
"Will no one bid," said England,
    "For their souls so pure and white,
And fit for all good or evil
    The world on their page may write?"

"We bid," said Pest and Famine;
    "We bid for life and limb;
Fever and pain and squalor,
    Their bright young eyes shall dim.
When the children grow too many,
    We'll nurse them as our own,
And hide them in secret places,
    Where none may hear their moan."

"I bid," said Beggary, howling;
    "I bid for them one and all!
I'll teach them a thousand lessons—
    To lie, to skulk, to crawl!
They shall sleep in my lair like maggots,
    They shall rot in the fair sunshine:
And if they serve my purpose
    I hope they'll answer thine."

"I'll bid you higher and higher,"
    Said Crime with a wolfish grin;
"For I love to lead the children
    Through the pleasant paths of sin.
They shall swarm the streets to pilfer,
    They shall plague the broad highway,
They shall grow too old for pity
    But ripe for the law to slay.

"Give me the little children,
    Ye good, ye rich, ye wise,
And let the busy world spin round
    While ye shut your idle eyes;
And your judges shall have work,
    And your lawyers wag the tongue,
And the jailers and policemen
    Shall be fathers to the young!"

Charles MacKay
"The Children's Auction"[1]

During the six years of its existence, the Illinois Woman's Alliance accomplished more in the way of practical reform and political education than many organizations that have lasted five times as long. Although it was founded and led by trade unionists and avowed socialists like Elizabeth Morgan and Corinne Brown, the Alliance drew in virtually every woman's organization in Chicago. Each of the thirty organizations that belonged sent three delegates to Alliance meetings, but press reports—the only record we have of the organization's work—make it clear that the left and labor delegates led the coalition: they headed the most active committees, were among the hardest workers, and were the source of most of the Alliance's programs. For this reason, the Alliance is a key example of the merging of the labor movement and the broad women's movement under socialist leadership. Perhaps because of its close connection with the labor and socialist movements, its work is seldom mentioned in history books.[2] It deserves to be remembered because it shows what a united front can achieve, even in such a nonrevolutionary situation as prevailed in Chicago's Gilded Age, where public policy was openly made by the corporations and implemented by one of the earliest and most highly developed big-city political machines. The Alliance bucked both in its campaigns for factory inspection, new schools, compulsory education, sweatshop regulation, public baths, an end to child labor, and no more police victimization of prostitutes.

The stimulus for the formation of the Alliance was a series of investigative reports entitled "City Slave Girls," published in the *Chicago Times* in the summer of 1888. At the August 18 meeting of the Ladies' Federal Labor Union, the members discussed little else. Lizzie Swank Holmes recalled her difficulties in organizing garment workers: "It is a hard point to get the girls to admit the exact conditions they are in, as they are proud and sensitive about letting anyone know how little they really earn and how wretched their lives are. They struggle on to the fainting point to keep up appearances." Elizabeth Morgan told how her sister had tried to live on the $2 a week she got making men's ties in a sweatshop; she had then worked around the clock in a succession of small tailor shops, only to find herself cheated out of her wage packet in five different places. "Until the *Times* took up the cause of working girls," she said, "not a hand was raised in their defense." Corinne Brown agreed: "We are in a position to know and the exposure of these truths touches us, members of women's organizations as we are, much closer than any others."[3]

They drew up a plan of action to take to various organizations and agencies, beginning with the Chicago Trades and Labor Assembly. The plan focused on three demands:

1. The enforcement of existing factory and inspection ordinances. Tommy Morgan had introduced such legislation ten years previously, but the labor men appointed to the inspectors' posts were paid $1,000 a year. Consequently, as the press pointed out, they never inspected anything except the salary attached to their office and their chances of holding onto it as long as possible; they spent their time doing electoral canvasing instead.[4]
2. The enforcement of compulsory education laws.
3. The appointment of women factory inspectors, "responsible to women's organizations."[5]

The CT&LA was enthusiastic and accepted a resolution that called for the formation of a united front against sweated labor, saying, that "inasmuch as the working classes are as yet too ignorant to use their numerical and political power for their own protection, therefore we respectfully request the humane element of the great middle class to lend their social and political influence to the agitation commenced by the *Times* for the protection of these poor, blind slaves of the industrial system."[6]

By October 6 the women had managed to convene a meeting at the Palmer House which was attended by delegates of twenty-five women's organizations. At this meeting was born the Illinois Woman's Alliance, a broad coalition united front of forces, including church groups, professional women's organizations, the labor movement, and the suffragists.[7] Its first coordinating committee consisted of Corinne Brown as chairman, representing the Ladies' Federal Labor Union; Caroline Hurling of the Cook County Suffrage Association; Annie H. White of the Woodlawn Reading Club; Elizabeth Morgan, representing the CT&LA; Jennie Howison of the Miriam Chapter of the Order of the Eastern Star, a Masonic organization; Dr. Harriet Fox of the Women's Physiological Society; Frances N. Owen of the Woodlawn Presbyterian Ladies' Aid; and Alva Perry of the South End Flower Mission.

The Alliance's manifesto, which it mailed out to 150 organizations with requests for help and endorsements, reflected the diversity of its members, combining an emphasis on social purity with a concern for sweated labor. "The sanitary conditions surrounding our working girls," the manifesto read, "are a blot upon the nineteenth-century civilization, are destructive to womanly purity, are dwarfing the physique, starving the intellect, and weakening the morality of our children, thus sapping the very life-blood of our nation by destroying the manly and womanly virtues on which our country was founded."[8]

Although Lizzie Swank Holmes was at early meetings of the Alliance, she soon dropped out. Her paper the *Alarm* was scornful of this motley united front: "The Alliance is composed of women delegates from twenty-six societies, Christians of all shades of orthodoxy, dress-reformers, women suffrage agitators, spiritualists, radicals and societies for almost every conceivable purpose." Equally ridiculous to the anarchists was the idea that any significant reforms were possible under capitalism: "I supose they imagine they can regulate the laws of supply and demand, nullify the baleful result of 'protected' competition and the iron law, and compel capitalists to pay living wages by this sort of agitation."[9]

Undeterred by such criticisms from the left, Alliance members developed innovative and sophisticated tactics for making their points. They picked up muckraking techniques developed by the progressives and successfully used both the labor and "capitalist" press. They sat in on meetings of the city council and the board of education, and haunted the police courts, issuing forth to deliver stinging denunciations. They took a leaf out of the ward bosses' book and, led by Dr. Fanny Dickinson, established their own precinct committees. They refused to disclose these committees' purposes but hinted darkly that they would spy upon the city's sanitary machinery, reporting gross misconduct to the Alliance.

The work of the Alliance fell into four main areas: its campaign against sweatshops; its efforts to protect children, including legislation against child labor and for a compulsory education bill; its inspection tours of state institutions ranging from asylums to police courts, in order to expose their abuses; and its drive to get public baths in the working-class districts of Chicago.

While the Alliance's inspection tours of public institutions carried on the charitable tradition of ladies visiting the poor, its campaign exposing abuses in the police courts had a different and more modern muckraking character. By focusing on police treatment of prostitutes, the Alliance could make both feminist and socialist points about the treatment of women, using every occasion to point out the discrimination against women inherent in the law. One member, for instance, told the press after visiting the Erring Woman's Refuge:

> The public, it appears, has not deemed it necessary to build a refuge to reform men who have betrayed these girls. . . . As the most of them are married men, it is presumed, I suppose, that within the sacredness of their homes the reform is to be accomplished by the pure and refining influence of their wives, whom they honor and cherish, and their little ones, whom they would shield from harm.[10]

The Alliance demanded that women no longer be convicted of prostitution unless the men involved were willing to come forward and bear witness against them, and that men as well as women be arrested for soliciting on the streets regardless "of the reputation of the woman solicited."[11]

Police abuses were flagrant in Gilded Age Chicago. The prime mover of the Alliance's police committee, Fanny Kavanaugh, decided to observe the police courts personally and what she witnessed made her blood run cold. Women of the working-class districts were randomly rounded up and arrested as prostitutes on no evidence. These women were then fined or charged bail by the court bail bondsmen and released, only to be rounded up again within a few days or weeks. The bail bondsmen would persecute those released—or blackmail them—until they got their money back. These bail bondsmen were often saloonkeepers from the area around the precinct station, appointed on the basis of their political ties; Judge Tuley, a reformer, called them "vampires." In one year, 1889, the police arrested and held over fifty thousand people, one-third of whom were "bailed out" the next morning and sent home without being charged. As Fanny Kavanaugh noted: "[The women] are arrested in droves and fined only according to their ability to earn, so that the bailer is sure of his fees, the shyster of his, and even the judge receives a small fee for signing the bond. After all the trouble of arrest and fleecing, the city usually gets about $1."[12]

She observed other abuses as well. One woman was jailed overnight when she went to buy medicine for her sick child—apparently any woman out alone was fair game for the police. Eight children were arrested for sleeping under the sidewalk, even though they had nowhere else to go. A woman came to the precinct to find her husband, who had been held all night; when she asked why he had not been booked, she was arrested and fined $1 for impertinence.[13]

The Alliance's revelations got sensational publicity and Fanny Kavanaugh was barred from the Harrison Street police station. With help from reformers like Judge Tuley and Judge John Altgeld (soon to be governor), she directed the press toward the fact that the constitutional rights of Americans—particularly that of *habeus corpus,* or the right to a trial—were being denied to those who were poor and female. A worker herself, a member of the LFLU Local No. 2703 and the first woman to be appointed to the executive board of the Chicago Trades and Labor Assembly, Fanny Kavanaugh was "very emphatic" in her belief that such matters as prostitution were the proper province of the labor movement. As she told a reporter:

First, as far as the women themselves are concerned, the public should remember that our terrible economic conditions, tending ever to lower women's wages, even to the starvation point, drive women and young girls rendered desperate by destitution annually by countless thousands into a life of shame. It is therefore the imperative duty of organized labor, until such time as our industrial conditions shall be readjusted upon a more equitable basis, to extend to these unfortunates the protection and assistance denied them elsewhere, and to see that in the police courts, to which for the purposes of plunder they are periodically and systematically dragged, they obtain at least the modicum of justice to which they are entitled.[14]

She was opposed to the Samuel Gompers type of pure-and-simple trade unionism, believing that unions should be the organized arm of the working class as a whole, responsible for guarding its economic, social, and political interests. This broad approach to class interests, combined with feelings of feminist solidarity and a concern for children, led the Alliance in 1891 to formulate its fundamental principles as follows:

1. The actual status of the poorest and most unfortunate woman in society determines the possible status of every woman.
2. The civilization of the future depends upon the present condition of the children.
3. Public money and public officials must serve public ends.[15]

One of the Alliance's most successful campaigns, begun in 1889, was for an improved compulsory education system, which it saw as the best way of dealing with the evils of child labor. The Alliance estimated that there were at least fifty thousand children between the ages of seven and fourteen in Chicago "who were unaccounted for, who did not go to school or work."[16] That meant that they were working in sweatshops or wandering about the streets. Upon investigation the Alliance found further horrors: at least ten thousand children were sleeping in the streets because they had no other home.[17] Furthermore, although the school board had $2 million in unspent money, it had built no new school buildings, while the existing schools were so dilapidated and the number of places in them so inadequate that thousands of children were on half-days.[18] To the women of the Alliance the need for both stricter enforcement and stronger laws was undeniable; public education was in a state of emergency.

But the issue was complex in ways the women of the Alliance did not fully take into account. To them the choices were clear: child labor or education, ignorance or literacy, the streets or the schools. Opposition to public education, however, came not only from those who employed children, but also from the parents of working children, who feared that the loss of their wages would mean starvation for the entire family. Concerned about the short-run effects of reform, some parents did not realize that child labor depressed adult wages: in the long run the standard of living of families with working children would be improved if they stopped. Other parents feared the "Americanization" programs in the schools: Why should their children learn to speak English instead of their parents' language? Why should they be taught different customs and beliefs than those of the old country? Why should they learn all kinds of highfalutin, impractical things rather than a trade? Still other parents preferred parochial schools for religious and cultural reasons, and although the campaign for public education was not aimed at children who were already in parochial schools, the Catholic and Missouri Synod Lutheran hierarchies opposed public education laws, fearing the imposition of secular standards—such as an English language requirement—on their own institutions.

Despite this disquiet among some working-class parents, public education was supported by most organized workers. They detested child labor. They wanted their children to be able to read, to do sums, to speak the language of the country they lived in, and to make a better future for themselves than their parents had. Public education was a thing to fight for.

The fight focused on two issues: the hiring of female school inspectors and graft at the board of education. Corinne Brown, head of the Alliance's education committee, led the campaign. A single-taxer turned socialist and a veteran of the city's school system, she had been a teacher for thirteen years and a principal for six, after which she married a broad-minded banker and retired to Woodlawn, spending her time in the feminist and socialist movements. She had been radicalized by the Haymarket affair, and was one of the founders of the Ladies' Federal Labor Union. Fellow socialist Gertrude Breslau-Hunt, a longtime friend, described her in a memorial tribute:

> Mrs. Brown was intellectually adventurous, afraid of nothing, "trying all things," discarding superstitions, speculations and conventional lies for science and practical sociology. She was keen and logical, warm-hearted and sympathetic, which fact was often hidden from the unobserving by her quick, sometimes abrupt manner and merciless stripping off of merely conventional husks of sentiment not backed up by serious effort to remove causes of suffering.[19]

Her vitriolic style was one of the things that endeared her to the press and gave the campaign for pubic education such panache.

The demand for inspectors who would represent the movement and not owe their jobs to the Democratic patronage system was part of the Alliance's strategy for uncovering abuses. They wanted female inspectors in both sweatshops and schools, and school inspectors with police powers in each ward. In response, two women, one a member of the Alliance and the other a member of the Chicago Women's Club, were actually appointed school inspectors, but the fact that they were given salaries raised a problem in the relations between the Alliance and the CT&LA.

Many of the middle-class women in the Alliance saw factory and school inspector jobs as ideal, since they combined financial independence with social service, and felt they had a right to them once they had called them into existence. The CT&LA, on the other hand, had had ten years of experience with paid inspectors chosen from their own ranks and was convinced that such workers inevitably became part of the political machine that ran the city. As the CT&LA secretary noted: "Union after union was brought under [the machine's] control. . . . All the important offices in the labor organizations were filled by office holders or their friends. . . . The factory, workshop and tenement house ordinance was dead, and every pretense of inspection made in its name was farce. . . ."[20] The CT&LA had passed a rule excluding any paid officeholders from membership; it urged the Alliance to do the same and also to forbid anyone running for office to use the name of the Alliance or its officers in any electoral petition.

The Alliance gave in, passing an amendment to its constitution that said no one could retain her membership while holding a public office, though she could regain it afterward. Reporting back to the CT&LA, Elizabeth Morgan noted with some annoyance that the Alliance also gave a vote of thanks to all those who had signed the electoral petition asking that two of its members be made school inspectors:

> This illogical action was due to the fact that, though the women insist upon political and social equality, they refuse to patiently listen to criticism or receive advice, claiming exemption because they are women and have a right to do as they please anyhow.[21]

The two new female school inspectors set to work energetically to uncover abuses. They did such a good job, in fact, that the board of education soon fired them. The *Chicago News* reported:

> Truant officers, under orders from the Board of Education, have stopped work. They were forbidden to pick up any more children from the street, to make house-to-house visits, or to threaten any with the reform school. Their efforts were to be confined to looking after truant children reported by principals of schools. Strange to say, these lists soon became so scant that truant officers found their work almost gone—a condition of affairs but one step removed from the present, when they are finally laid off duty altogether.[22]

The Alliance concluded that the inspectors were fired for doing their jobs, and when one was reappointed a few months later, Elizabeth Morgan noted, "We fear that the reappointed inspector will (after this course of discipline) have a clearer official comprehension of the value of official inactivity."[23]

As a result of the firings, the Alliance decided that one of its priorities would be to get more than one woman on the board of education so that they could at least know what was going on. They laid out their arguments in a letter to the mayor:

> The greatest responsibility of the domestic life is the training of children, for upon that depends the full development of that individual character which is the bulwark of the nation. When it was brought to our notice. . . . that there were many children of tender age being deprived of an education and forced to work in shops and stores, we became convinced that woman's whole duty could not be performed when confined within home walls.

For thirty-three years men alone have served on the Board of Education, appointed especially for their financial ability, and it may be well to look at the condition of the schools at the end of that time. To begin with, the whole school property was valued at $12,000,000 and there was to the credit of the board nearly two millions in available cash, and despite this there were 60,000 children on the streets, in shops and stores, who, according to law, should have been in school. Notwithstanding the ample funds, children were crowded into damp and dark basement rooms, as in the Franklin school, many even waiting their turn to claim a seat in the lower division. . . . There were more than two hundred half-day divisions. . . .

We do not want to be understood as censuring the men who have managed the schools. They have done the best they could. But as we cannot expect to find the best example of domestic discipline in a home solely under a father's care, neither do we expect to find it in schools managed by men alone.[24]

This argument represents a combination of feminism and social uplift that became standard among that part of the feminist movement most influenced by the settlement houses. It is an interesting contrast to the kind of argument that was used by Elizabeth Morgan and Fanny Kavanaugh in the sweatshop and police court campaigns where feminist thinking was combined with a much stronger class orientation.

The mayor disregarded the Alliance's petition and the women decided to appoint their own watchdog committee to report on board of education meetings. To the press, at any rate, the reason for the mayor's recalcitrance was clear: protection of graft. "Certain male members of the Board of Education of Chicago and Cook County claim that the reason they are opposed to having women on the Board is because they cannot understand the intricacies and mysteries of the morals involved in the financial matters that the Board has to deal with, and their presence makes them very uneasy when financial affairs are under consideration."[25]

The Alliance did, in fact, continually uncover graft. On one occasion the women petitioned the city council to ask the board to answer the following questions:

1. Why does the board during each of six months of the school year defer for one week payment of the teachers' salaries?

2. Where is the money deposited?
3. Why does the board during the months of January, February, and March withhold until the last of April 25 percent of the teachers' salaries?
4. Does the money thus kept back from the teachers' salaries draw interest and for whose benefit?
5. Why is no mention made of this practice in the annual report?[26]

The board declared itself extremely insulted that it had not been addressed directly, but did not deign to answer the questions, its main line of defense being, "Who are these people who are asking these questions? . . . Never heard of them before!" One reporter declared that from the look on the women's faces board members would be lucky if they didn't hear of them again.[27]

The women continued to press their demands for more school buildings, the enforcement of the truancy law, equal pay for women teachers and inspectors, and the appointment of three women to the board. The board reacted to this pressure with temper tantrums and by breaking all the appointments it made with Alliance members. It told the press that "the Alliance is possessed of a curious idea that it can fully grasp the subject [of schools] by an attendance of its agents for two hours every two weeks at the formal meetings of the board."[28] Corinne Brown responded in her most acid tone:

> No, gentlemen; inexperienced and credulous we may be, but we have never been so void of ordinary intelligence as to expect to learn from the board anything of the public schools. We have attended your meetings to become acquainted with you and to find out how you succeed in doing so little. Our interest is centered upon the children, the moral protection and the methods of teaching afforded them, subjects which you severely let alone.[29]

One of the women's most substantial victories in the campaign for public education came early, when a bill they sponsored in the state legislature passed with surprisingly little opposition and was signed into law in May 1889. It provided for a twelve- to twenty-four-week school year for children between seven and fourteen (the variation being due to the different conditions on farms and in the city), though it had many loopholes for child labor with parental consent. In March of the following year the Alliance noted with satisfaction that at least sixteen hundred more children were in Chicago schools than had been there the year before. And by February 1891, when Elizabeth Morgan summed up the work of the Alliance, the record was undeniably impressive:

> In regard to education and child labor the Woman's Alliance has proved itself far more active and effective than the trade and labor unions. Through the efforts of the Alliance the educational laws of the state have been improved and the laws more strictly enforced. Truant officers have taken thousands of children from the streets and placed them in the schools.
>
> Female factory inspectors have been appointed at the request of the Alliance, and their work promises to bring about valuable and permanent improvements in the environment of the wage-workers of Chicago, and tends to render the employment of children under 14 years of age unprofitable, if not wholly impossible. Moreover, through the organization and activity of the Alliance, a more intimate knowledge of the conditions under which females and children are forced to work in the industrial and commercial hives of the city has not only been obtained by its members, but through them the organizations they represent and the general public have derived a clearer comprehension of that greatest of all questions: the labor question.
>
> The investigations of the Alliance have also added further proof that low wages and the general unfavorable conditions of employment are the primal cause of prostitution and crime.[30]

When Corinne Brown, Elizabeth Morgan, and others had organized the LFLU Local No. 2703 in 1888, they had immediately come up against the increasing problem of sweatshops; this was the impetus for the formation of the Illinois Woman's Alliance. How could women workers so concentrated in the "sweated industries" be unionized, while whole families were forced to labor twelve and fourteen hours a day for less than a living wage in tenement house workshops, spread out in a vast number of scattered buildings? Not only were the workers difficult to find, they lived so near the margin of starvation and were so dependent on each small fluctuation in the industry that it was nearly impossible for them to maintain an organization.

The conclusion was inescapable: before women could be organized into stable trade unions, child labor and sweatshops had to be eliminated. The sweatshops must be brought under one roof; employment must become yearlong, not seasonal; and the children must go to school, not work.

The Alliance's first approach to both child labor and sweatshops was their campaign for factory inspectors. In May 1889 the Alliance committee, with support from the CT&LA, asked the city council for five inspection badges; it further requested that an equal number of men and women be appointed as volunteer inspectors. The mayor did not respond. After a month, a committee of thirteen women from the Alliance invaded a city council health committee meeting. The health committee passed the issue to the legal committee, which brought it up at the next city council meeting, where a spirited debate broke out on the issue of inspectors serving without pay. Some aldermen were for this, on the ground that the need for reform was great and there was no money for salaries. Alderman Cullerton, noted for his opposition to the eight-hour legislation that had just been extended to public works programs, tried to get the matter sent back into committee; when this failed, he successfully proposed that the inspectors should be paid $50 a month out of health committee money.[31] Many Alliance members were pleased; they were glad to get badges for women and hopeful that the mayor would choose from their list of nominations, thus making clear his support for their work. The CT&LA held to its antisalary position and noted that the object of getting volunteer inspectors was to pressure those who were already paid to do their duty; the new measure would only create more professional officeholders.

In fact, the mayor was in no hurry to appoint either paid or volunteer women. By the following October he had chosen only one inspector. He then asked the Alliance to provide him with new names, preferably those of widows, so that the city could help them support their children. The Alliance indignantly responded that they would stick by the names they had already submitted, and that while they regretted that any woman should be bereaved, they did "not think it right to use a public office as a means of relief."[32] One newspaper accused the Alliance of "extraordinary heartlessness" and "inexcusable snobbery," sarcastically remarking that "only ladies needing no salary may make application. Ladies with carriages and footmen are preferred."[33] Alliance members replied that their object was to clean up the sweatshops, and women with no patronage ties would do that most relentlessly.

It was for one of these jobs that Mary Kenney O'Sullivan, busy writing letters to the board of health about dirty restrooms, was only briefly considered because she had no friends with influence. Of course, she was not a widow either. Only one of the Alliance's nominees, Dr. Rachel Hickey, was ever appointed; though it was an achievement to have won women the right to be factory inspectors at all. But it soon became clear that two or three factory inspectors could do little, particularly when they were chosen by the Democratic machine. In the end, the exposures of sweatshop conditions that led to change did not come from city inspectors, but from the labor movement itself, at first alone and then with the added help of the social workers and progressives around Hull House.

In August 1891, in response to a request from Abraham Bisno's striking cloakmakers, the CT&LA decided to make its own investigation of sweated labor in the garment industry. A committee composed of labor racketeer Skinny Madden, CT&LA secretary Mark Mitchell, and Elizabeth Morgan set out, followed by a crowd of newspapermen and journalistic artists with sketchbooks. Although some of the "sweaters" had been warned of the invasion and had closed up shop, others were taken by surprise. In one shop, a journalist interviewed the child workers:

> "How old are you, Ida?"
> "Eleven years."
> "How many hours do you work?"
> "From 7 until 9."
> "How much do they give you?"
> "One dollar a week. I only work half a day on Saturday, though. Yes, of course I work on Sunday. Fourteen hours is a day's work in this shop. No, I don't get any board. I live with mother. I have a brother who earns a little money. They put me to work when I was 9 years old. I am three years in this country and have been working ever since. I get 10 cents a dozen for making knee pants."[34]

Other children were afraid to speak up—one girl of thirteen

trembled uncontrollably and said, "For God's sake don't put my name in the paper. They will kill me. It is worse than slavery."

The worst shops were those subcontracted by philanthropist J. V. Farwell, known as a pillar of the church. One was a tiny 10-foot-square basement room where ten men and thirteen young girls worked. Some of the girls earned only $3 for a sixty- to seventy-hour week making velvet cloaks for the luxury trade. It was at this shop that Mark Mitchell of the CT&LA burst out: "They are Jews. The thing that cuts me is that they are all my people, and I love my people. They talk of bringing millions of Jews here from Russia to avoid the persecution of the Czar. Is this what they propose to bring them to? The tyranny of the Russian administrative system is preferable to their condition here. They are simply slaves—these my poor countrymen and women."[35]

The committee visited thirty sweatshops and its findings were widely circulated in the press and in a CT&LA pamphlet entitled *The New Slavery: Investigation into the Sweating System . . .* , published with a special vote of thanks to Elizabeth Morgan.[36] Many of the leaders of the Chicago labor movement had, like the Morgans, been child laborers in the British Isles. They were horrified to see the sweatshop system that had stolen their childhood, and had then been brought under control by the British ten-hours bill and the inspection acts of 1847, being introduced into the United States. After describing the indignities of the sweating system and referring to the example of Britain, the CT&LA pamphlet went on:

> The sweat shop may now be found only here and there, hid away from public view on only an occasional block, but the system is developing rapidly, and unless stamped out it will extend until whole sections of this city will be swallowed up by it, and the degradation of labor will then be complete.[37]

The CT&LA pamphlet appealed to the community's sense of human decency, as well as to its fear of contagion: the glaucoma, scarlet fever, diptheria, and smallpox that infested the sweatshops would inevitably spread throughout the community on the clothes made there. Settlement workers like Florence Kelley who were concerned with public health used this argument repeatedly, especially after the smallpox epidemic of 1894. Abraham Bisno of the cloakmakers' union found other arguments more pressing but recognized that different emphases were the basis of a united front:

> The assault we made on home work, too, was inspired by different motives. The public sought to guard itself against contagious disease, normally prevalent in the homes of the poor families doing the work. In our case, we wished to abolish home work because it was possible for us to organize our people much more efficiently when large numbers of them were working in the larger shops. So while the newspapers and churches were agitating for one set of motives, the unions who supported the bill were mainly inspired by the economic motive.[38]

In January 1892 Florence Kelley, a socialist, a friend of Friedrich Engels, and the translator of his *Condition of the Working Class in England in 1844,* moved to Chicago in order to get a divorce—the Illinois law was more permissive about women retaining custody of their children than that of her native Pennsylvania. While working in Philadelphia Florence Kelley had become familiar with the work of the Illinois Woman's Alliance and had formed a similar but smaller organization, the Workingwomen's Society of Philadelphia, in March 1889. Its object was to help women form organizations for

> self-protection, enlightenment, mutual aid and benefit, and for obtaining and enforcing legislation in the interest of the working class, by (1) gathering into a central society all those devoted to the cause of organization among wage-earning women; adopting a label, collecting statistics, publishing facts, furnishing information and advice; (2) founding organizations in trades in which they do not already exist, and cooperating with existing societies to the end of raising wages, shortening hours, and improving conditions of labor.[39]

Florence Kelley moved into Hull House and had a major role in turning the settlement away from its purely social service and cultural uplift orientation to one embracing social action as well. She was aided by Alzina Stevens, who had returned to Chicago and also lived in Hull House. The two plunged into the sweatshop campaign, and in April Florence Kelley wrote Engels in great excitement:

We have a colony of efficient and intelligent women living in a workingmen's quarter, with the house used for all sorts of purposes by about a thousand persons a week. The last form of its activity is the formation of unions of which we have three, the cloakmakers, the shirtmakers and the bookbinders. Next week we are to take the initiative in the systematic endeavor to clear out the sweating dens. There is a fever heat of interest in that phase of the movement just at present. Senator Sherman Hoar is travelling about the country looking into the dens at night and unattended. The Trades Assembly is paying the expenses of weekly mass meetings, and the sanitary authorities are emphasizing the impossibility of their coping, unaided, with the task allotted to them. So we may expect some of the palliative measures pretty soon.[40]

A three-pronged legislative strategy was developed. It included enforcing existing sanitary ordinances; strengthening and enforcing child labor, truancy, and compulsory education laws; and passing an eight-hour bill for women. The first two demands came from the labor and women's movements; the last came primarily from the legislature, with heavy support from Hull House. Although the Chicago labor movement had been agitating for an eight-hour day for many years, notably in 1886, it had not envisioned that it would come about through state legislation: many trade unionists and radicals thought they would win the eight-hour day through large-scale social agitation combined with a general strike, while a few thought revolution would be necessary. (Indeed it should be noted that the eight-hour day is more a fiction than a reality even today, when compulsory overtime prevails in heavy industry, and many workers would question whether time-and-a-half compensates for a sixty- or seventy-hour week and its effect on family life.)

Senator Hoar's visit to Chicago in April 1892, his sweatshop tours, led by Elizabeth Morgan and Florence Kelley, and their testimony before his committee all caused a furor in the press and focused the national spotlight on conditions in Chicago. Such publicity could not escape the notice of the state legislature, which proceeded to climb on the bandwagon. In February several state legislators came to Chicago for the famous tour and one told the press he was preparing legislation on the eight-hour day. Governor Altgeld had just been elected, and a reforming spirit was in the air. Anything seemed possible.

Considering that labor had been virtually unregulated until this time, the bill that was introduced contained a number of startling provisions. All of them would make sweated labor far less profitable than it had been: children under the age of fourteen could not be employed in manufacturing; women and children could only work an eight-hour day; employers were required to have on file a physician's certificate of health and an affidavit of age for all children between fourteen and sixteen; the board of health was empowered to search and confiscate goods found in tenement workshops that violated the sanitary code. And finally, manufacturers were required to furnish the names and addresses of their subcontractors and workers, thus enabling unions to find and organize them.

The CT&LA, the Illinois Woman's Alliance, and Hull House joined to lobby for the bill, holding countless meetings and sending delegation after delegation of workers and reformers to Springfield. One Chicago mass meeting drew twenty-five hundred people; on the stage next to the union banners hung a man's shirt with a placard showing the effects of sweated labor: "Paid for making, per dozen: in 1890, $1.55. In 1893, 90 cents." A large and varied group sat near the podium, including labor racketeers Skinny Madden and Billy Pomeroy; Senators Hoar and Noonan; Tommy and Elizabeth Morgan; reformer Henry Demarest Lloyd; Florence Kelley and Ellen Gates Starr of Hull House; and a large number of clergymen. Mary Kenney chaired the meeting.

The speeches reflected the varied composition of this united front. Reverend V. P. Gifford gave the keynote speech. After discussing the dangers of contagion and the need for good samaritans, he ended: "The man should make the money and the woman remain at home to care for it. Work should not be added to her burden of childbearing"—a statement that any number of the women present must have resented. Henry Demarest Lloyd, on the radical end of the spectrum, presented a large number of resolutions on sweated labor and tenement housing, and went on to say that if these evils were not cured, the garment industry should be nationalized. He called for pressure on the legislature and the formation of consumers' leagues.[41]

Much to the surprise of all concerned, particularly the manufacturers of Illinois, the eight-hour bill passed the state assembly with little opposition. Outraged at this invasion of their prerogatives, the employers quickly formed a manufacturers' association to agitate against the bill and have it proven unconstitutional in court. Under this pressure the united front of women and labor began to disintegrate. The damage was particularly marked in the Illinois Woman's Alliance.

There had been struggles between the labor delegates and the middle-class reform elements in the Alliance before—over the question of payment for city inspectors and the issue of charity work. Some of the wealthier members of the Alliance saw both labor reform and orphanage visits as part of the same tradition of "friendly visiting" and philanthropic service. In the heat of the campaign for improved public school facilities, for instance, the Women's Club, some of whose members also belonged to the Alliance, devoted most of its energy to a drive to collect clothing for poor school children. While this was a worthwhile endeavor, it was quite different from the political exposures and agitation favored by Corinne Brown, Elizabeth Morgan, and Fanny Kavanaugh.

Although the Alliance did not try to prevent its member organizations from doing such work, in May 1889 it voted not to engage in fundraising or other charity work. Caroline Hurling of the Cook County Suffrage Society, then president of the Alliance, argued that the Alliance had been formed to change the laws and win practical reforms rather than to do philanthropic or service work:

> We want to put ourselves on record concerning this charity matter right now. Why should private charities do, and continue forever to do, what rightfully should be done by the State? The City has money, and so has the State, to do these things and they ought to do them. Let us get at the source of the evil rather than palliate its results.[42]

As the Alliance's work developed, contradictions in members' goals and outlook came increasingly to the surface. In November

1891 there was a fierce struggle over whether to support the women shoemakers who were on strike at Selz Schwab. Corinne Brown offered a resolution in support of the strike which passed only after much debate and by a small majority. Those opposed felt the resolution was "an endorsement of strikes generally and hence contrary to the spirit of the Alliance."[43] This was a slap in the face for both Elizabeth Morgan and Mary Kenney, who had organized the union at Selz Schwab, the former as a member of the Ladies' Federal Labor Union, the latter during her tenure as AFL organizer.

Corinne Brown then declined to serve as president of the Alliance again, and Elizabeth Morgan resigned from the board. Fanny Kavanaugh had nearly resigned from the police committee a few months before when she was told that "the Alliance no longer believed her reports on police matters."[44] Some members apparently felt her work was being treated sensationally in the press while other Alliance work was ignored. The tide was clearly changing. The labor members had stressed economic questions and structural remedies for social wrongs, but many of them were missing Alliance meetings in order to work for the eight-hour law. In their absence, a shift in tone became apparent in reports of Alliance meetings, and factional activity and backbiting increased.

At one meeting in 1892, for instance, the main topic of discussion was the liberalization of the divorce laws, a subject of general interest. This was, however, followed by a discussion of a resolution "that some of the present cooking utensils are unfit for use and should be replaced by new ones better adapted to cook fruit than the tin vessels heretofore used" presumably on the grounds of health. After this came a debate on whether female nurses should be expected as part of their duties to bathe helpless male patients, and another on the overcrowded state of the streetcars, which was making rush hour hard for working women and children; the Alliance decided to try to get women shoppers to travel at off-hours.[45]

The manufacturers' campaign against the eight-hour law intensified existing differences among Alliance members. A number of people who had been involved in the sweatshop campaign began to work on enforcing the new law; Governor Altgeld ap-

pointed Florence Kelley chief factory inspector, and she hired
Abraham Bisno, Alzina Stevens, and Mary Kenney as deputies.
They all did an enormous amount of work seeking out and
publicizing illegal working conditions, but they soon found their
efforts undermined: they could not get the city to take action
against the offenders. Florence Kelley took the district attorney a
case involving an eleven-year-old child who had been employed
gilding picture frames and had lost an arm because of the poi-
sonous fluid he used at work. The district attorney rebuffed her:
"You bring me this evidence this week against some little two-by-
six picture-frame maker, and how do I know you won't bring me a
suit against Marshall Field next week? I'm overloaded. I wouldn't
reach this case inside two years."[46]

In an effort to combat this subversion of the new law, members
of the Women's Shoemakers' Union introduced a resolution at an
Alliance meeting in February 1894, "strongly condemning the
manufacturers of this city for combining to nullify the State laws."
They stated that, as women workers, they unanimously approved
of the law and "pleaded for its maintenance and enforcement."[47]
The Alliance voted not to support the resolution.

We can only speculate as to why this happened. Perhaps the
Alliance had been taken over by an antilabor clique. Maybe it had
been less solidly prolabor from the beginning than it appeared,
and had merely been drawn into doing good things by the charis-
ma of Elizabeth Morgan and others, who had now turned their
attention to other matters. Perhaps members of the Manufacturers' Association had bribed, blandished, terrified, or used
husbandly influence to make Alliance members take their side.
There are no answers in the record.

It is clear, however, that at least one new officer of the Alliance,
a Mrs. Fixen who was serving as corresponding secretary, had ties
to the Manufacturers' Association. At the meeting after the unfortunate vote against the eight-hour law, Elizabeth Morgan
stormed in and asked, on behalf of the Ladies' Federal Labor
Union, to see the minutes; she demanded that the Alliance recon-
sider its position. This was done, and a new pro–eight-hour
resolution was passed without much open opposition. But instead
of officially informing the Ladies' Federal Labor Union of this

development as she was supposed to, Mrs. Fixen "by some mistake addressed her communications to the Secretary of the Manufacturers' Association,"[48] who wrote and asked the Alliance to give him equal time to present the manufacturers' side. When the Alliance agreed, it became clear to some of its members that it was no longer the prolabor force it was intended to be, but had become a neutral body which was planning to coolly consider each side of the case and judge between them.

In an ineffectual attempt to wipe the slate clean, the Alliance then challenged the Manufacturers' Association to a public debate on the eight-hour law. The meeting was held in April, and more than a thousand people attended. Elizabeth Morgan chaired the meeting, and speakers included Henry Demarest Lloyd; Ellen Henrotin of the General Federation of Women's Clubs, a devoted advocate of the bill; Dr. Bayard Holmes; and Tommy Morgan. The representatives of the Manufacturers' Association failed to show up, however. Instead, they sent a letter explaining that they opposed the eight-hour law because Illinois industry would be put at a disadvantage and would leave the state, and because the law would "supplant female with male labor," robbing women of one-fifth of their earnings and all their freedom of contract.[49]

Soon after this meeting, the factory legislation the Alliance was trying to support perished, struck down by the Illinois Supreme Court in the spring of 1894. The Illinois Woman's Alliance did not long outlive the eight-hour bill. Many labor organizations had already withdrawn from it because of "petty differences and personal spites. . . . Strongminded females with axes to grind [were in control of the organization and] the results are chaos and failure."[50]

The final episode in the Alliance's demise seems to have been its opposition to Kate Bradley's candidacy for the board of education. She was an Alliance member who was strongly supported by the CT&LA, which had gathered 40,000 petition signatures on her behalf. The Alliance opposed her, according to the labor press, "for the ridiculous reason that she had been reared in a convent."[51] After this final affront, the Ladies' Federal Labor Union withdrew from the Alliance, charging that it had "publicly and unnecessarily antagonized the organized labor movement" and that their objective in founding the Alliance, "the protection of women and children . . . now appears to have [been] entirely forgotten."[52]

There seems to have been little disposition on the part of labor and socialist forces to stay and fight for leadership of the organization, although only two years earlier it had been the major reform voice in the city on issues concerning women and children. When serious contradictions arose within the united front of women, its labor and socialist members, feeling disappointed and betrayed, turned away in disgust. In October 1894, the Ladies' Federal Labor Union called a meeting of delegates from "every union organization in the city composed wholly or in part of women," as well as the few Working Girls Clubs. They wished to form an organization to replace the Alliance, but this time there would be no middle-class members; the working class would go it alone:

> The object of the council is to concentrate action for the improvement of the condition of women, girls, and children. The prime movers in the plan were at one time members of the Woman's Alliance, but on the control of that organization passing into the hands of a class not interested in the betterment of conditions for members of their own sex, the delegates from trades' unions withdrew . . . [and] a small clique of the members reigned supreme.[53]

Elizabeth Morgan announced that the new organization would be at work by the following legislative session, but her prediction proved overly optimistic. Other splits in the labor movement intervened and prevented the new coalition from coming into existence. At the December 1894 AFL convention, the Morgans and other radicals suffered a severe defeat; they had come close to getting a socialist program passed but were outmaneuvered by Gompers, whose brand of pure-and-simple trade unionism was consolidated in the AFL from that time forward. Furiously disappointed, Tommy Morgan joined other members of the Socialist Labor Party in forming a dual union, the Socialist Trades and Labor Alliance, to be made up only of revolutionary workers. This move effectively isolated the left wing of the labor movement from the masses of workers within it. After such a split the idea of a broad federation of women workers in Chicago could be only a dream. When the labor movement as a whole was divided, the female workers could hardly be united.[54]

At its peak, the Illinois Woman's Alliance demonstrated the strengths of a united front of women. It brought together most of Chicago's women's organizations under the leadership of working-class and socialist women, with strong support from the labor movement, and it worked to improve the general conditions of working-class women and children. But its very success provoked the opposition of the manufacturing class, and this in turn brought the class contradiction within the Alliance to the surface. The charity-mindedness of many middle-class members and their failure to show solidarity with the women of the labor movement at a moment of crisis made a struggle for leadership of the movement necessary, but rather than engage in that struggle, the socialist and labor women withdrew from the Alliance, just as their male counterparts were to withdraw from the AFL when their program was defeated. The Alliance could not exist without them and soon disappeared from history.

A united front, with its internal contradictions, always contains the possibility of betrayal, and struggle within it is inevitable. While it may be human to react to this by leaving, much is sacrificed by those who do so without a fight. It may be that even if the trade union and socialist women had stayed and fought for hegemony over the Alliance they would have lost. But one thing is certain: where there is no battle, there can be no victory; and when leadership of the whole women's movement is voluntarily turned over to its bourgeois members, they will certainly take it.

Part III
Fragmentation

In 1905, Lizzie Swank Holmes summed up her early work in an article for the AFL magazine, the *American Federationist*. She was proud and confident of the future of women in the labor movement.

> Chicago is said to be the best organized city in the United States for women workers. . . . But that handful of humble, earnest, working women who laid the foundation of the present excellent organization, who "broke the ground," as it were, who introduced the idea of solidarity to the indifferent, scoffing, or apathetic working women of thirty years ago, are never mentioned in the records of labor's achievements. But they do not mind the neglect. They did not work for glory, but for the rights of poorly paid, toiling women and children, and they rejoice today to know that the *class* is recognized, and that the necessity of union and of mutual helpfulness is so well understood by working women in general.[1]

She had good reason to be proud of the work of the 1880s and 1890s, for the situation of women in Chicago's labor movement was unique. Over thirty-seven thousand women were organized (as compared to five thousand in New York)[2] in mixed and all-female locals. In 1903 Lou Grant, assistant secretary of the Illinois Bureau of Arbitration, found separate women's locals among men's clothing workers, paper box makers, school teachers, bindery girls, cracker packers, twine workers, rubber workers, shoe workers, can makers, telephone and switchboard operators, women's clothing workers, knitters, janitresses, feather duster makers, woven wire mattress makers, picture frame makers, candy dippers, core makers, horse nail makers and novelty workers. Women were also in mixed locals of the printers, cigarmakers, commercial telegraphers, and post office clerks.[3] It was an impressive achievement.

But it was short-lived. The industrial depression of 1907–1909 devastated these women's unions, driving the women—the most marginal and lowest-paid workers at best—out of the labor force or forcing them to keep their jobs on their employers' terms. By 1909 the results were clear: the president of the Women's Trade

Union League estimated that the number of women in Chicago unions was reduced to ten thousand, and there was not a single all-female local left.[4]

This decline in the number of female unionists was not matched by a similar decline in the number of men in unions, a number which remained constant throughout the period. Industrial cycles and employer persecution affected both sexes but affected them unevenly, because of women's more insecure place in the work force and the fact that much of their value to the employer depended on their remaining marginal.

Employers were hostile to unions in general but found women's unions intolerable—and not only because they were new. Industries that had not yet reached the monopoly stage, such as the garment industry with its thousands of small "cockroach" manufacturers, depended on the cheapness of female labor. If they had been compelled to pay women a living wage, many such manufacturers would have gone under. And the chief reason for the women's cheapness was their lack of organization. Andrews and Bliss summed up the situation in their government report of 1911:

> The low wages at which women will work form the chief reason for employing them at all. . . . A woman's cheapness is, so to speak, her greatest economic asset. She can be used to keep down the cost of production where she is regularly employed. Where she has not been previously employed she can be introduced as a strike breaker to take the place of men seeking higher wages, or the threat of introducing her may be used to avert such a strike. But the moment she organizes a union and seeks by organization to secure better wages she diminishes or destroys what is to the employer her chief value.[5]

In times of depression when jobs were scarce, the argument that a woman's place was in the home had considerable force among laboring men, who were often dubious at best about the need to organize women and did not recognize that women had joined the industrial work force to stay. The men had themselves only recently begun to form stable unions, and in many industries these were also hard pressed. The AFL was becoming increasingly conservative, and radical influence on its leadership was declining, particularly after a large part of its left wing seceded again in 1904 to form the Industrial Workers of the World, and began to build revolutionary industrial unions among the unskilled workers that the AFL had neglected. It is impossible to know whether or not the male unions could have sustained women's locals if they had given them more assistance, since they barely tried. As Alice Kessler-Harris has noted, the end result of the AFL's attitude was "to divide the working class firmly along gender lines and to confirm women's position as a permanently threatening underclass of workers who finally resorted to the protection of middle-class reformers and legislators to ameliorate intolerable working conditions."[6]

Other things changed with the turn of the century. The socialist and feminist movements became too divided to do consistent united front work. In 1901, disgusted with the sectarianism of the Socialist Labor Party, a number of influential radicals formed the Socialist Party. This in turn developed a gap between its left and right wings that by 1912 had become unbridgeable. The feminist movement was dominated by the mainstream National American Women's Suffrage Association, and radical feminists from the Congressional Union (later called the National Woman's Party) had split off to develop more militant tactics in the suffrage battle. Another sector of the feminist movement, often called the social feminists, led by settlement workers like Jane Addams, remained concerned with working women and was instrumental in the formation of the Women's Trade Union League. The League could occasionally muster support from the whole united front of women, as in the 1909 shirtwaist makers' strike, but these moments became increasingly rare and fragile. Because of all these schisms, those who were trying to organize working women could no longer assume the kind of united support that had helped Elizabeth Morgan and Corinne Brown.

The following chapters examine the united front of women in this period of fragmentation, with particular emphasis on the Women's Trade Union League, the Industrial Workers of the World, and the Socialist Party as they dealt with the question of alliances across class lines or, in the case of the IWW, unity between housewives and working women.

5
Leonora O'Reilly and the Women's Trade Union League

Long have we lived apart,
   Women alone;
Each with an empty heart,
   Women alone;
Now we begin to see
How to live brave and free,
No more on earth shall be
   Women alone.

Now we have learned the truth,
   Union is power;
Weak and strong, age and youth,
   Union is power;
On to the end we go,
Stronger our League must grow,
We can win justice so,
   Union is power.

For the right pay for us,
   We stand as one;
For the short day for us,
   We stand as one;
Loyal and brave and strong,
Helping the world along,
For end to every wrong,
   We stand as one!

Charlotte Perkins Gilman
anthem of the Women's Trade Union League[1]

The Women's Trade Union League was founded in 1903 and lasted until 1950. It marked a renewed attempt to build a united front of women centered around working women, and, particularly in its early years, it did valuable pioneer work in demonstrating various ways these women could be reached, especially in the garment industry.

The impetus behind its formation came from William English Walling, a socialist intellectual and settlement worker who had been excited by a similar organization in England. On his return in 1903, he contacted Mary Kenney O'Sullivan in Boston. Though now a widow with young children, she was as full of energy as ever and had maintained her connections with both the AFL and the settlement movement. Together the two decided to try to create a new organization at the 1903 AFL convention, and since the trade union women there numbered a dismal four, they called upon various settlement workers to represent the sex. A few—a very few—male trade unionists participated as well.

By the end of the convention, the new women's organization had officers,[2] a constitution, and a program consisting of five demands: (1) the organization of all workers into trade unions; (2) equal pay for equal work; (3) an eight-hour day; (4) a minimum wage scale; and (5) woman suffrage.[3] It was decided to set up local leagues in Boston (where Mary Kenney O'Sullivan played a leading role), in Chicago (with help from the women at Hull House and the University of Chicago Settlement), and in New York, where William English Walling immediately contacted a one-time shirtwaist maker turned settlement worker, Leonora O'Reilly.

A charismatic speaker and organizer, Leonora O'Reilly seemed to the League's middle-class members—usually called "the allies"— a miraculous example of working-class spirituality; no one who met her ever forgot her, and one of her oldest friends described her as "one of those rare nun-like spirits whose only adequate medium of expression is divine service to mankind. And this service she achieved, not through remarkable intellectual power, a quality much more common, but through the divine fire, the infinite tenderness and compassion of her own spiritual life."[4]

Leonora O'Reilly in fact embodied all the contradictions of the united front of women in her own person. She was eager for education and culture, yet defiantly proud of the strengths of her own class. Hating the condescension of her female allies and the indifference of male trade unionists with equal passion, and torn by her own ambivalence and sharp perceptions, she was to find no peaceful haven in the Women's Trade Union League. She was a searcher, an idealist, a positivist practicing "The Religion of Mankind," at various times an active member of the Knights of Labor, the Henry Street Settlement, the Women's Trade Union League, the suffrage movement, the Friends of Irish Freedom, the National Association for the Advancement of Colored People, the Socialist Party, the support movement for the anti-imperialist struggle in India, and the pacifist movement. She was in turn a shirtwaist worker, a sewing teacher at the Manhattan Trade School, a settlement worker in Brooklyn, and a full-time organizer for the WTUL until—her heart weakened by years of child labor— she lapsed into illness, depression, and a slow death at the age of fifty-seven. She was in many ways the soul of the WTUL, the only one beloved by all factions. Something in it died with her.

Leonora O'Reilly grew up in a household of Irish rebels on the Lower East Side in the 1870s and 1880s, at a time when the neighborhood teemed with every kind of radical. Marxist exiles from Bismarck's Germany, Italian revolutionaries in red Garibaldi hats, Jewish anarchists and socialists from Russia, and survivors of the Paris Commune, all mingled with American adherents of the "cooperative commonwealth," trade unionism, free love, votes for women, and every conceivable kind of deism. Leonora O'Reilly was deeply influenced by two friends of her family, both survivors of the Paris Commune, Jean Baptiste Hubert and Victor Drury. Drury, an acquaintance of Karl Marx, had also been one of Mazzini's soldiers in the war for Italian independence from the Austro-Hungarian Empire. Leonora O'Reilly drank in her friends' stories of "self-sacrifice, of renunciation of all those personal ties held dear by most of us, all their splendid, heroic deeds."[5] She went to work in a shirtwaist factory when she was eleven, and when she was sixteen, Hubert recruited her into the Knights of Labor, to which her mother already belonged.

In that same year Leonora O'Reilly became part of a small group that called itself the Working Women's Society. It included Ida Van Etten, a woman of independent means who had taken up the cause of working women and had worked with Eva McDonald

Valesh in 1892 to persuade the AFL to hire a woman organizer. Its leading spirit was Alice Woodbridge, who had worked for many years as a retail clerk and led the new group in investigating and exposing conditions in the stores. What they found was so dreadful that they took the facts to a group of women philanthropists, including Josephine Shaw Lowell, noted for her interest in the labor movement, Dr. Mary Putnam Jacobi, and Louisa Perkins; they all joined the Society.[6]

Possibly because of the influence of its middle-class members, the Working Women's Society was uninterested in organizing women into unions. Like the Illinois Woman's Alliance, it was a transitional form between the charity organizations of the nineteenth century, which sought to ameliorate bad conditions through private means, and the trade union organizations and government agencies of the twentieth century. The members of the Society decided that trying to organize a union of salesclerks would be fruitless: the clerks were all women and "consequently usually timid and unaccustomed to associated action;" they were young and therefore inexperienced and flighty; and they were unskilled and therefore easily replaced.[7] The Society decided instead to direct a barrage of appeals to the female consumer:

> It is the *democratic demand* for cheapness that keeps alive this sad condition of things. It is *our* needs and *our* desires that regulate a large part of production. In our eagerness to make our little money go far, are we not too careless about the claims of those who make for us, or stand behind the counter which we face? When a neatly made garment is offered to us as "cheap," do we stop to ask at whose expense is the cheapness? . . .
>
> Are we not all sisters one of another, and should not a woman's heart thrill at being called on for help? . . . Where it is a possible thing, let the buyer come into personal contact with the worker. Let each woman buy her material . . . as our ancestors did. Then let her go to the home of the workers, and pay a fair price for the making, giving loving and sisterly interest and sympathy into the bargain.[8]

When this effort to turn back the clock, along with attempts to get women to shop early so that clerks would need to work only eight hours,[9] proved insufficient, the Society turned to legislation. Samuel Gompers supported their proposal for a state eight-hour law for women and children—although he did not believe in similar legislation for men—and a bill for women factory inspectors. The former failed, the latter passed in 1890.

The main work of the Society, however, was in consumer education, and its work in this area became the basis for the Consumers' League, founded in 1890, an organization for middle-class consumers only (neither workers nor employers were eligible for membership, to ensure that the society be "nonpartisan") that sought to reform working conditions through public pressure. In 1899 Florence Kelley came from Hull House to head the Consumers' League.[10]

Leonora O'Reilly was a factory worker, and she was more interested in organizing and educating workers than in consumer groups. She, Alice Woodbridge, and the other working-class women in the Society began to concentrate more on legislative and strike support work than on consumer education.[11] She was, however, deeply influenced by some of the middle-class women in the Society, particularly her close friend Louisa Perkins, who felt that the socialist emphasis on class conflict was too narrow and that enlightened people of all classes should work together to create a fair society: "I know and you know, that the perfect engine with which to bring about radical reforms is to be composed of strong disinterested men and women, representatives of the varied industries and interests of society, grouping money, trained intellect, practical experience and noble insight."[12] This strategy for change—one of the main ideas of the Progressive Era and almost a textbook description of an elite—was to have great influence in the Women's Trade Union League.

Although she worked twelve hours a day, and had become a forewoman by her mid-twenties, Leonora O'Reilly wanted to be as educated and cultured as the middle-class radicals she met. She was the only female factory worker in the Social Reform Club, a study circle that covered everything from economics to Dante to Comte and the "religion of humanity," and that included Edward King, a pioneer in workers' education on the Lower East Side; Lillian Wald of the Henry Street Settlement; Felix Adler, founder of the Ethical Culture Society; and Arthur Brisbane of the *New York Journal.* On her own, she learned shorthand and went to the

YWCA gym. As she wrote a friend, "I am studying every night in the hope of making something more out of my life than a mere manager to make money for someone else to spend."[13] She yearned to leave the factory and find more scope for her talents, even though Louisa Perkins told her that she could make her job as forewoman into a work of Christian charity, "real mission work of the noble kind. That place must always be filled and if you can stand as a middle man of righteousness, faithful and just to the interests of all, you can not only help your own shop, but set a higher standard for the place or position everywhere. And you must be supremely careful to be just to the employer."[14]

Most of Leonora O'Reilly's settlement friends found it "incongruous" that such a brilliant creature should spend ten hours a day in a shirtwaist factory.[15] In 1894 some of these women— Louisa Perkins first among them—raised the money to buy her a year's freedom. She and her mother went to live next to the Henry Street Settlement, and she took on two new tasks: running a model shirtwaist factory to teach girls how to do quality sewing, and organizing a women's local of the United Garment Workers. But her health was already failing. Even as she was beginning her new life, she wrote in her diary: "June 28. O most wretched day. Hardly able to crawl around. I wonder if this means that I am breaking down. True I have worked hard enough to break down some people but then I ought to be made of better stuff than that. What an awful thing, if just now when I have found freedom if I could not use it."[16]

The experimental "little shop of the new idea" was based on the belief that if young girls could be taught to do fine sewing and make complete garments instead of mere pieces, they could make more money. This idea was not a realistic one, considering the way the garment industry was becoming increasingly rationalized and tasks in it divided. When the model shop ended after a year and a half, the girls went back into the factories, able only to earn a few dollars more because of their increased skill. The work the little shop turned out was too fine to be marketable except at a very high price, and the cooperative did not even pay for itself.

At the same time that they experimented with their model workshop, Leonora O'Reilly, Lillian Wald, and a few other settle-

ment women were trying to organize women garment workers
into Local No. 16 of the United Garment Workers. The UGW was
in general indifferent to the fate of unskilled women clothing
workers, and particularly so in New York.[17] Local 16 was organized
in the spring of 1897, and excerpts from Leonora O'Reilly's diary
show some of the difficulties she faced in trying to organize
women's locals in shops where there were already men's locals:

> The W.W.G.U. #16 met tonight. The meeting was not so large as it
> ought to be. The men sent word, that, as yet, they are too busy with
> contractors to spare a minute to strengthen the organization of
> either men or women; but this week will end the strike. . . .
>
> *June 24.* . . . Mr. Cohen the official walking-delegate and organizer
> of the G.W. now on strike accepts the proposition that when he
> starts out to organize the men, a woman from the W.G.W. branch
> shall go with him and organize the women for Local #16. . . .
>
> *June 29.* . . . Miss Persky just saw Mr. Cohen who says they are
> organizing men at the rate of twenty-five shops a day. The women
> laugh at him or refuse point-blank to attend. This will not do says
> our Com[mittee]. Miss Wald dispatches a letter at once . . . stating
> that our Com[mittee] is ready to help the men organize the women
> as agreed to by the men with our body and in their contract with
> the bosses. . . .
>
> *June 30.* Got the cards from the printer, went to Mr. Schoenfeld's
> office, received the list of shops which are already organized as far
> as the men are concerned; but not organized for women. In the
> morning L. O'R visited sixteen of these shops; most of them had
> three women employed, all of whom were given the cards, asking
> them to attend Wednesday night meetings. Some of the women
> responded. Others looked as if they feared even to touch the
> foreign thing: the ticket.[18]

Seven women came to the first meeting; none but the organizers
came to the second. The committee again resolved to "go to the
meeting of the different branches of the trade and see if the men
can be stirred up to a consciousness of their duty to help the
women to see the need for organization."[19] And so it went. New
York was a far cry from Chicago in this period.

Without more assistance than this from its union, a woman's
local could not survive for long. In the late 1890s, Local 16 filed a
formal resolution at the United Garment Workers' convention,

censuring the union's executive board because "the female garment workers have not been given the necessary cooperation by the other tailor unions of the United Garment Workers of America in order to improve their conditions."[20] No help was forthcoming, and Local 16 gradually faded out of existence.

By 1903, when the Women's Trade Union League was founded, the working-class women who joined it—Leonora O'Reilly, Mary Anderson, Agnes Nestor, Rose Schneiderman, and others—had all had experiences of this sort. They knew that they would get less help than they needed from their brothers in the AFL, but it took them some years of testing various approaches to realize exactly how little help they could indeed expect.

From the beginning the AFL gave the WTUL lip service rather than money, organizers, or practical assistance. League delegates went to the 1907 AFL convention to ask the executive board to appoint a woman organizer and waited two weeks without even getting a hearing. The only money the WTUL ever got from the AFL was $150 a month in 1912, and this was cut off when the League strayed slightly from the path laid down by the United Garment Workers during the controversial Lawrence strike. Margaret Dreier Robins, the League's national president, went to the AFL convention every year with little or no result. After a meeting with Gompers in 1915, she reported back:

> We met Mr. Gompers. He stated . . . that the Exec. Council of the American Federation of Labor recognized the need of organizing women, but they did not think women were qualified to organize women, that, in the first place, women were very difficult to organize, if they could be organized at all; that, secondly, women organizers were rarely worth anything, that they had a way of making serious mistakes—and used some other language which, frankly, I don't want to repeat.[21]

Most members of the League were sure that the reason the AFL would not appoint women organizers was that its leaders wanted all the jobs for themselves, despite the evidence that women workers could be more easily organized by other women than by men. Margaret Dreier Robins told the AFL executive board:

> I know the average man feels that organization is his job and that the woman is an interloper, and, in addition to that, I know that it is

really serious for you to put a woman in a man's place, because the man does represent a political entity and the woman is a disenfranchised human being. Just as soon as Brother Duffy [leader of the carpenters' union] will help vote for the enfranchisement of women the sooner . . . we will be a little more on a footing with the men in the labor movement.[22]

The AFL leaders were suspicious of the WTUL because of the allies: they believed in pure trade union organization, not reform amalgams. On the other hand, they themselves were less than active in promoting unionism for women, and they realized that this left a vacuum that made it difficult to criticize the League. They frequently took the tack of recommending the League follow the example of the Union Label League, a women's auxiliary to the AFL whose only function was to persuade consumers to buy union goods. The Union Label League gave organizational form to the idea that, even in the labor movement, woman's place was in the home: it neither organized women workers nor educated housewives in the principles of trade unionism, and since most women workers were unorganized, the union label goods that women were supposed to buy were almost all made by men. The song of the United Garment Workers, "The Union Label Man" by M. Y. Lane, expressed the AFL's attitude toward the "flighty" woman as well as toward the label: once she catches her man, the heroine forgets all about the needs of organized labor.

> I met a little maiden down at Coney by the sea
>> She wasn't very tall, she wasn't very small.
> I said to her, and took her hand, "Now you must marry me."
>> She said, "I'm not so sure at all.
> You see I am a fac'try girl in dreary shop all day,
>> We girls must bend o'er our machines and work our lives away;
> For living wage, the Union Label is our only guarantee.
>> Is it on ev'ry thing you wear?" I smiled and said, "just see."
>
> CHORUS
> "I wear the Union Label on my coat and pants and vest,
>> I wear it on my collar and my tie.
> To help the girls who made them and the one I love the best,
>> I ask for it on everything I buy.

I wear it on my overalls, my shirt, and on my hat,
   I wear it on the insole of my shoe,
I wear the Union Label wherever I am able,
   And now I'll Union Label you."

A year had sped and we were wed and one day I espied
   No label on the broom. I glanc'd about the room,
"No label on the crackers, bread or cereals," I cried,
   And threw them out unto their doom.
My wife was cutting out a dress, the pattern was unfair,
   And as she rose I also found no label on her chair,
No label on the stove, the toilers' long and weary day.
   "Have you forgot the workers, dear?" I cried, then smiled to say:

CHORUS[23]

Not surprisingly, women in the WTUL felt that the Union Label League was no answer to the problems of organizing working women, raising class consciousness, or promoting solidarity between men and women workers. As Robins noted:

> Can't you see that we cannot go on using women just for the service they can render men? That the purpose of women is to be of service to themselves and their sisters, and what we are especially organized to do is to make possible an organization of women in the industries. We are pledged to help the women and children, to help little girls, not to help iron workers.[24]

This was a particularly telling comment because the ironworkers had a clause in their constitution reading: "Any member, honorary or active, who devotes his time in whole or part to the instruction of female help in the foundry or in any branch of the trade, shall be expelled from the union."[25] Elizabeth Gurley Flynn of the IWW pointed to the same problems with label leagues in one of her many criticisms of the AFL approach:

> Men unionists are not themselves stirred to great enthusiasm over the label on shoes, hats, overalls, cigars, etc. . . . How much less can we expect of the women in the homes, many of whom know nothing of the significance of the label, to demand it on the countless purchases they make. No special efforts have ever been made

seriously to interest the wives in what the men consider "man's affairs." Many a wife hasn't the remotest idea what the union that John goes to every night consists of.[26]

The AFL leadership countered such criticisms by pointing accusingly at WTUL tendencies to suffragism and socialism. The latter was a particular fear, raised during the League's tiny show of sympathy for the IWW-led Lawrence strikers and made credible by the fact that on certain political questions the League was more progressive than the AFL. In 1909, for instance, the League condemned the Asiatic immigrant exclusion bill that Gompers believed to be the one defense U.S. labor had against the "Yellow Peril"; demanded that the size of the U.S. Navy not be increased; and called on the AFL to form a labor party. Gompers took note of this "problem" in his autobiography, in a unique equation of middle-class "egotism" with socialist ideology, the implication being that, while honest working people would have nothing to do with socialist ideas, the middle class is vulnerable to them in its search for self-aggrandizement:

> To these efforts [of the League] to help women, interested women of means contributed funds. This sort of subsidizing created a problem of control—whether wage-earning women or those interested in wage-earning women should guide the movement. I had to be on guard constantly to help maintain the balance for trade unionism. It is hard for those who have not been a factor in real production enterprises, to appreciate the nature and self-efficiency of economic power. A trade union movement is inherently a self-dependent movement. The friendly outsider may contribute advice and assistance, but there is no opportunity for him to play a conspicuous part. Consciously or unconsciously, it is personal egotism that leads him to decry trade union methods and inclines the outsider to Socialism in which he may have a leading part.[27]

If problems with the AFL were acute on the national level, they were devastating when the fate of a local union of women, or a woman organizer, was involved; the AFL did not use its power to organize women workers, but to keep them unorganized.[28] AFL leaders would say women could not be organized because they were unskilled and the AFL charter was only for skilled workers. They would then refuse to allow women to become apprentices and so learn a skill. Or the national leadership would refuse to decide which international (there was one for each craft) had the right to organize a group of workers. If a group of women workers applied for admission to the international in their craft and the international turned them down, they would appeal to the AFL leadership, who would reply that they had no control over the decisions of any international in the federation. If the women then asked the AFL to charter them as an independent local union, the AFL would refuse on the ground that this would violate the jurisdiction of the international in that craft. The buck would be passed back and forth until the women's organization disintegrated in sheer demoralization. Sometimes an international would consent to organize women workers, but would organize separate locals for men and women in the same factory, and a joint committee would negotiate with the company. The women usually got the worst of such negotiations.

A few craft unions, mainly in the garment industry, did try to organize women. They included the International Ladies' Garment Workers' Union and the Amalgamated Clothing Workers. With the help of the Women's Trade Union League, these unions called general strikes of all the workers in one industry, a tactic that had much in common with industrial unionism and was very different from the usual AFL methods. But the women's participation in running locals was not particularly encouraged, even in the garment unions, and as a result women were seldom found in leadership positions above the lowest level.

The AFL stand on women workers had a devastating effect on the labor movement as a whole. Manufacturers were able to hire women at lower wages than union men, and thus undercut the wage level of the entire working class. Women workers often had no alternative but to scab. The workers were divided among themselves and their ability to fight for improved conditions was weakened.

In the absence of support from the mainstream labor movement, it was inevitable that working women would turn increasingly to their middle-class female allies for help and leadership. The allies were for the most part drawn to the Women's Trade Union League by their sense of feminist solidarity, though a few, like Helen Marot, were deeply interested in labor. Most of them were professional women or were independently wealthy: they were the wives and daughters of well-to-do professionals and small capitalists, with an occasional maverick like Margaret Dreier Robins' husband Raymond, who had struck it rich in the Alaskan gold rush. Many of the allies were breaking new paths for women, finding ways to live collectively in settlement houses, often eschewing the bonds of family, husband, and children that would have held them back from social activism. Leonora O'Reilly admired their independence: she valued their work on eight-hour and child-labor legislation, on improving schools and housing, and she saw that they were trying to serve the labor movement selflessly. But she found in them the same denial of the realities of class, of struggle, of her own experience, that she had seen in Louisa Perkins ten years earlier. Their denial of the class struggle was well expressed by Jane Addams, the first vice-president of the League: workers did not need their own movement; rather, the goal should be to merge labor organizations into a general movement of universal progressivism.

> There is a temperamental bitterness among workingmen which is both inherited and fostered by the conditions of their life and trade; but they cannot afford to cherish a class bitterness if the labor movement is to be held to its highest possibilities. A class working for a class, and against another class, implies that within itself there should be trades working for trades, individuals working for individuals. The universal character of the movement is gone from the start, and cannot be caught until an all-embracing ideal is accepted.[29]

Although Leonora O'Reilly also had high ideals, her experience as a factory worker from childhood had taught her the meaning of class struggle in a way that women like Jane Addams, however well intentioned, could never fully understand.

Some of the working women who came into the League and remained there were strong individuals who fought their way into the trade unions, often as the first women in their locals. Others were—like most of the female work force—young girls living at home who had energy and enthusiasm but lacked political experience. A few members had risen against considerable odds to become union officers, and some of these went on to become full-time staff members for the League.[30] Because of the difficulties of combining marriage and children with political work, most of these, like the settlement women, were single; they tended to drop out of the League when they got married.

The League was thus a united front organization of women from different classes and different occupational and ethnic groups. Its members were united by their feminism and by their desire to organize women workers. They believed this would be possible only if they worked through the AFL to enlist women in craft unions; they feared industrial unionism because of its association with the radical IWW. Only in its second decade did the League begin to relinquish this goal and give more emphasis to legislative work than to organization.[31]

Within the framework of the League's general unity, there were substantial political differences. Some of these arose from the varying class origins of its members, but they were not reducible to class alone. On certain questions, such as favoring organizing over legislative work, the League's working-class members would tend to be on the same side; on others they would split along ethnic or political lines. One hotly debated issue, for instance, was whether the New York League should stress organizing the downtown Jewish workers or the uptown "American girls." Struggles over such questions were probably sharpest in New York, where the League's socialist element was strongest. Although most of the League's socialists believed that the revolution would come about peacefully through an accumulation of reforms and electoral victories, rather than through a general strike or uprising, they nevertheless stressed class consciousness and militancy and believed that more fundamental changes were needed than those that could come about solely through unity among women. This sometimes set them in opposition to both the allies, who usually agreed with Jane Addams, and the AFL leadership, which was increasingly opposed to mixing politics with economics.

These differences occasionally came into the open, as in the election for the executive board of the New York League in 1913. Rose Schneiderman, a Jewish socialist who had taken a leave of absence to do suffrage work, was running against Melinda Scott, a feminist hat trimmer who was rather conservative politically. She was one of the few members of the League to side with the AFL leadership and vote for Chinese exclusion from the United States. She was also identified in the New York League with the policy of dropping organizational work among the Lower East Side Jews in order to concentrate on the Irish and American-born workers uptown. The electoral battle was bitter and factionalized. As Pauline Newman, a close friend of Rose Schneiderman, saw it, the allies campaigned for Scott while the workers were for Schneiderman. She wrote Rose Schneiderman after the election:

> I hardly slept last night, and am still excited. For the reason that the vote was so close. Linda got 58, and you 54. Think of it! And please don't think me excited when I say I don't think the Counting was right. . . .
> . . . [Helen Marot] went to the teachers who happen to be members of the League and told them that "Miss Schneiderman is interested in Suffrage more than in Trade Unionism." But we got hold of these people and they did not come at all. Mary [Dreier, president of the New York League] too, told Nel. [Eleanor] Schwartz that it would be too bad were you elected as she needs you so much in the suffrage work. Nel. told this to Mary Van Kleeck, but Mary told her that Rose is needed for a bigger job, than suffrage, and therefore she will vote for Rose. Mrs. Laidlaw [the auditor of the National American Woman Suffrage Association in 1911–1913, Harriet B. Laidlaw] came in to vote, and in talking to me she said that she is going to vote for Linda because she does not want to lose you. So you see, that nothing was left undone by them to line up a vote for Linda on the grounds that you were a Socialist, a Jewess, and one interested in suffrage. With all that, Linda got only four votes more.[32]

On the surface the battle may have been fought on the issue of suffrage versus trade unionism, but there was behind-the-scenes opposition to Rose Schneiderman because she was a socialist. This is clear in a letter Raymond Robins wrote his sister-in-law Mary Dreier:

> I think I would patently make it an issue that the W.T.U.L. must support the general policies of leaders like Miss Scott. . . . She is working all the time to organize working women for their industrial freedom. Most of the others are working for a socialist millen-

nium. They have a perfect right to work for this end, but they have no right to do so under cover of the W.T.U.L. Rose is the only one of the socialist group in your league for whose ability I have any respect. I would keep Rose and fire the others if I could. If she would not stay than I would fire all the paid workers that will not play steady with Melinda. Either this or resign.[33]

There were from the beginning differences of interest and politics between most of the allies and the trade union women. As early as 1905 Gertrude Barnum, a Chicago judge's daughter who was the League's first national organizer and one of the allies least sensitive to class issues,[34] reported: "It has not been simple to keep a 'fair game' between Trade Unionists—who chafe at the inactivity of allies, and allies who criticize the activities of the Unionists."[35] Despite a formal provision in the League's constitution that a majority of its executive board were to be current members of trade unions, its founders foresaw a division of labor that gave trade unionists the role of technical advisors rather than policymakers. The minutes of the organization's first meeting are quite clear on this point: the purpose was to "unite College women to give ideas, women of social position to give influence to create a social sensitiveness, and Women of the Trades to supply the practical information."[36] The idea was not to transform existing class relations but to duplicate them while creating a benevolent elite that would function on behalf of the masses of working-class women.

The organizational principle of building an elite and the educational ideas that developed from it ran directly counter to the democratic impulses and ideas of class solidarity that drew working women into the trade-union movement to begin with. This contradiction created a fundamental problem in the work of the League. When women in the garment industry were swept into its unions through mass strikes, they joined not only for practical reasons, but also because of their desire to develop both as people and as a class. Chicago garment worker Anna Rudnitsky expressed this complex of feelings in the League's magazine, *Life and Labor:*

> What bothers me most is time is passing. Time is passing and everything is missed. I am not living, I am only working.

But life means so much, it holds so much, and I have no time for any of it; I just work.

In the busy time I work so hard. . . . I am too weary for anything but supper and bed. Sometimes union meetings, yes, because I must go. But I have no mind and nothing left in me. The busy time means to earn enough money not only for today but to cover the slack time, and then when the slack time comes I am not so tired, I have more time, but I have no money, and time is passing and everything is missed. . . .

I have been thinking. First we must get a living-wage and then we must get a shorter work-day, and many many more girls must do some thinking. It isn't that they do not want to think, but they are too tired to think and that is the best thing in the Union, it makes us think. I know the difference it makes and that is the reason I believe in the Union. It makes us stronger and it makes us happier and it makes us more interested in life and to be more interested in life is oh, a thousand times better than to be so dead that one never sees anything but work all day and not enough money to live on. That is terrible, that is like death.[37]

This messianic vision of the labor movement was not reflected in the methods or the leadership philosophy of most allies. Many working-class women who took part in mass strikes experienced trade unionism as something that transcended their everyday lives. They were uplifted and transformed by their sense of class and female solidarity. But the allies had no such experience. Their main contact with transcendence was through art, and they did their best to communicate its beauties, often by leading the sort of "outing" to a museum or the opera that Mary Kenney O'Sullivan had deplored in her early experience with the Working Girls Clubs. While many of the working women tended to think, in the phrase of Eugene V. Debs, of rising *with* their class not *from* it, the allies thought in terms of improving conditions for the many while uplifting a special few.

An exchange between Leonora O'Reilly and Laura Elliot, an ally who was for a time head of the New York League's education committee, illustrates these differences. Laura Elliot's plan for her committee emphasized culture—trips to the opera, lectures on art; this was very different from either political education or the industrial training that Leonora O'Reilly thought essential.

Leonora O'Reilly, who had been exposed to Dante and Comte and "high culture" extensively in her own early contacts with middle-class reformers, had spent years studying only to find out in despair that her labors had not even equipped her to pass the civil service examination. She found letters such as this one from Laura Elliot maddening:

> Society does not mean to me just *one* producing class. I believe, with all of those men who have had the divine leisure to develop the evolutionary spirit of man, in the *cross fertilization of culture* as one of the greatest factors in growth and progress. . . .
>
>   . . . You cannot push me out, and you cannot make me afraid of any working girl sister, or render me *self conscious* before them. I refuse to be afraid to tell them that I can teach them music, that I can take them to the Metropolitan Museum and *teach* them and help them. . . .
>
> Dear Sister, get into the Cosmic Band Wagon and be a Monist, and hear the Human Counterpuntal Symphony, where every *point* is sustained by every other *point,* then you will see that it takes all kinds of men to make and run a world. . . .
>
> Leonora O'Reilly, do you honestly, honestly, honestly believe in Evolution, believe in Karl Marx, and *that the time has come or is coming when the wage earning dog is to have his day.* . . . Sometimes I feel that you do not see any future for your sister and brother wage-earners.
>
> You, like the Jews, seem to be so oppressed with oppression. I have never heard you *say* that you believed relief was coming. And yet I thought this was the meaning of Socialism—the coming to power of the working classes.
>
> Sometimes I seem to stand quite alone meditating upon some dream. Am I lying to these girls?[38]

By the time Leonora O'Reilly came to the Women's Trade Union League, she had been thoroughly exposed to this kind of fuzzy-minded uplift and had rejected it. She knew the value of what she was. Some notes she made for a speech to the YWCA in 1908 show the attitude that often made her a center of controversy: "The work which makes people stand on their own feet is the work that counts—the dignity of labor—teach labor to be self-respecting. Contact with the 'lady' does harm in the long run—gives a wrong standard—No use preaching Christianity until you are ready to live it—Brotherhood of man only possible through the brotherhood of labor."[39]

The allies, on the other hand, tended to view the working

women who came to the League as cultural raw material. The League's policy was to train working-class women to take the reins of leadership from the hands of the allies—when they were ready. The allies would select those who were particularly promising, according to their own standards, from the various working-class specimens who came forward. They would train them, polish their manners, somehow find the money to put them on staff or send them to school—in short, transform them from working-class activists to female labor leaders who could with comfort take tea on the White House lawn, as did Rose Schneiderman.

One of the prime examples of this process, Rose Schneiderman came to the League in 1907, a young rank-and-file capmaker fresh from organizing a local in her industry. She was soon offered a choice between a scholarship which would have enabled her to become a schoolteacher and a job on the staff of the New York League. She chose the latter and worked her way up. By the time she became president of the national organization in 1927 she had been working in the New York office for twenty years, as well as holding other staff positions in the garment unions and the suffrage movement. She was poised and polished; she disavowed her socialist ideas and left her capmaking days far behind. The WTUL frequently held her up as a model of the way working girls were trained for leadership.

In 1913 the national WTUL set up a school to train young woman trade unionists as organizers. It included courses at the University of Chicago and at Northwestern University (courses that eventually developed into a full-fledged summer school at Bryn Mawr), as well as training in office work. An early class issued a sharp criticism of the school's fundamental policy, which appeared to be one of remolding the workers:

> We believe most profoundly that the School as it is being administered must fail of its avowed purpose, i.e., the training of trade union girls for leadership among their fellow workers. We cite the following reasons:
> 1. Because initiative and the qualities that make for leadership are neither permitted nor encouraged to develop.
> 2. Because past experience and knowledge of the movement are discounted and ignored; we resent being made over.
> 3. Because the treatment accorded us as students in the School has

not been that of equals and co-workers in a great cause, but
rather that of distrust and condescension.

4. Because on no matter, great or small, are we considered capable
   of making a decision for ourselves, although every one of us has
   for many years been not only permitted but forced by circumstances to meet her own problems and make her own decisions. . . .

We submit that office routine work is distinct from organizing
work, and that training in the former makes no contribution to the
value of the latter.[40]

At issue was the development of the female part of the working
class: Should the allies make it in their own image and produce
that strange amalgam, the working-class "lady," or should the
League's educational policies be directed toward industrial and
political education and the creation of experienced organizers
who were still one with their class? Trade unionists were the
majority on the League executive board after 1907, but numerical weight and political weight are not the same. Apart from such
matters as the selection and development of certain workers for
leadership positions, an imbalance was created by the fact that
most of the working women in the League lacked the allies'
self-confidence, poise, organizational experience, and verbal skills.
Moreover, they were much younger. How could they be expected
to lead the organization?

If power is measured by the opinions that carried the most
weight, the politics that tended to prevail, and the people who
chose the leadership, the allies held the balance. This comes out
clearly when the League's strike-support propaganda is contrasted
with that of the IWW or of other trade unions. The League's
literature always emphasized the poverty of the strikers, their
youth, helplessness, femininity, the way they were victimized by
the employers and the state. It presented a picture of the working
class as pitiful, a suitable object of charity. There is no message of
class solidarity in their material, no sense that the working class
was potentially strong. The message was "Help these helpless
girls, victims of cruel employers," rather than "Help these workers who are fighting cruel employers; their cause is just."

Helen Marot, longtime secretary of the New York League,
must have been thinking about such differences of emphasis

when she wrote her book *American Labor Unions* in 1914. She discussed the class dynamic that can develop in a united front of trade unionists and allies:

> The reformers dominate and the labor men are in the position . . .
> of being auxiliaries to others concerned with the administration of
> labor affairs. . . . They accept positions of vice-presidents while the
> reformers assume, quite naturally, the positions of presidents. The
> reformer is equipped for the campaign with a sort of training and
> experience which is not labor's and with which labor is unfamiliar.
> The reformers formulate their theories and observations of labor
> conditions with a marvelous precision which they can execute pre-
> cisely because they are impersonal.[41]

While the allies' power derived in part from their verbal skills and their confidence in political maneuvering, it also came from the power of the purse. They were able to donate large sums of their own money and raise money effortlessly from their own social circle. Neither of these options was open to the working girl. Large donors always have power, but in an organization that exists on donations they need not even threaten to withdraw their money for that possibility to be present in everyone's mind.

Mary Dreier and Margaret Dreier Robins, independently wealthy sisters from an upper-middle-class German family, served as both public leadership and financial mainstays of the organization. They were brought into the movement by Leonora O'Reilly, who had met them when she was a social worker at Asacog House in Brooklyn. Margaret Dreier Robins moved to Chicago and became the League's national president in 1907. During her tenure, which ended in 1924, she virtually supported the national office; a few years after she resigned it collapsed financially, never to regain its old strength. Mary Dreier played a similar role in New York: the balance sheet included in the League's 1908 report showed that the main source of funds was individual contributions, which totalled $3,539. There was only $158 collected in dues, and of course, the AFL was no help.[42] Over a third of the contributed money—enough to cover almost all the staff's salaries—came from the Dreier family.[43]

This was hardly a stable way to finance a labor movement, and it was bound to affect the work of the League. In 1911 Pauline

Newman analyzed its effects on the organization in Chicago in a
letter to Rose Schneiderman.

> Mrs. Knefler [president of the St. Louis League] is perfectly right
> when she says the League is owned and controlled by one per-
> son. . . . I find that Mrs. Robins pays everybody's salary, all other
> necessary expenses, and as a consequence she has no opposition in
> the entire organization.
>
> Mrs. Robins means well I am sure, but in the end it is bound to
> suffer. She does not give the girls a chance to use their brains, she
> does not want them to think, but wants them to agree with every-
> thing she does. And unfortunately they do; they have to; she pays
> their salaries. . . . A good many organizations here look on them as
> a philanthropic bunch. They do mingle too much with the other
> side. The girls here are not imbued with the spirit of Unionism—
> but philanthropy. What would become of the League as an organi-
> zation were Mrs. Robins to leave them—is easy to imagine.[44]

The class conflicts within the League were noted by the allies
as well as the trade unionists. In her 1909 report to the executive board Mrs. Robins discussed political differences within the
organization. The two groups she mentions are clearly allies
and unionists:

> Some members looked upon the purposes of the League as largely
> educational, feeling that the investigation of industrial conditions
> among women workers, looking to the securing of legislation, and
> the interpretation of trade unionists and allies to each other, con-
> stituted its most important functions. Other members felt that to
> organize women into trade unions, and to strengthen women's
> unions already in existence by developing leadership among the
> working women themselves, were more important; and that, al-
> though the two theories were not at all incompatible with each
> other, the resources of the League necessitated deciding upon one
> policy or the other at the present time.[45]

Because Leonora O'Reilly was older, more self-confident, and
more experienced in united front work than the other working-
class women in the League, she inevitably became a storm center
of such class conflict. As early as 1904 she made a note to herself to
tell William English Walling that the allies "must drop the attitude
of lady with something give her sister, altogether—it never goes

deeper than the skin."[46] She never hesitated to speak up when she felt an ally was being insensitive to class issues, and she resigned or nearly resigned from the League several times, the cause in 1905 being an "overdose of allies."[47] The ally she had had a surfeit of at that time was Gertrude Barnum, who felt impelled to lecture Leonora O'Reilly about her resignation:

> I do wonder that while there is a free hand for you to help in organizing girls in the garment trades in New York, you would resign from a commitee which is ready to work and a League which would help.
>
> I shall not resign myself until I am driven by actual hunger and cold—that is until it is proved that I cannot raise enough money in or out of "the job" to keep me alive to do the work.[48]

The two women also disagreed about Dorothy Richardson's *The Long Day,* a book depicting the lives of working women, supposedly by one of their number, that Gertrude Barnum admired and Leonora O'Reilly found insufferably condescending and distorted. O'Reilly felt so strongly about it that she wrote a long diatribe, which was never published, for the *New York Journal:*

> The book sells like hot cakes at a fair—Ministers preach sermons on it. Critics vie with each to review it. It becomes the topic of afternoon teas. . . . [It appeals to those] who could not be paid to listen to the patient, plodding every day life of the working woman until she is made picturesquely immoral, interestingly vulgar, and maudlinly sentimental. . . .
>
> No, good Mr. Editor, Mr. Publisher, Mr. Sensational Minister and Lady Bountiful of afternoon teas, you may have paid your money for a *real* working girl sensation, but you did not get the *real* thing.
>
> No working woman ever wrote like that about her class. . . .
>
> No, we do not pull each other's hair and enjoy the fight—Nor do we "spit in and bloody each other's face something fierce."
>
> Neither do Salvation Army women who are at the same time factory employees drink gin in the corner liquor store and trade on their Redeemer's name generally.
>
> The "so long" of the working woman is no more to be commented upon than the "upper register" tones of the wouldbes that come among us—language, intonation, and enunciation being largely a matter of environment. The working woman while she may

imitate the "upper register" of the lady for fun passes her verdict on it as "different"—while the intellectual lady with less modesty and more egotism calls the one Right and the other Wrong. . . .

That all working women are notoriously clean in their conversation save when led on by certain types of mind who are soon spotted and stamped for what they are worth, I assert positively without fear of contradiction after an experience of over twenty years daily intercourse with them *as one of them*.[49]

Gertrude Barnum responded to such criticism (on League stationery, with Leonora O'Reilly's name crossed off the letterhead):

If you keep getting off every committee in which every member does not agree with you in every respect, you will not contribute much to any constructive work! But that's your business. You may be right about the Long Day. . . . I should have liked to have read the Long Day with you. It might have helped make me worthy to espouse the Trade Union Cause, which I sincerely wish to do honestly and democratically and faithfully and well. Fortunately everyone does not abandon us "allies" as soon as they disagree with us and we may be useful yet.[50]

One of the issues which caused friction between the allies and the working women was legislation for a minimum wage for women. Mary Dreier, who was head of the New York Minimum Wage Commission as well as of the New York League, suggested in 1914 that the League support the Commission's bill. She was outvoted, with Leonora O'Reilly, Melinda Scott, and Helen Marot firmly opposed, believing with Samuel Gompers that a minimum wage would become the ceiling rather than the floor wage in a given industry. But the allies were firmly committed to the minimum wage, particularly since the League's progress in organizing women had slowed considerably and would continue to be problematic without increased help from the AFL. Women workers could not live on the salaries they made, and the allies felt that a minimum wage law was necessary for their survival; they were also furious at the AFL's opposition to the legislation. Margaret Dreier Robins wrote Leonora O'Reilly:

We are going to have a National Executive Board meeting in Philadelphia in November at the same time as the A.F. of L. meets. I am so eager that we should bombard the A.F. of L. with women and women delegates and force it upon their attention that *there is a woman's cause* in this day and generation. If I could but tell you how their arrogance to and contempt of the working women makes me boil!! If only I could get the rank and file of working women 1/10 as mad as I am, something would be doing. . . . In the June and July numbers of the *Federationist* Mr. Gompers opposes vigorously minimum wage laws as well as laws limiting the hours of work for women as for men on the plea of freedom of contract! How much freedom of contract did you have Leonora dear when you went to work and how much freedom of contract has any child of 14?[51]

Mary Dreier saw it as a clear feminist question, resting upon the issue of suffrage: "What gets me, is that the men decide this question negatively without consulting the trade union women!! But we must be gentle with them if we want them to act with us—they have the votes! . . . I am greatly concerned with Gompers opposed and the New York men weak or opposed the girls and women will continue to be crushed between the upper and nether millstones—it does sometimes seem to be a rotten world for the women."[52]

Apart from its support work for the mass strikes that unionized the garment industry, the League's major contribution was to prove that different kinds of organizational work were necessary to reach working women than those standard among laboring men. Theresa Wolfson made this point in 1926, and it is as valid today as it was then:

The contribution of the Women's Trade Union League to the technique of organization was a realization of the special problems besetting women workers and the initiation of methods . . . and social activities that women understood. Women organizers, women speakers, women trade unionists were developed and encouraged by them to work in a field of organization that had generally been considered hopeless.

. . . [the] male organizer may have acquired a method of approach in his work with men which he cannot transfer to the organization of women, because they are primarily not interested in . . . the same [topics] and [he] failed to take into consideration the psychology of the women workers—their habits of thought.[53]

Most unions met in saloons, where respectable girls would not go; they met late at night when women, overburdened with housework and lacking baby-sitters, found it hard to get out. Equally, male organizers found it difficult to get into women's boarding houses to recruit for the union. All this was perhaps obvious, but not to the AFL; and, although the League often saw what was needed, it did not have the resources to do it. Its report on organizing work in 1912, a peak year, says it all. Requests for help poured in from across the country, but the League had few people to send and those who did travel could not stay anywhere long enough to set things up properly. The best the League could do was build local chapters and send occasional organizers to help in time of strikes:

> In the few instances where we have been able to go to the help of girls in other cities we have really been able to do something. In Sedalia, Missouri, for instance, the girls protested against low wages and other wrong conditions in the overall factory. It was impossible to win the strike but we helped them to open a Union Shirt Co-operative Factory which has up to the present been very successful. . . . What we need is money to engage organizers from among the trade union girls and choose from among the many different nationalities. If in Chicago we could do with the Bohemian and Italian groups what we have been able to do with the Hart, Schaffner and Marx workers we would lay a real foundation for the abolishment of the sweating work in the home.[54]

The money, which could only have come if the rest of the labor movement had seen the importance of organizing women, was not forthcoming. As a result, the emphasis of the League gradually shifted from organization to legislation and lobbying. Those workers who had remained in the League cast off their early class struggle ideas and began, with the allies, to believe in the gradual reformation of capitalism through solid legislative work. This was as true of women like Rose Schneiderman who were reform socialists, as it was of women like Melinda Scott who opposed socialism. By 1915 Rose Schneiderman—having been won over, along with the other working women in the New York League, to support minimum wage legislation for women—had come to believe that legislation was more than a palliative. It was a way to help women unionize since it would make it easier for them to take risks by giving them more money. She spoke of legislation almost as the equivalent of a share in state power: "the government can be made to be our own government, that we can do what we want with it, make legislation that we want, and not accept what the masters want us to take."[55]

The League's tendency to look to the federal government as a major source of support increased during World War I; William O'Neill estimates that by 1919 members of the Women's Trade Union League held thirty-eight government posts.[56] Agnes Nestor, a one-time glovemaker from Chicago, was on the federal Women's Committee, and Mary Anderson, a Chicago shoe worker, became head of the Women's Bureau. Such developments contributed to the League's sense that the federal government was a reliable ally when compared to the AFL, which had never appointed any of them to anything.

Conditions for working women had changed enormously since the early days. It was by now clear that women were not transients in industry but were a permanent part of the work force, and unions for women began to become respectable. Before the WTUL was founded a career as a female trade union organizer didn't exist. Women who organized for unions did so as a vocation, a calling they could not resist. So Mary Kenney O'Sullivan described her own decision to stop being a bookbinder and become an organizer: "Someone must go from shop to shop and find out who the workers were that were willing to work for better working conditions. I must be that someone."

The League encouraged the transformation of one section of the female working-class movement into a group of professional labor leaders or government representatives of labor. Under these new circumstances, being a union organizer ceased to seem as dangerous and radical as it had in the days of Haymarket, and became almost a job like any other. In a 1933 pamphlet entitled "Careers for Girls," the League firmly put forward the ideal of a "career"—as opposed to the ideals of solidarity and struggle, of serving the people.

> Sometimes it is necessary for the organizer to take a job in a shop, so as to become acquainted with the workers. She distributes circulars advising the employees of the benefits of trade union organization,

acts as intermediary between workers and employers, arranges conferring committees and arbitration committees, and negotiates with employers. . . . She endeavors to draw favorable public opinion by speeches and by interviews with the press. She must also play with the women with whom she works—dance with them if necessary and otherwise make herself agreeable so as to win their complete confidence. . . .

From the position of organizer in one locality or one branch of an industry, a woman may work up to the position of national organizer, covering the entire country or the industry as a whole. Furthermore, there are notable examples . . . of woman organizers being appointed to administrative positions in the labor departments of State and Federal Governments. . . .

The obvious satisfactions are those that come from having any considerable share in the quickening of social progress; the molding of opinion, and watching it change lives; the practising of leadership, only to develop it in others and pass it on.

The obvious disadvantages are the long and irregular hours; the excessive demands on physical and spiritual endurance; the collapse of promising successes, and reconstruction from the bottom up.[57]

The women who built the WTUL created the conditions that made it possible for women to do trade union organizing as a career, but with this possibility came careerism. Thus, along with the development of trade unionism among women to the point where it could sustain professional organizers, came the development of the woman labor leader—never a complete equal in the labor aristocracy because she was a woman, but nevertheless able to find her place in its ranks.

The influence of the AFL was decisive in this process. Not only was it the only stable model for union organizing, but it also blocked other avenues of development. Had the labor movement at this period been more open and democratic, more eager to struggle, less dominated by the increasingly bureaucratic leadership of the AFL, the history of the Women's Trade Union League might have been different. The influence of the allies was important, but the principal reason the League developed as it did was the authority of the AFL.

Not everyone in the League waited to see this drama played out. In 1915 Leonora O'Reilly represented the League at the state

AFL convention and plunged into black despair as a result. As long as the AFL continued to dominate the labor movement, she decided, there was no future for her, for women workers, or for the League. She wrote Mary Dreier:

> Now, don't drop dead, but this is my last labor Convention. Also my hands are off the Trade Union job in New York. I shall leave the movement for the movement's good. My mind is made up. . . .
>
> Trade Unions are necessary. They must be worked for in season and out. Women must be organized better than men are organized. The powers that be in the Labor movement of New York State do not and will not recognize an outside body's right to help with the work. Worse than that they attribute their own shortcomings to the outside body's disinterestedness. They use its work to influence personal animosity or worse still to cover up their own crookedness. The crookedness will sooner become known to the rank and file when the outside body is not there as a scapegoat. By keeping in the struggle we shall hinder more than help the rank and file from getting real light as to who it is that is playing foul in the game. . . .
>
> Wages, minimum or maximum regulated by law, the whole damn business is done for at this end of the rope.[58]

Mary Dreier's reply to her friend urging her not to give up was sensible enough, but Leonora O'Reilly was beyond the reach of common sense; she felt her whole life added up to nothing. She had one last stab at intensive political work, going on Henry Ford's peace ship to an international conference of women against the war, held in Europe and called by women in the countries already fighting to show the horrors of war in the hope that its spread might be prevented. O'Reilly, who was the sole representative of the U.S. working class at the conference, was profoundly moved by its spirit of international solidarity. When she returned, she was refused the opportunity to speak about the conference at the AFL convention; the leadership felt there were "sinister influences" behind the peace movement.[59]

She was from then on only sporadically active in the League. A close friend spoke of the bitter depression she suffered:

> There was in Nora's life a period of terrible disillusionment, of a cruel awakening from her world of roseate dreams so fearfully different from life as it was. . . . Even to her consecrated mind, it

gradually had evolved that in the actual work about us, there was a great deal of selfishness and ugliness. All her life she had thought of herself last, had given so unstintingly of her time, of her energy, all the beauty that was herself! And often, for her harvest, she gathered only selfishness, malice, and hardness. How that seared her sensitive soul! For two or three years, all the sweetness, all the sunlight seemed to have gone out of her heart. Often would I hear: "Pigs, pigs! All of them!"[60]

In Leonora O'Reilly's youth she dreamed of making a special contribution, of becoming an apostle of truth and culture who could bring together women of all classes in common service to working women and in unity with working men. All these dreams had become dust, and what she called the "religion of labor" had turned to the worship of false gods. She was in many ways the purest spirit in the League and much of its idealism went with her when she left. Over the years, the League was to become only a shell of a real organization, a staff operation without a mass base. Despite this decline, the Women's Trade Union League has an important place in the history of the united front of women. It pioneered new methods of organizing women workers and gained a permanent toehold for women within the palace of organized labor. Perhaps it was only a toehold, but that was better than no hold at all.

6
Rebel Girls and the IWW

Yes, her hands may be harden'd from labor,
And her dress may not be very fine;
But a heart in her bosom is beating
That is true to her class and her kind.
And the grafters in terror are trembling
When her spite and defiance she'll hurl.
For the only and Thoroughbred Lady
Is the Rebel Girl.

That's the Rebel Girl, That's the Rebel Girl,
To the working class she's a precious pearl.
She brings courage, pride and joy
To the fighting Rebel Boy.
We've had girls before
But we need some more
In the Industrial Workers of the World,
For it's great to fight for freedom
With a Rebel Girl.

Joe Hill
"The Rebel Girl,"
written for Elizabeth Gurley Flynn (1915)[1]

The Industrial Workers of the World represented a new kind of unionism in the United States. Organized by industry rather than by craft and rejecting the exclusionary practices and jurisdictional wars of the AFL, it engaged in a fight to the death with the capitalist class, a fight for power rather than for bread alone. The general strikes it led in the textile mills of the East—Lawrence in 1912, Paterson in 1913—showed it could mobilize masses of working women. By addressing their problems as class problems rather than purely workplace ones, the IWW linked workers in the textile industry with the rest of their community—their husbands and wives, their ethnic organizations and churches, and workers in other industries—to build a working-class army strong enough to lead embryo revolutions.

The IWW's founding conference in 1905, called by an assort-
ment of revolutionaries from the Western Federation of Miners,
the Socialist Party, and the Socialist Labor Party, and including
only one woman, Mother Jones, laid out its principles with unmis-
takable clarity:

> The working class and the employing class have nothing in com-
> mon. There can be no peace as long as hunger and want are found
> among millions of working people, and the few, who make up the
> employing class, have all the good things of life.
>
> Between these two classes a struggle must go on until the workers
> of the world organize as a class, take possession of the earth and the
> machinery of production, and abolish the wage system. . . .
>
> It is the historic mission of the working class to do away with
> capitalism. The army of production must be organized, not only
> for the every-day struggle with capitalists, but also to carry on
> production when capitalism shall have been overthrown. By or-
> ganizing industrially we are forming the structure of the new
> society within the shell of the old.[2]

Only when the working class was organized into one big industrial union with revolutionary politics would it have the unity and
muscle it needed to fight the capitalist class, becoming stronger
and stronger until it seized power through a general strike that
would paralyze the country. All the workers in the United States
would occupy their workplaces and put their hands in their
pockets. Powerless without them, the capitalists would stop making money, the government would be deprived of revenue, and in
a month at most, the state apparatus would simply collapse.

Although this vision was unquestionably more of a revolutionary
fantasy than a well worked-out strategy, the IWW's emphasis on
class solidarity was real—in practice as well as in theory. Unlike
the AFL, the IWW or Wobblies, as they were often called, organized women and men on an equal basis, just as it organized blacks
and whites together in a South ruled by lynch law and the Ku
Klux Klan. The IWW organizers declared, "No longer will we
allow the Southern oligarchy to divide and weaken us on lines of
race, craft, religion and nationality."[3] But at the same time, the
IWW firmly maintained that there was no "race problem. There
is only a class problem. . . . The economic interests of all workers,

be they white, black, brown or yellow, are identical, and all are included in the program of the IWW."[4] In line with this approach, the IWW seldom acknowledged the existence of women's oppression as distinct from class oppression. The problems of working-class women, like those of men, were to be solved by the abolition of wage slavery and the class system.

This economism—thinking that all the problems of the working class were economic in origin and could be solved in one simple stroke—was a severe weakness in the IWW's work. Despite it, the IWW was able to reach out in an extraordinarily sensitive way to women in many strike situations, leading vast uprisings of the entire working-class community—men, women, and children—in isolated, poverty-stricken, one-industry textile or mining towns. Disregarding the contemporary stereotypes of female delicacy, the Wobblies had a keen appreciation of the fighting qualities of women:

> The advent of women side by side with men in strikes, will soon develop a fighting force that will end capitalism and its horrors in short order. As one of them remarked to the writer not long since, in the language of Kipling, "The female of the species is more deadly than the male." It is also well to observe that the male becomes more "deadly" in the presence and with the aid and encouragement of the female. The industrial union movement seeks to develop the fighting quality of both sexes.[5]

Strikers' wives became active in the IWW-led mass strikes because, unlike the AFL unions, the IWW made a deliberate attempt to involve them and to support them against the indifference or opposition of their husbands, fathers, and ministers. It enlisted the wives of male strikers in the IWW local itself, rather than relegating them to "union label leagues" or women's auxiliaries. Moreover, these women had their own reasons for wanting to fight. In the company towns and migrant labor camps of the West, people were oppressed as members of family units rather than as individuals. The wives of the Mesabi iron miners, the Eastern European steelworkers in Pennsylvania, the Italian fishermen in California, or the Western loggers all had grievances of their own and could be organized by any union sensitive to their concerns.[6]

In the iron mines of the Mesabi, for instance, mine bosses insisted on getting sexual access to a miner's wife or daughter in return for giving him a safe place below ground. It is no wonder that miners' wives and daughters were active in the great iron strike of 1916.[7] In a number of company towns, the workers lived in company-owned housing and were evicted during strikes. In such cases the whole family inevitably became involved, the women often fighting off scabs with rolling pins, brooms, and pokers. They were proud of such activism. In a fishermen's strike in Pittsburg, California, when the fish dealers tried to renege on the price they had agreed to, the women went after them with rocks. An IWW organizer foolishly told them to be quiet and go home, and they retorted, "We will make a revolution here, and who are you?"[8] Entering the industrial struggle gave these housewives enough collective strength and confidence so that they could, at least momentarily, resist the patriarchal authority of priests, husbands, and even IWW organizers.

Time and again the IWW proved its ability to mobilize masses of women during strikes; it was, moreover, the only labor organization to raise the non–workplace-related issue of birth control. But it never did the follow-up, the day-to-day organizing, or the special work around the oppression of women that would have enabled it to hold onto them as members. This was only partly because of the kind of crude male chauvinism inevitable in an organization so largely made up of men, which Elizabeth Gurley Flynn criticized from time to time in her speeches:

> I know a local where members forbid their wives speaking to an IWW woman, "because they'd get queer ideas!" I heard a member forbid his wife, who had worked nine hours in a mill, from coming to the meeting, "because she'd do better to clean the house!" When I suggested an able woman as secretary of a local, several men said, "Oh, that's a man's job! She couldn't throw a drunk out!"[9]

Such chauvinism could be overcome, because most members realized that it violated their principles of solidarity. The economism that lay behind their failure to develop special campaigns around the oppression of women was harder to fight, since IWW theory supported the idea that such efforts were unnecessary even as its practice showed the opposite. Organizational measures like special locals for women's work would have been seen as transgressions against solidarity, and campaigns around women's rights were believed to disrupt class unity.

In 1907 a rank-and-file member of the IWW, Sophie Beldner, wrote a letter to its Western newspaper, the *Industrial Union Bulletin,* suggesting a new approach to organizing women workers. She had worked in the garment industry in New York and San Francisco and had found a low level of consciousness among the women she worked with. As they repeatedly told her, "We have no use for a union. We're going to get married before long." While this sort of attitude led many male unionists to conclude that women were not worth organizing, she had a different opinion:

> But as women are a little behind, and a greater amount of energy is needed to call them to action, therefore I would suggest that a literature fund be established in one of the industrial centers where there are enough active women to take the initiative to carry out this plan. . . .
>
> Meanwhile, IWW women would contribute articles to *The Bulletin,* bearing on the question of industrial unionism and working class emancipation.
>
> The local in charge of the fund would select the best articles and publish them in leaflet form with the sanction of the general administration of the IWW.
>
> This, in my opinion, would be the only means by which we could reach the women in factory and at home, and make out of them a powerful factor in the onward march of the working class.
>
> We must also take into consideration the women that are out of the shop, the slaves of the slaves—that we can reach only through literature. On the other hand, there are many class-conscious women who feel and know the necessity of revolutionary education, but not being in the proper conditions to agitate or having no talent to convince others, remain inactive. Supplied with literature which they could distribute, they would benefit the organization just as much as their active factory sisters.[10]

Suggestions like these were raised from time to time but nothing came of them. The result was that the IWW had few women members. Joe Hill, the IWW songwriter and martyr, spoke to this problem in 1914:

The female workers are sadly neglected in the United States, especially on the West coast, and consequently we have created a kind of one-legged, freakish animal of a union, and our dances and blowouts are kind of stale and unnatural on account of being too much of a "buck" affair; they are lacking the life and inspiration which the woman alone can produce.

The idea is to establish a kind of good fellowship between the male and the female workers, that would give them a little foretaste of our future society and make them more interested in the class struggle and the overthrow of the old system of corruption. I think it would be a very good idea to use our female organizers, Gurley Flynn, for instance, EXCLUSIVELY for the building up of a strong organization among the female workers.[11]

Perhaps in response, Elizabeth Gurley Flynn tried that same year to bring into being a "live group" to do "propaganda among women."[12] Again, nothing happened. Two years later, Frank Little, the half-Indian organizer soon to be lynched by vigilantes, suggested that a "special literature be created for women workers, that space for articles concerning female workers be provided in our papers, and that a league for women, with lecturers, be formed to carry on a special agitation for the benefit of women."[13] Once again, there were no results. The IWW strategy for women remained one of workplace organizing alone. In a period where relatively few women worked outside the home, this strategy was bound to affect its ability to organize women. It never solved the organizational problems involved in recruiting housewives; the IWW charter, in fact, stated that only wage earners were eligible for membership. Another irate letter to the *Industrial Union Bulletin* from Sophie Beldner in 1908 asked what this meant the organization thought of working-class housewives:

1. Is a married woman of the working class a chattel slave or a wage slave?
2. Has she the right to belong to a mixed local of the IWW?

I ask these questions because objection has been raised by some members of the Denver local to the effect that a married woman, a housekeeper, has no right to belong to a workingmen's organization. . . .

Some assert that we have no grievance against the capitalist class, therefore we have no place in the union. Our grievance is against our husbands, if we are dissatisfied with our condition.

I believe the married woman of the working class is no parasite or exploiter. She is a social producer. In order to sustain herself, she has to sell her labor power, either in the factory, directly to the capitalist, or at home, indirectly, by serving the wage slave, her husband, thus keeping him in working condition through cooking, washing and general housekeeping.

For being a mother and a housekeeper are two different functions. One is her maternal, and the other is her industrial function in society. I believe the wage slave's wife has got a right to belong to a mixed local. I think it should be encouraging for working men to see women enter their ranks and, shoulder to shoulder, fight for economic freedom.

Civilization denies us the right of expressing our political opinion at the ballot box. Will the economic organization, the IWW, our only hope, exclude us and deny us the right to record our discontent against the capitalist system?[14]

The editor replied that he could see no reason why a married woman could not belong to a mixed local (a local of workers from more than one industry), but that he had no idea what would become of housewives once the mixed local had enough members from the various industries to divide into industrial unions. "It is a matter to which the next convention will give attention,"[15] he wrote—but the next convention did not deal with it.

As we have already seen, it was a widespread fallacy in the working-class movement that workingmen's conditions were declining because women were going into the factories and driving down wages. In the socialist movement this took the form of saying that while women had to be wage slaves under capitalism, after the revolution they would be able to return to their happy homes and would not have to work for wages any more. One female IWW member wrote a spirited rebuttal to this fantasy in 1910:

Fellow Worker Man Toiler: You say you want us girls to keep out of the factory and mill so you can get more pay then you can marry some of us and give us a decent home. Now, that is just what we are trying to escape; being obliged to marry you for a home. And aren't you a little inconsistent? You tell us to get into the IWW, an organization for wage workers only? We haven't heard of any Household Drudge's Union, not even in the IWW. Going from the factory back into the home means only a change in the form of servitude, a change for the worse for the woman. The best thing that ever happened to woman was when she was compelled to leave the narrow limits of the home and enter into the industrial life of the world. This is the only road to our freedom, and to BE FREE there is not anything to be desired more than that. . . . So we will stay in the factory, mill, or store and organize with you in the IWW for ownership of the industries, so we can provide ourselves with decent homes, then if we marry you it will be because we love you so well we can't get along without you, and not to give you a chance to pay our bills, like we do now.[16]

Despite such polemics, there were never sufficient numbers of women within the IWW to mount a sustained recruitment campaign for women. Although the records do not indicate percentages by sex, many locals seem to have had only one or two women members, with women sympathizers grouped more loosely around them. But these members were too isolated to have much impact on the organization as a whole, and there were very few women in leadership they could look to for support. The IWW had only three women organizers: Lillian Forberg, very briefly in 1907; Matilda Robbins (Rabinowitz), between 1913 and 1916; and most importantly, Elizabeth Gurley Flynn, between 1908 and the 1920s, who took a special interest in the oppression of women and frequently wrote and spoke on the subject.

One barrier to organizing women into the IWW was the organization's composition. Although it focused everywhere on those dispossessed workers the AFL rejected—the unskilled, immigrants, blacks, Asians, migrants—there were crucial differences between the East Coast and West Coast membership, and it was the West that was dominant. Charles Ashleigh, an English-born member, explained these differences:

In the eastern industries women and children are employed. It is common for a whole family to be working in the same mill, plant or factory. This makes for family life; a debased and deteriorated family life, it is true . . . but nevertheless, marriage, the procreation of children and some amount of stability are assured by the conditions of the industry. . . .

As we journey westward we mark a change. We leave the zone of great industry and enter country in which capitalism is still, to some extent, in the preparatory stage. . . . All of these three principal occupations of the unskilled workers of the Pacific coast—lumber, construction work and agriculture—are periodical in their nature. . . . The result of this is the existence on the coast of an immense army of unskilled or semi-skilled workers, of no fixed abode, who are forever engaged in an eternal chase for the elusive job. . . .

The striking feature of the Pacific country is that it is a man's country. Conditions render it impossible for the worker to marry. Long terms in isolated camps produce the same phenomena of sex perversion as exist in the army, navy and monastery. The worker is doomed to celibacy with all its physical and moral damaging results. The brothel in the town, between jobs, is the only resort.[17]

Many Western Wobblies felt that their lack of family and job ties made them the vanguard of the working class, the "militant minority" that would lead the downtrodden, hagridden masses of the East to freedom. As one put it:

The nomadic worker of the West embodies the very spirit of the IWW. His cheerful cynicism, his frank and outspoken contempt for most of the conventions of bourgeois society, make him an admirable exemplar of the iconoclastic doctrine of revolutionary unionism. . . . He promptly shakes the dust of a locality from his feet whenever the board is bad, or the boss is too exacting, or the work unduly tiresome, departing for the next job. . . . No wife or family encumber him. . . . Nowhere else can a section of the working class be found so admirably fitted to serve as the scouts and advance guards of the labor army.[18]

Other Wobblies disagreed, feeling that the organization would be stronger when its vanguard members learned to stay on the job, pointing to the example of the Lawrence strike, where "the workers who were oppressed the most fought the hardest and stood the brunt of the battle—the women, encumbered with babes and husbands."[19]

When the Western Wobblies did attempt to organize women, their lack of familiarity with the living conditions of most women workers sometimes made their approach very odd indeed. The author of the following appeal seems to have believed that there were hundreds of footloose rebel girls wandering about the land, jumping freight trains in search of work:

> We need you women workers. If you have decided to spend the winter on the Pacific coast, come to Seattle and help us organize the women houseworkers!
>
> Agitate in a quiet way. Make the public employment office your headquarters and spread the union idea. Discontent is great among women here, and liable to come to the surface at any moment. We need you, and badly, to exploit this discontent.
>
> Remember that the value of organization—industrial unionism— is the most necessary lesson the women workers of Seattle need. Birth control and other side issues will regulate themselves, once the I.W.W. has job control in the industries, and then only.[20]

Faced with this level of male incomprehension, it is a wonder that there were female locals in the West, especially since the organization's ideas about solidarity discouraged separation along sex lines. Nevertheless, in one of the more curious chapters of U.S. labor history, the housemaids of Denver organized themselves under the leadership of Jane Street in 1916.

Domestics were traditionally the most isolated and subservient of workers, tucked away in the attics and basements of the rich, unable to leave the house except for an afternoon once every two weeks, with mistresses who acted like parents and spies as well as employers. Such working conditions bred resentment, but it was seldom expressed in collective action; more often, domestic workers flitted from job to job, in a pattern known among employers as "the servant problem."

Jane Street, an independent-minded Colorado domestic worker, felt that of all the kinds of labor, hers bore "the deepest taint of chattel slavery handed down from the time when it was a disgrace for a member of the master class to lace his own boots." She was determined to give the "ladies on the hill" in Denver a real servant problem by building a union of modern revolutionary house-maids who "don't believe in mistresses or servants. They would do away with caste altogether. They believe in removing the degra-dation from domestic service by teaching their employers to look upon the hands that feed them and wash for them, and scrub for them with respect or fear and humility."[21]

By March 19, 1916, after three months of intensive organizing, Jane Street had contacted enough domestic workers to hold a secret mass meeting, where they spoke of their grievances and formulated demands for the future: $12 a week, no work on Sundays, shorter hours, and better treatment. In a letter to a fellow Wobbly woman, Jane Street described the way she had gone about organizing this meeting:

> My method was very tedious. I worked at housework for three months, collecting names all the while. When I was off of a job I rented a room and put an ad in the paper for a housemaid. Sometimes I used a box number and sometimes I used my address. The ad was worded something like this, "Wanted, Housemaid for private family, $30, eight hours daily." [This was an unusually high wage.] I would write them letters afterwards and have them call and see me. If they came direct, I would usually have another ad in the same paper, advertising for a situation and using my telephone number. I would have enough answers to supply the applicants. Sometimes I would engage myself to as many as 25 jobs in one day, promising to call the next day to everyone who phoned. . . .
>
> I secured 300 names in this way. I had never mentioned the I.W.W. to any of them, for I expected them to be prejudiced, which did not prove the case. I picked out 100 of the most promising of the names and sent them invitations to attend a meeting. There were about thirty-five came. Thirteen of the thirty-five signed the application for a charter.[22]

The new local had several tactics for raising wages and bettering conditions. It planned to build up a card file of all domestic jobs in Denver and make this information available to anyone looking for work. It would thus act as its own employment bureau and drive the "employment sharks" out of business. It would focus on recalcitrant employers, making it impossible for them to get help unless they met the union's demands. And it would start its own boarding house, an organizing center where women could stay and leave their baggage while they looked for work. Jane Street was confident of success; as she told her fellow workers, "You have one great advantage over your mistress. She must have you in her home. She won't wash her own dishes. You can get your rights by working on the individual woman."[23]

The local at first met with great success. Its list of jobs grew from 300 in March to 2,000 in May and 6,000 in November.[24] When there was an advertisement for a maid, dozens of "union maids" would respond and demand the same price until the prospective employer was convinced that it was the going rate. The union also took up the IWW's militant language and tactics, including the threat of sabotage: "It is almost uncanny the way dishes slip out of that girl's hands," reported the *Rocky Mountain News*. "Picture father putting on his favorite soft shirt to find that the new laundress 'sabotaged' it by using plenty of starch."[25] Another weapon was the use of songs, such as "The Maids' Defiance":

> We've answered all your door bells and we've washed your dirty kids,
> For lo, these many weary years we've done as we were bid,
> But we're going to fight for freedom and for our rights we'll stand.
> And we're going to stick together in one big Union band.
>
> CHORUS
> It's a long day for housemaid Mary, it's a long day's hard toil.
> It's a burden too hard to carry, so our mistresses' schemes we'll foil.
> For we're out for a shorter day this summer
> Or we'll fix old Denver town.
>
> We've washed your dirty linen and we've cooked your daily foods;
> We've eaten in your kitchens, and we've stood your ugly moods.
> But now we've joined the Union and organized to stay,
> The cooks and maids and chauffeurs, in one grand array.
>
> CHORUS[26]

As the local grew stronger, opposition began to come from the rich women of Denver, seconded on one side by the YWCA and on the other by employment bureaus whose businesses the union had destroyed. The YWCA urged the housemaids to join its ranks instead of the union. The employers organized their own group, called the Housewives' Assembly. According to the IWW it was

made up largely of the female politicians and members of the
Colorado Law and Order League, an organization formed during
the Colorado coal strike of two years ago to oppose the coal miners
in their fight against Rockefellerism and wage slavery. They are the
same gang of society parasites that applauded the Colorado National Guard and lionized its officers after they had massacred
women and children of Ludlow.[27]

The methods used by the employment sharks were more devastating. When the local had first organized, the employment
agencies had descended upon its meetings in pursuit of "white
slaves" for the whorehouses of the Far West. The girls appealed
to their fellow workers in the IWW mixed local in Denver, who
rose to the challenge with enthusiasm and "foiled the white slavers
and drove them away from our meetings. These fellow workers,
though repeatedly threatened with bodily violence at the hands
of the gang of white slavers, stood their ground and defended
the girls."[28] But the underworld was not defeated so easily. In
November 1916, the "sharks" raided the union's office and cap-
tured its card file of employers:

> The robbery occurred in the early morning when Secretary Jane
> Street had stepped out of the office to go to the wash room on the
> floor above. Fellow Worker Street had been sleeping in the head-
> quarters at night with a "gatt" under her pillow and a section of gas
> pipe within easy reach guarding against just such an occurrence.
> She locked the door when leaving and upon her return found the
> list gone with the exception of a few cards scattered over the floor
> that the thief had apparently been in too great haste to pick up.[29]

The loss of the card file was a serious setback, but it did not
destroy the local. A year later Jane Street wrote a fellow organizer
in Tulsa that they had moved into a new office and were growing
stronger every day.[30] And the union was spreading across the
country: domestic workers in Salt Lake City organized in June 1916,
followed by those in Duluth, Chicago, Cleveland, and Seattle.[31]
Until World War I and the accompanying repression of the IWW
interrupted the union's progress, its future looked bright indeed.

Although male Wobblies had been willing to defend the women
from white slavers, the question of sexuality divided the Denver
IWW itself, as it did the labor and revolutionary movements as a

whole. Some members of the IWW mixed local appeared to believe that the domestic workers' local was there to provide them with girlfriends and were enraged when they were barred from the women's clubhouse. They were no doubt outraged to begin with by the existence of an all-female local, a deviation from the IWW norm. Jane Street thought their objections more personal than principled, as she wrote a fellow Wobbly woman in 1917:

> I would advise you strongly against trying to have your head-quarters in connection with the other I.W.W. local there. . . . Sex can come rushing into your office like a great hurricane and blow all the papers of industrialism out the window.
>
> The Mixed Local here in Denver has done us more harm than any other enemy, the women of Capital Hill, the employment sharks and the Y.W.C.A. combined. They have cut us off from donations from outside locals, slandered this local and myself from one end of the country to the other, tried to disrupt us from within by going among the girls and stirring up trouble, they gave our clubhouse a bad name because they were not permitted to come out there, and finally they have assaulted me bodily and torn up our charter.[32]

At the beginning of the century issues of sexual behavior were perhaps more controversial than any others. The IWW was considerably more radical in its sexual ideas and analysis of society than was the population at large, but in a period when the sexual double standard was rigidly enforced and the penalty for straying was frequently devastating for women, "sexual freedom" was bound to be more expensive for them than for men.[33] This is vividly revealed in the memoirs of Chicago cloakmaker Abraham Bisno. One passage describes the aftermath of an affair he had with the wife of a comrade whose husband encouraged the romance. His experience of the affair was completely different from the woman's, as he points out, because of the different opportunities available to them:

> A friendship between men and women is not only a friendship but also a sex act, which in my opinion is essential to the friendship. Once [there was] a real friendship, the natural consequence would be a sex life together and to be honest with oneself, sex satiation. . . .
> I therefore made approaches to my woman friends with no moral

compunctions and no sense of that conduct being binding for
continuity, while the effect on my friend's wife was different. It was
an experience of an instinct acquiesced in because of my pressure as
well as her husband's. Once the experience was over, she needed
continuity because her field of opportunity was so limited as compared with mine or that of her husband. . . . She was hungry for me
as well as lonesome, while I loved her just the same but loved others
and was neither hungry nor lonesome. That situation which was
not the same for her as for me formed a feeling of resentment in
her. I had done her an injury, the result of which caused her great
suffering. I had done myself no injury at all, the result of which only
left in me a pleasant memory of a very comfortable experience.[34]

Sexual radicalism was all too frequently a mask for sexual
opportunism among men. As one socialist wrote in the *New York
Sunday Call* in 1911:

Certain party members, principally males, either believe or profess
to believe that they have "advanced" ideas concerning love and
marriage. Reduced to essentials, these theories generally indicate
that the men in question do all in their power to escape marriage,
but persistently exert every effort to have as many love affairs
as possible.
    These men are not novices at all in the art of interesting bright
young girls intellectually. The girl's interest once enlisted . . . the
"advanced" theories are trotted out. . . . More often than not her
surrender is brought about because she is made to believe that she
has been ungenerous—taking all and giving nothing.[35]

Such bitter observations were supported by the testimony of some
of the men. Floyd Dell, a Greenwich Village writer, described the
way his fellow bohemians dealt with a woman's guilt feelings
about engaging in premarital, or "free," sex:

There were three ways in which these feelings of guilt were com-
monly exorcised—first, and most completely of all, by the emotions
of self-sacrifice. . . . Any tenth-rate free-verse poet could find a
capable and efficient girl stenographer to type his manuscripts, buy
his meals and his clothes, pay his rent and sleep with him; the
maternal emotion sufficed instead of a marriage ceremony. . . .
The other spiritual hocus-pocus which sufficed instead of a wedding-
ring to give a girl a good conscience, seemed to consist in quotations

and arguments from Edward Carpenter, Havelock Ellis, and other modern prophets, arguments designed to show that love without marriage was infinitely superior to the other kind, and that its immediate indulgence brought the world, night by night, a little nearer to freedom and Utopia.[36]

Some women did take up the cause of sexual radicalism. Emma Goldman and Margaret Sanger espoused free, expressive sexuality for women as well as for men, reinforced by the protection of birth control. The few women in leadership positions in the IWW were also able to be unconventional, even anticonventional, in their love lives: Elizabeth Gurley Flynn lived for many years with Italian anarchist Carlo Tresca, who had a wife and children elsewhere; Matilda Robbins had a protracted, difficult relationship with Ben Legere, a fellow Wobbly, who was also married with children. When asked her opinion of "free love," Elizabeth Gurley Flynn exclaimed magnificently, "What is the other alternative? slave-love? Then I believe in *free* love, at all costs."[37] But not all women in the IWW felt similarly. In 1915 a rank-and-file woman, Mrs. Floyd Hyde, wrote *Solidarity* expressing her concern about propaganda favoring free love:

> Once on the other side of what present day society considers decency, the woman who has taken this step is not only branded by the world as lewd, but she has lost her guide post of experience which leads to a well organized personality. She has launched herself out into the world with a lot of abstract, aimless ideas which tend to disintegrate all her organized effort. She is shifted here and there by the impulse of her emotions, till more often the end is, that she sinks beneath the swell of her passions, ruined, lost.[38]

Ben Williams, the editor of *Solidarity*, responded like a good dialectical materialist:

> The ethical code of the future society will not spring full-blown with the advent of that society. On the contrary, it finds its roots immediately in the general movement of today whose goal is economic freedom. And just as there are political and industrial martyrs to the cause of the new society, so there have been, are, and doubtless will be, sex martyrs to the cause of the new morality whose full fruition can only result from the economic freedom of woman.

He added however, that this was something each woman had to decide for herself, and a "mere man" was not justified in "butting in" with advice.[39]

Mrs. Floyd Hyde responded that, unfortunately, men were "butting in" and insisting on being paid sexually for teaching women about politics and admitting them as equals into the revolutionary movement:

> Since the days of the hetaerae [courtesans], or freed women of Greece, men have demanded a price for all these new interests [of women]. Woman must pay with her sex for all she receives. These women of Greece became poets, artists, and learned in political affairs, while their virtuous sisters remained ignorant slaves to the men for whom they bore children, but these women of hetaerae were public women. If one of these women had reserved her right of choice she would have been thrown out from her world of opportunity. So we find women of today with broad minds, hungering for the social intercourse of other minds congenial with theirs, giving their sex as the price of this association. Not because their sex feeling has become so strong that they must exhaust it in this manner, but because they are willing to sacrifice their sex feelings to supply their intellectual demands.
>
> It is the innate disposition of every man to expect a woman to pay with her sex for all the benefits she receives from him, social, intellectual, or otherwise. The woman who refuses to pay this price, but battles in the face of it for her place in the intellectual world, has a harder battle to fight than if she committed the usual social sin.[40]

Women like Elizabeth Gurley Flynn tended to overlook such problems—at least until they impinged upon their own personal lives—and sometimes spoke as if sexual freedom, once a woman was financially independent, could be accomplished by an individual exercise of will:

> The only sex problem I know is how are women to control themselves, how be free, so that love alone shall be the commandment to act, and I can see but one way, through controlling their one problem of how to live, be fed and clothed—their own economic lives. . . . Sexual enslavement . . . follows economic enslavement, and is but a gentle way of saying prostitution, whether it be for one night or one whole life.[41]

The disjunction between the views of Elizabeth Gurley Flynn and Mrs. Floyd Hyde are one aspect of the difference between the few women who became leaders in the IWW and the masses of women who had some relationship to the organization. The demands on all IWW leadership were severe in terms of poverty and risk, and these were particularly hard on women; a defiance of conventional sexual morality was but one item in a list of particulars that made the life of the organizer strikingly separate from that of most working-class women. Women organizers who traveled for the trade unions, the Women's Trade Union League, and the Socialist Party faced similar problems: few had stable marriages, few had young children. Being an organizer for the IWW was, however, far more hazardous than any of these because of the explicitly revolutionary character of the organization, which was from its inception under attack by employers, local police and vigilantes, the federal government, and the Pinkertons, not to mention the AFL. Certainly no woman with a traditional family life could have been a full-time IWW organizer. If Elizabeth Gurley Flynn had not had a devoted mother and sister who cared for her baby after her marriage broke up, for instance, she could never have gone on the road as she did, while Matilda Robbins gave up her job after she had a child, although she had additional reasons for doing so, and saw her life as a struggle between her political commitment and her unhappy but demanding love affair.

Elizabeth Gurley Flynn did her best to develop an understanding of the oppression of women that went beyond the general economism of the IWW, but she was isolated in an organization with so few active women in it, and found little support for this aspect of her work. Her interest in feminist issues was, however, encouraged by her friends in the Heterodoxy Club, a consciousness-raising organization that was founded by Marie Jenney Howe in 1912 and lasted into the 1930s; the only membership qualification was that one had to be a woman with unorthodox opinions. As Elizabeth Gurley Flynn described the club's luncheon discussions, their effect on her point of view was considerable:

The subjects dealt mainly with women and their accomplishments. All the members were ardent suffragists, some were quite extreme feminists. All were people in their own right in many and various fields of endeavor. No one was there because her husband or father was famous. . . . I had worked almost exclusively with men up to this time and my IWW antipolitical slant had kept me away from political movements. It was good for my education and a broadening influence for me to come to know all these splendid "Heterodoxy" members and to share in their enthusiasms. It made me conscious of women and their many accomplishments.[42]

Inez Haynes Irwin, a writer and militant suffragist, recalled some of the discussions at the Heterodoxy Club in her unpublished autobiography:

Sprinkled among meetings came a series of what we called "background" talks. A member told whatever she chose to reveal about her childhood, girlhood, and young womanhood. They ranged in atmosphere from the middle-western farm on which Leta Hollingsworth's childhood was spent, where all her dresses were made from flour bags which had the manufacturer's name printed on them, through a life of inherited rebelliousness, like that of Charlotte Perkins Gilman; from the cool, faded elegance of the great house on the Hudson, in which Alice Duer Miller was raised; to the fiery shadow of Emma Goldman, in which Stella Comen Ballantine—who was her niece and adoring partisan—lived, was brought up on the theory of philosophic anarchy and listened to the discussion of all the rebellious movements in the world. . . .

I have never listened to such talks as these backgrounds. . . . A statement of one of our members immediately gave me to think. She was telling simply but frankly the story of her love affair and her marriage. She ended: "But I would not have married him if I had not lived with him for a year to find out whether or not I cared enough for him to marry him." This was the first time that I had ever heard any woman make a statement that, in my childhood and girlhood would have been described as "compromising." . . . But later I reflected with a great surge of feministic triumph that most of the women in Heterodoxy were—through their own efforts—economically independent. Many of them with established and impregnable reputations. They were as independent of their own "compromising confession" as any man.[43]

If her ties with women outside the organization helped Elizabeth Gurley Flynn to maintain her concern with women's liberation during her years in the IWW, her own background and parentage were an even greater influence. Annie Flynn, her mother, was an extraordinary woman, an Irish revolutionary and member of the Knights of Labor who had supported her entire family as a tailor when she was young and who continued to work even after she married and had children. This was extremely unusual at the time, as was her insistence on having only female doctors during her pregnancies. Annie Flynn hated "household drudgery," as she called washing, ironing, dishwashing, and cleaning; she preferred to read and go to lectures in her spare time. A poem that Elizabeth Gurley Flynn clipped and pasted in her scrapbook when she was fifteen expressed her own views on the subject:

> From a kitchen, good Lord, deliver me!
> And from sweeping and scrubbing dirty floors,
> Rescue me, O Lord, from eternally washing dishes and baking little
>   paltry messes!
> From building little insignificant stove-fires, and churning with an
>   insignificant little churn O save me!
> And from dusting useless furniture! And moving around other
>   useless property! And doing things on a small scale.
> Lord, I would fain give all this work to machinery, and of what that
>   cannot do I will willingly do my share![44]

Other women associated with the IWW thought it was terrible that Elizabeth Gurley Flynn was not better at housework because it made her one-sided, a defect caused by too early and too exclusive an immersion in movement work.[45] They did not, needless to say, make the same criticism of male agitators.

If Elizabeth Gurley Flynn got her feminism from her mother, she got her outspokenness and her love of travel from her father, Tom Flynn, a stone quarrier from New Hampshire who had lost the sight of one eye and most of his male relatives to the quarries. Determined to get out while he could, he passed the entrance examinations to Dartmouth College and began to train as an engineer. Although he had to leave school before completing his degree in order to support his brothers and sisters, Tom Flynn was able to find work in this profession—on and off. He was always losing his jobs, however; either the company failed or he was fired for his outspoken views on such issues as the Spanish-American war. He understood imperialism because he knew how the British had treated Ireland; he was an early member of the Anti-Imperialist League, which opposed the growing overseas involvement of the United States, and to the day of his death he never mentioned the word "England" without adding "God damn her!"

Because he kept losing jobs, the Flynn family moved around a lot, going from New Hampshire to Ohio to Massachusetts to New York City. There, in 1900, Annie Flynn put her foot down and said she would go no further. She had four schoolage children who needed to stay put.

The Flynn family moved into a cold water railroad flat in the South Bronx, where the only heat came from the stove. A few years later they moved to another tenement a few blocks away, at 511 East 134th Street, where they remained for the next twenty-seven years. There they fought the usual heroic battles of the poor against roaches and rats, dark and dirt, hunger and cold. They had only one set of underwear each, and Annie Flynn had to wash all of it each night. Elizabeth Gurley Flynn always felt that it was their extreme poverty, along with their Irish background, that made them receptive to the socialist ideas they encountered in New York.

The Flynns got door-to-door leaflets about Sunday night forums being given in Harlem by the Socialist Labor Party, and the family began to attend. Elizabeth took to these events like a duck to water, but the other children—Tom, Kathy, and Bina—were too young. They would go to sleep on the benches that lined the walls and wake up at refreshment time.

To all the Flynns, but especially to Elizabeth and her father, Marxism came like a light, making sense of everything that had happened to them. As Elizabeth Gurley Flynn wrote later:

> When I began to accumulate scientific Socialist literature, my father seized upon it. He read everthing by Marx and Engels he could lay his hands on. His knowledge of mathematics helped him to master them easily. He read them aloud to his family. He talked and argued about them with anyone who would listen—in the saloon, in the park, on the job. Scientific Socialism came as a balm to my

father's spirit. It exposed the capitalist system in all its ugly naked greed, and its indifference to human welfare. It showed how it enriched the few and impoverished the masses of people. It explained what caused depression, "bad times," economic crises.[46]

She was reading avidly herself, gulping down Edward Bellamy's *Looking Backward*, Kropotkin, Upton Sinclair's *The Jungle*, as well as *The Communist Manifesto* and other works by Karl Marx and Friederich Engels. She read widely on the position of women, especially Mary Wollstonecraft and August Bebel's *Woman and Socialism*, the main theoretical work at that time.[47] Someone at the Harlem Socialist Club heard that she was on her high school debating team and invited her to make a speech at one of their forums. Her mother encouraged her, but her father was against it; he disapproved of women speaking at meetings and also felt he should have been asked to speak instead. She compromised by choosing a topic her father would think too unimportant to be jealous about—"What Socialism Will Do for Women"—and made her first public speech on January 31, 1906. She was sixteen, in a short schoolgirl dress that came down just to the top of her boots, with her hair streaming down her back like Alice in Wonderland. Her speech was not childish, however. She blamed the oppression of women on organized religion, culture, and laws, as well as on women's lack of education and submissiveness. One of the high points of her speech was an attack on the idea of chivalry:

> Men cant of chivalry, they carry a little bundle or umbrella for a woman, but seldom carry a baby. They give up a seat to a fast, gaudily-dressed butterfly woman, but let a poor working girl stand, they take the pretty girls home from a party or club while the less attractive ones must trot off alone, they tell their wives of their simpering, silly adoration for them, but clasp their pocketbooks with an iron hand, they are willing to do all the foolish little nothings that a sensible woman doesn't want, but refuse to give us our rights, and they talk of chivalry. . . .
>
> I do not argue that woman is higher than man, but I do argue she is his equal. She is to the man and the man is to her as the two parts of a pair of shears are to each other. Together they are useful, separately they are worthless, but they are equal.[48]

At about this time, she cut out another poem for her scrapbook,

"The New Woman" by Elizabeth Cardozo, which describes a cold feminist who works for social progress and looks down on love as unimportant. The poem ends with her stepping down from her pedestal to "forfeit all just to look up and love." Elizabeth Gurley Flynn scribbled in the margin in red ink: "Don't do it! Don't *look up* to *any* man!"[49]

In the summer of 1906 she began to talk from a soapbox near Times Square and at the corner of Seventh Avenue and 128th Street in Harlem. The press made much of her youth, her extremism, and her loveliness. In August she was arrested for blocking traffic at 38th Street and Broadway. The judge discharged her, suggesting that she should finish high school before trying to teach others. Her previously straight-A record was going downhill fast, however, as a result of nightly meetings. She was sick of school, which she criticized in one of her speeches for divorcing theory and practice, preparing for college rather than life and work, and giving too much homework.

She began to frequent radical meetings on the Lower East Side, where everyone was talking of the revolution then going on in Russia, and she went to her first mass demonstration, protesting the czar's massacre of 1,500 workers on Bloody Sunday, 1905. Soon she was swept up in the agitation around the trial of the officers of the Western Federation of Miners (Haywood, Moyer, and Pettibone), who were being held in Colorado on murder charges as part of an effort to break up their union. At one meeting, she met Irish revolutionary James Connolly, later martyred during the 1916 Easter uprising. He was living in New York, publishing *The Harp* to publicise the struggle for Irish freedom, and organizing for the IWW on the docks. Through Connolly and the Haywood-Moyer-Pettibone trial she learned of the work of the IWW, which she joined in 1906. Although IWW bylaws restricted membership to wage earners, she, like other women, was allowed to join because the organization needed women, because of her youth and working-class background, and because she did full-time movement work.

Her local elected her as its delegate to the national convention in Chicago in 1907. It was her first train trip alone and she was terribly excited, expecially when she made a speaking tour in the

West after the convention. From then on high school seemed duller and duller, and she became increasingly unable to tolerate her father's attempts to run her life.

She began corresponding with Jack Jones, an IWW organizer in the Mesabi iron mines that she had met at the convention. He was a handsome man in his early thirties, a man of action who seemed exciting compared to the New York intellectuals she knew. When he invited her to speak on the Mesabi range in December 1907, she quit school over her mother's protests and was off. A few weeks later she married him. She was seventeen. As Vincent St. John, then filling the IWW leadership post of General Organizer, joked, "Elizabeth fell in love with the west and the miners and married the first one she met."[50]

No sooner were they married than Jones was arrested on a phony dynamite charge. Though he was released, he lost his job. He found another working on the Duluth railroad tunnel and brought Tom Flynn to work there as an engineer, but both men did so much on-the-job agitation that they were quickly fired. Elizabeth Gurley Flynn recalled:

> All three of us went to New York, and I can see my mother's pale face as this unemployed army appeared with suitcases full of dirty clothes. It was a hard summer. We were all very poor. The men remained out of work.
>
> My mother resented Jones' presence. She felt he should not have married me, so young a girl, so far away from home, without the knowledge of her parents, though she felt guilty for letting me go alone. She hated poverty and large families and was fearful that my life would become a replica of her own. It was bad enough to have one man around the house out of work, spouting ideas and reading books while she toiled to keep our small crowded quarters clean and make ends meet—but to have two of them was just too much. It was an unhappy time for all of us.[51]

Jones became restless in this situation and the couple moved to Chicago to look for work. She was already pregnant. They moved into a rooming house where two other IWW members, Joe Ettor and Ben Williams, also lived; they were all very poor, living on free barroom lunches, but they managed to get an egg and some milk every day for Elizabeth Gurley Flynn because of her "delicate condition." Nevertheless, poor nutrition probably contributed to the death of her baby, which was born prematurely. Both she and Jones were grief-stricken. Vincent St. John came to their aid: he found Jones a job in the West and sent Elizabeth Gurley Flynn on her first cross-country tour as a paid organizer. They were reunited in Missoula, Montana, where she became pregnant again.

At this time the IWW was trying to organize Western migratory workers in the employment centers of the logging industry, the railroads, the fields, and the mines. They did this by speaking on street corners in the transient workers' districts. To prevent such organizing, the Missoula city government outlawed street-speaking in 1908, and the IWW tested the law in mass civil disobedience campaigns similar to those of the civil rights movement of the 1960s:

> We sent out a call to all "foot-loose rebels to come at once—to defend the Bill of Rights." A steady stream of I.W.W. members began to flock in, by freight cars—on top, inside and below. As soon as one speaker was arrested, another took his place. The jail was soon filled and the cellar under the firehouse turned into an additional jail. But the excrement from the horses leaked through and made this place so unbearable that the I.W.W. prisoners protested by song and speech, night and day. They were directly across the street from the city's main hotel and the guests complained of the uproar. The court was nearby and its proceedings were disrupted by the noise. . . .
>
> Eventually, the townspeople got tired of the unfavorable publicity and excitement. The taxpayers were complaining of the cost to the little city. . . . An amusing tussle then ensued between the I.W.W. and the authorities as to who should feed our army. We held our meetings early so the men would go to jail before supper. The police began to turn them out the next morning before breakfast. . . .
>
> Finally, the authorities gave up. All cases were dropped. We were allowed to resume our meetings. We returned to our peaceful pursuit of agitating and organizing the I.W.W.[52]

Elizabeth Gurley Flynn did not remain in Missoula long, for another free speech fight began in Spokane, Washington, and she was called off to help—despite her pregnancy and the disapproval of her husband, who would not go with her or even visit her. He thought it was time for her to start acting like a normal wife.

Spokane was the center of all the industries in the Pacific Northwest that used migrant labor. After picking the crops or laying rail in the summer, the workers would come into Spokane to spend their pay in its cheap flophouses, bars, and brothels, and then proceed to the local employment agencies to find new jobs. These agencies were run by racketeers, or "sharks." The workers would have to pay a shark a commission to learn where the job was, usually the distance of a day's travel or more from the city. When he got there, however, the worker would find that the job did not exist; or he might be fired after a day or two so that the shark could send out another worker and split the commission with the foreman. The individual worker, without a union or legal protection or other means of finding work, would have to travel back to Spokane and try again. Consequently, Spokane had a large skid row area full of angry workers who were receptive to the IWW's call.

The sharks were also the major organizers of prostitution in the Northwest. In 1908 C. F. Sebring, an officer of Peerless Agency, was convicted of shipping out fourteen- to sixteen-year-old girls for the purpose of prostitution. The scandal implicated a number of other agencies as well, but, as the IWW speculated, since only one man was brought to trial and the city clearly knew what was going on, Sebring "may have been imprudent or lacked money."[53] The IWW local concentrated on the sharks' abuses, urging the workers to come to the union hiring hall instead of the employment agencies. It gathered recruits by street corner speaking and by the spring of 1909 it had at least twelve hundred members and was publishing its own paper, the *Industrial Worker*.[54] In March 1909, the city council, acting on complaints from the sharks and the chamber of commerce, passed a law against street speaking by anyone but the Salvation Army, on the grounds that the IWW was attacking religion and government. The IWW responded with its usual tactic: a free speech campaign, as soon as the heavy work seasons of spring and summer were over. On October 25, James Thompson was arrested for speaking without a permit. On November 1, the union began continuous soapboxing, with a new speaker replacing each one who was arrested. A police raid on the IWW hiring hall caught whatever leadership was there, including the editors of the paper. Four hundred people were arrested during the first week in October. Most were sentenced to thirty days; when they were released they spoke again and got another thirty days—those whose health could stand more than one stay in the Spokane jails, that is. Spokane's treatment of IWW prisoners was designed to kill or maim rather than to punish by due process or reform. Groups of twenty-eight men would be forced into a seven-by-eight foot cell, called a "sweat box"; it took four policemen to push the door shut. Then the police would turn up the steam heat until the men passed out, after which they were put in ice-cold cells and given the third degree, including brutal beatings. Three men died after their discharge from the Spokane jail and many were permanently injured.[55]

Elizabeth Gurley Flynn spent only one night in the jail before the IWW raised bail for her, even though it was set unusually high because of her fame as a class warrior. Her comrades were concerned about her health as well as her safety, for she was noticeably pregnant. Although she felt she could be more useful out of jail than in, she rather resented her comrades' solicitude, feeling that they were "fussy old guys" who were motivated as much by prudery as by concern.[56] This was a period in which pregnant women were not supposed to be seen outside their homes but were to emerge after nine months bearing an infant who had arrived by mysterious means. A number of men in the Spokane local felt that it did not look nice for her to be seen speaking and worried that she might have her baby right on the platform; they had restricted her activities to out-of-town fundraising meetings and to work on the paper.

Elizabeth Gurley Flynn used her night in jail to tremendous effect for the IWW; her story was picked up coast to coast. She had been put in a cell with two prostitutes. In the middle of the night, the warden came and took the younger one out of the cell. She was gone for a long time, and it appeared that she had been taken downstairs to see a "sweetheart"; she was later taken out to visit another and subsequently explained that a third man would have been brought to her cell except that the warden did not entirely trust the new prisoner. "Taking a woman prisoner out of her cell at the dead hours of night several times to visit sweethearts looked to me as if she were practicing her profession inside of jail as well as out."[57] As a result of Flynn's revelations, the Spokane feminist movement got involved in improving jail conditions and a matron was installed in the jail for the first time.

Money poured into the IWW, and the Spokane free speech fight ended in victory for the union, although at a considerable cost in health and life. The city was spending $1,000 a day on repression, but this campaign showed no signs of destroying the IWW. When a negotiating committee went to see the mayor, he agreed to stop enforcing the anti–free speech law and to let the IWW reopen its hiring hall, sell its paper, and hold street corner meetings in the near future. The city also revoked the licenses of the worst of the employment sharks and released IWW members who were in prison. The Wobblies could now organize migrant workers in Spokane.

When the Spokane struggle ended, Jones came to get his wife. He demanded that she give up speaking and traveling and live in one place with the baby and him. But she did not want to settle down:

> A domestic life and possibly a large family had no attractions for me. My mother's aversion to both had undoubtedly affected me profoundly. She was strong for her girls "being somebody" and "having a life of their own." I wanted to speak and write, to travel, to meet people, to see places, to organize for the I.W.W. I saw no reason why I, as a woman, should give up my work for this. I knew by now I could make more of a contribution to the labor movement than he could. I would not give up. I have had many heartaches and emotional conflicts along the way but always my determination to stick to my self-appointed task has triumphed. But it wasn't easy in 1910.[58]

Despite the advanced state of her pregnancy, she took the first cross-country train home to her mother, who was delighted with her decision. Her mother and her sister Kathie helped take care of the baby, Fred, from the hour of his birth; Annie Flynn even rented a room in Lawrence during the 1912 strike so that her daughter could see the child at any time. Elizabeth Gurley Flynn stayed home only until Fred was weaned, and then she began to speak occasionally in New York. The IWW paid her a wage as a part-time organizer, but the family was very hard up and she refused to take money from Jones. As the baby grew older she began to travel again, leaving Fred in her mother's care and concentrating on strike towns, where she could be most useful. She had been getting $19 a week plus expenses from the IWW; after Fred was born she got $21. The rent on the Flynn apartment was $18. The younger Flynns worked while in school to help out, but the family budget was still very tight.

Although the life of a traveling organizer was strenuous and dangerous, Elizabeth Gurley Flynn loved it. She had a wanderlust and a deep interest in regional conditions and differences. She learned to know the lives of working people intimately, to analyze them, and to make use of local examples whenever she spoke.

> I stayed at homes wherever I went. I knew the lives of working people first hand. In those days no travelling Socialist or I.W.W. speaker went to a hotel. It was customary to stay at a local comrade's house. This was partly a matter of economy, to save expenses for the local people, and partly a matter of security for the speaker in many outright strongholds of reaction, like one-plant company towns.
>
> But, more than all else, it was a comradeship, even if you slept with one of the children or on a couch in the dining room. It would have been considered cold and unfriendly to allow a speaker to go off alone to a hotel. It was a great event when a speaker came to town. They wanted to see you as much as possible. People came from all around to socialize at the house where the speaker stayed. They heard about other parts of the country while the speaker could learn all about the conditions in that area. It was hard on the older speakers, but while I was young and vigorous I did not mind it.[59]

Elizabeth Gurley Flynn quickly emerged as a major agitator, and as one of the more important voices for women's liberation in her time, though this aspect of her work has since been neglected. It is true that Flynn was part of a largely male organization; nevertheless, her wide range of experience, her Marxism, and her own concerns as a woman made her able to express the problems of women vividly. She was quick to defend women against the widespread charges of being "backward" and "impossible to organize" that were used to justify neglect:

I have heard revolutionaries present a large indictment against women, which if true, constitutes a mine of reasons for a special appeal based upon their peculiar mental attitudes and adapted to their environment and the problems it creates.

Women are over-emotional, prone to take advantage of their sex, eager to marry and then submerged in family life, are intensely selfish for "me and mine," lack a sense of solidarity, are slaves to style and disinclined to serious and continuous study—these are a few counts in the complaint. Nearly every charge could be made against some men and does not apply to all women; yet it unfortunately fits many women for obvious reasons. It is well to remember that we are dealing with the sex that have been denied all social rights since early primitive times, segregated to domestic life up to a comparatively recent date and denied access to institutions of learning up to half a century ago. Religion, home and child-bearing were their prescribed spheres. Marriage was their career and to be an old maid a life-long disgrace. Their right to life depended on their sex attraction and the hideous inroads upon the moral integrity of women, produced by economic dependence, are deep and subtle. Loveless marriages, household drudgery, acceptance of loathsome familiarities, unwelcome child-bearing, were and are far more general than admitted by moralists, and have marred the mind, body, and spirit of women.[60]

For all these reasons, Flynn agreed with the rank-and-file women in the IWW that special forms of propaganda and special kinds of organization suited to the conditions of women's lives had to be developed if the IWW were to successfully organize them. She opposed the tendency to address general appeals to the whole working class and then blame women if they did not flock to the organization's banner:

> We of the IWW must study our material and adapt our propaganda to women, if we expect a ready response. Some of our male members are prone to underestimate this vital need, and assert that the principles of the IWW are alike for all, which we grant with certain reservations. They must be translated for foreigners, simplified for illiterates, and rendered into technical phrases for various industrial groups.[61]

Similarly, they must be specially directed toward women.

In a speech she made in 1911, Elizabeth Gurley Flynn laid out her ideas and feelings with a passion that clearly places her in the struggle for women's liberation as well as the class struggle:

> Multitudes of wives and mothers are virtually sex slaves through their direct and debasing dependence upon men for their existence, and motherhood is all too often unwelcome and enforced, while the struggle for existence even in homes where love and affectionate understanding cast their illuminating rays is usually so fierce that life degenerates into a mere animal existence, a struggle for creature comforts, no more, and it is impossible for love to transcend the physical. The mental horizon of the average housekeeper is exceedingly limited, because of the primitive form of labor in the household, the cooking, cleaning, sewing, scrubbing, etc., for an individual family. How can one have depth or mental scope when one's life is spent exclusively within the four walls of one's individual, composite home and workshop, performing personal service continually for the same small group, laboring alone and on the primitive plan, doing work that could be better done by socialization and machinery, were not women cheaper than machines today.
>
> We are driven to the conclusion . . . that much more than the abstract right of the ballot is needed to free women; nothing short of a social revolution can shatter her cramping and stultifying sphere of today. Yet I have a firm and abiding conviction that much can be done to alleviate the lot of working class women today. . . . I feel the futility, and know that many other Socialist women must, through our appreciation of these sad conditions and our deep sympathy for our sister women, of extending to them nothing more than the hope of an ultimate social revolution. I am impatient for it. I realize the beauty of our hope, the truth of its effectiveness, the inevitability of its realization, but I want to see that hope find a point of contact with the daily lives of working women, and I believe it can through the union movement.[62]

Notes that Elizabeth Gurley Flynn made for a speech about women sometime during World War I clearly show both her feminism and her Marxism. She focused on the growing tendency of women to leave the home and enter industrial production, believing that it laid the economic basis for a real struggle for equality. But she was no mechanical materialist, relying on economic developments alone to liberate women. She saw reproductive and sexual freedom, exemplified by birth control, as the "most fundamental of all the claims made by women," for only a woman's "right to her own body—Sex independence in and out of marriage" could bring about "equality in the home" and the "breakdown of that modern and bad institution, the man-supported family." She pointed to the necessity of "solidarity among women to achieve these ends."[63]

Although she agreed with the IWW that the struggle for woman suffrage diverted women from their true needs, she knew that women were oppressed by culture as well as economics, and applauded the efforts of the feminist movement to break down the genteel trivialization that afflicted the lives of even working-class women at this time:

> To the girl industry is a makeshift, a waiting station for matrimony. "Get married," "have your own home," "won't need to work," is the litany she hears daily at home and in the shop. Dances and social affairs, the marriage marts of the poor, become her haunts, dress and artifices to beauty, her interests. The profound biological instinct of the young to mate, artificially stimulated by mercenary motives and social stigmas, produces many unhappy marriages. . . .
>
> Mis-education further teaches girls to be lady-like, a condition of inane and inert placidity. She must not fight or be aggressive, mustn't be a "tomboy," mustn't soil her dresses, mustn't run and jump as more sensibly attired boys do. In Scranton recently, I heard a boy say to his sister, "You can't play with us, you're only a girl!" I hoped she would beat him into a more generous attitude, but in her acquiescence was the germ of an pitiable inability to think and act alone, characteristic of so many women. In the arrogance of the male child was the beginning of a dominance that culminates in the drunken miner, who beats his wife and vents the cowardly spleen he dare not show the boss! Feminist propaganda is helping to destroy the same obstacles the labor movement confronts, when it ridicules the lady-like person, makes women discontented, draws them from sewing circle gossips and frivolous pastimes into serious discussion of current problems and inspires them to stand abuse and imprisonment for an idea. A girl who has arrived at suffrage will listen to an [IWW] organizer, but a simpering fool who says, "Women ain't got brains enough to vote!" or "Women ought to stay at home," is beyond hope.[64]

Elizabeth Gurley Flynn and other IWW leaders were far in

advance of most of the feminist and socialist movement in their understanding of the importance of female reproductive freedom. As Linda Gordon points out in her important book *Woman's Body, Woman's Right,* the Socialist Party refused to take up the issue of birth control organizationally—some members felt it was too risky and controversial, while others thought it was immoral. Most probably agreed with Kate Richards O'Hare, who responded to the women who flooded her paper, the *National Ripsaw,* with requests for birth control information (then illegal): "We are not in a position to wage this battle at present. We have too big a job on hand fighting capitalism to take time to go to jail for swatting one phase of the system. Instead of writing us, write a letter to your Congressman or Senator. Demand that the law be repealed."[65]

Nor did the mainstream feminist movement take up the issue: to them the only issue was woman suffrage. As Carrie Chapman Catt, leader of the National American Women's Suffrage Association, wrote Margaret Sanger, "Your reform is too narrow to appeal to me and too sordid."[66] Birth control was first turned into a political issue not by any organization, but by individual militants acting as a loose, unorganized movement. The anarchists, particularly Emma Goldman and her lover Dr. Ben Reitman, did early and consistent agitation around the question. Important work was done by socialist activists in New York: Maud Malone, Anita Block, Dr. Antoinette Konikow, Rose Pastor Stokes, and Jessie Ashley. A few feminists, like Mary Ware Dennett and anthropologist Elsie Clews Parsons, became deeply involved in birth control work; and there was a cluster of people who came from socialist backgrounds but became identified with birth control as a single issue: Margaret Sanger, her first husband William Sanger, Dr. William J. Robinson, Sanger's sister Ethel Byrne, and her young allies Fania Mindell and Agnes Smedly (later to win fame for her work in support of the Chinese revolution). From the IWW came Elizabeth Gurley Flynn, Georgia Kotsch, Caroline Nelson, and Dr. Marie Equi, a West Coast Wobbly who was an open lesbian and probably the main distributor of contraceptive information to workers in the Pacific Northwest during this period. All of them broke the law, risked prosecution, and in some cases were actually tried and jailed while attempting to bring birth control information to working-class people.

To some, birth control was primarily a feminist issue, a way women could gain greater control over their lives. To most it was also a weapon in the class struggle, a needed reform that could lessen the poverty and hardship of working-class life, especially for women, and enable them to be freer to fight. Intensive agitation about the need for information about contraception began during the depression of 1914–1915, when the sufferings of the poor were especially severe. Elizabeth Gurley Flynn made birth control the subject of one of her main speeches on her 1915 lecture tour and was gratified by the response:

> It was an agreeable surprise on my lecture trip last year, that a number of applications for the lecture "Small Families: A Working Class Necessity," were made. It proved one of the most effective topics, yet a few years ago it was a tabooed subject in America, classified as "vulgar and obscene" both by law and public opinion. The radical change in attitude which now permits and invites a frank and serious discussion of this subject, is largely due to the indefatigable efforts of one woman, Mrs. Margaret Sanger....
>
> Birth control among the workers, not as a solution to the class war, but as a valuable contribution towards that end, is a logical conclusion for a woman of Mrs. Sanger's varied experiences.[67]

Margaret Sanger, a visiting nurse on the Lower East Side, was a left-wing socialist and a follower of the IWW, who had been active in strike support work in Lawrence and Paterson. Although in later years she advocated birth control for purposes of limiting and purifying the world's population and staving off revolution, in this period she saw contraception as a way to help working-class women, bring about a sexual revolution, and make the working class as a whole more fit for combat. Encouraged by Bill Haywood, one of the leaders of the IWW,[68] she went to France in 1913 to investigate the means of contraception being used there. The French working class was celebrated for having a declining birth rate despite the power of the Catholic Church and the government's policy of paying family allowances to people that bore many children.[69] Margaret Sanger collected many home birth control techniques in France, where "mothers prided themselves on their special recipes for suppositories as much as on those for *pot au feu* or wine."[70]

She returned to the United States in 1914 to start her own magazine, the *Woman Rebel,* which was circulated through IWW locals and by anarchist friends like Emma Goldman.[71] Margaret Sanger printed the IWW preamble in her first issue, as if to declare affiliation. Her purpose, she said, was "to stimulate working women to think for themselves and to build up a conscious fighting character."[72] Apart from its feminism, the magazine bore a strong resemblance to those of the anarchist fringe of the IWW, where there was a great emphasis on being a pure-spirited militant minority with, in Margaret Sanger's phrase, "a burning faith and a faith in burning."[73] The U.S. Post Office soon indicted her for an article that was "a philosophical defense of assassination,"[74] despite the fact that the magazine's main message was sexual freedom for women, including freedom from "forced motherhood":

> Our fight is for the personal liberty of the women who work. A woman's body belongs to herself alone. It is her body. It does not belong to the Church. It does not belong to the United States of America. . . . The first step toward getting life, liberty and the pursuit of happiness for any woman is her decision whether or not she shall become a mother. Enforced motherhood is the most complete denial of a woman's right to life and liberty. . . . Once the women of the United States are awakened to the value of birth control, these institutions—Church, State, Big Business—will be struck such a blow that they will be able only to beg for mercy from the workers.[75]

When Margaret Sanger was indicted, she decided to flee the country and do further research into European techniques of birth control; she planned to turn her trial into a political forum when she returned. As she fled she released her pamphlet *Family Limitation,* a popular digest of information about contraceptive techniques she had gathered in Europe: douching, condoms, pessaries (diaphragms), sponges, and suppositories. It contained arguments against *coitus interruptus* as being harmful to the nervous condition of the woman involved, and pleaded for mutual sexual fulfillment rather than the forcible exercise of the husband's conjugal rights. It suggested that "the working woman can use direct action by refusing to supply the market with children to be exploited, by refusing to populate the earth with slaves."[76]

One hundred thousand copies of the first edition of *Family Limitation* were printed clandestinely by IWW printer Bill Shatoff, and it was distributed primarily through IWW locals. Margaret Sanger recalls:

> At first I had thought only of an edition of ten thousand. However, when I learned that union leaders in the silk, woolen, and copper industries were eager to have many more copies to distribute, I enlarged my plan. . . . Bundles went to the mills in the East, to the mines in the West—to Chicago, San Francisco, and Pittsburgh, to Butte, Lawrence, and Paterson. All who had requested copies were to receive them simultaneously.[77]

In the next few years, 10 million copies were printed and many more were mimeographed, typed, or hand copied. When Margaret Sanger returned for her trial, she reported that "boys in the North Woods, lumberjacks, bereft mothers, all sent sums of from one to ten dollars out of their meagre savings to help me carry on the fight. Miners from West Virginia wrote that their wives had for the first time in 5, 8, or ten years been free from pregnancy. . . . Miners had walked five miles to read the pamphlet. Others had had it copied by friends who could write."[78] Elizabeth Gurley Flynn wrote Margaret Sanger, suggesting that the IWW form Sanger defense committees. She reported that the IWW had printed five thousand leaflets in Chicago containing extracts from her book, and that "one girl told me the women in the Stockyard district kissed her hands, when she distributed them."[79]

Despite the efforts of a number of IWW women and some men to make birth control a political issue, and despite the eagerness of IWW members for the information, there was considerable passive resistance to the issue inside the organization. In 1916 Elizabeth Gurley Flynn sharply criticized the bulk of the male membership for their lack of enthusiasm:

> The majority of women readers will agree on the vital importance of birth control propaganda. Although some of our men are opposed to it they are usually single. . . . few men can understand the hopeless hapless condition of an involuntary mother, who bequeathes a heritage of submission and despair to her children. I

met the wife of a miner recently, mother of six children, the oldest, eight, the youngest a nursing baby. She was suffering from general debility due to excessive child-bearing, and when I said, "I hope you'll soon be better," she reproached me scornfully by saying, "I hope I die soon." Certainly there would be more vigorous rebellion in our people if this crushing burden were lifted from the women. I am beseiged by women for information on this subject, and this opens up another avenue of assault upon the system, yet whenever the subject is selected by a local it is always amazing how few I.W.W. workers bring their women folk to the meeting. It is time they realized that the I.W.W. stands for a larger program than more wages and shorter hours, and the industrial freedom we all aspire to will be the foundation upon which a different world for men and women will be reached.[80]

With the coming of the war and the IWW's subsequent repression and disintegration, the organization was unable to agitate forcefully for birth control, even if all its members had been behind the issue. Because IWW members saw workplace-centered economic exploitation not only as the fundamental cause of class oppression, but as virtually its only manifestation, they did not understand the operation of the political machinery of class rule: the state. Despite the police harassment they were continually subjected to, despite the way troops were used against their strikes, they still took a lighthearted approach to state repression. They kept their organization loose, their membership lists were completely open, and they had no means of communicating with each other besides those offered by the U.S. Post Office. Consequently, when the government decided to destroy the IWW during World War I, it was able to suppress its publications and sweep almost all its active members up in a dragnet with little effort. Work with women—in fact, all IWW work—became a dead issue.

Margaret Sanger turned to other allies, while the women who had been active in the IWW went their separate ways. Matilda Robbins had a baby and became inactive. Dr. Marie Equi was sent to jail for treason—she had called American soldiers "dirty, contemptible scum," and charged that the ruling class owned the army and navy. The prosecuting attorney called her an "unsexed woman."[81] When she was released after a year in San Quentin, her health had deteriorated and she ceased to be politically active.

Elizabeth Gurley Flynn continued to do defense work for political prisoners, during the war and after, but she developed a heart condition and had to retire for a time when she was only thirty-six years old. During this period she went to live with Dr. Marie Equi. When she re-emerged in the 1930s and joined the Communist Party, her sense of urgency about the specific oppression of women had become muted by her desire to become more active again in general.

In the years of its strength, the IWW made two significant contributions to the theory and practice of organizing women in the United States. It found new ways of connecting the workplace and the community: in the heat of its great mass strikes, housewives came out of the isolation of their kitchens and joined their husbands and working women in the fight for survival on the picket line. In doing so, they created new space for their own struggle as women, new bargaining power in the home, new political understanding for the future, as well as doubling the size and strength of the working-class army. These moments did not last: after the strike, the community women returned to their kitchens and the wage-earning housewives sank once more under the unrelieved drudgery of their two jobs. And not only the women were demobilized: since the IWW's fervor was considerably more developed than its organizational understanding, its locals often fell apart after a successful strike. Nevertheless, the heights reached in IWW strikes were significant peaks in the historical experience of the whole U.S. working class. Only in the general strikes of the garment workers were women equally active—and the women in the garment industry did not stay mobilized either.

The IWW's second major contribution to work with women was its effort to integrate women's fundamental demand for reproductive freedom with the general class struggle, to take the demand for birth control into the labor movement and bring out its class aspects. Not only did the IWW agitate around the need for access to birth control information; it actively distributed such information at a time when to do so was to court arrest. This was a significant departure from its general economist outlook on the oppression of women and stood in startling contrast to the rest of the labor movement's avoidance of the dangerous issues of reproduction and sexuality. Even while its theory denied the necessity of special campaigns around women's rights, IWW practice on the birth control issue showed that it could be militant about the needs of women as well as about economic issues. By bringing these two realms together, the IWW added a new dimension to both the labor movement and the movement for women's liberation.

7
Socialists and Suffragists

We will not wait for the Social Revolution to bring us
the freedom we should have won in the 19th century.

Crystal Eastman
"Feminism" (1919)[1]

In the early years of the century the influence of U.S. socialists—
broadly defined to include the anarchists and Wobblies at one end
of the spectrum and the reform and Christian socialists on the
other—was as great as it has ever been. These same years saw the
development of a vast women's movement symbolized by and
centered upon the struggle for the vote. Yet the socialist movement did not have much effect on the millions of women who
mobilized for suffrage. Why?

Since Aileen Kraditor laid out a critique of the racism, class
bias, and political opportunism of the suffrage movement fifteen
years ago in her ground-breaking book *The Ideas of the Woman
Suffrage Movement 1890–1920*, its conservatism has been well
known. More recently, Ellen DuBois, in *Feminism and Suffrage*, has
traced the origins of the movement's conservatism to its relations
with the abolitionists, trade unionists, and Republican and Democratic parties. But these early influences do not explain why the
women's movement remained so conservative. It is true that it
developed in the same period as the emergence of U.S. imperialism, and that it was increasingly under the leadership of women
of the bourgeoisie—but why was their leadership so little challenged? To understand this, we must turn directly to what might
have been the left wing of the women's movement and see why it
had so little influence on the character of the movement as a
whole. The organizational weakness of the trade union suffragists,
the IWW's sectarianism towards the suffrage movement, and the
Socialist Party's poor understanding of united front work offer
some clues as to why the mainstream of the women's movement
remained politically backward in a climate of general social up-

surge, and why the radical feminists who eventually emerged as that movement's left wing were so concentrated on the single issue of suffrage.

There is a tendency today to go to the other extreme and overlook the critical importance of the demand for woman suffrage, or to assume that the suffrage movement's class base was so bourgeois that no radical influence was possible. In the hindsight of history, the suffragists' belief that the vote would bring not only full equality for women but also peace on earth seems a pitiful delusion. In fact, like other oppressed groups women could only learn the strengths and limitations of such rights through their own experience, and the most important consequence of the development of the women's movement was not the achievement of the franchise but the experience of building a movement itself. So Ellen DuBois points out:

> It is certainly true that the Nineteenth Amendment did not emancipate women, and that rediscovering the revolutionary hopes that feminists had for the ballot has a bitter edge for us today. However, it is a mistake to conclude that the woman suffrage movement was a useless detour in women's struggle for liberation because the vote did not solve the problem of women's oppression. The vote did not have the inherent capacity to emancipate women as individuals, isolated from the collective struggles of their sex. Like all institutional reforms, it required an active social movement to give it meaning and make it real. Approached as a social movement, rather than as a particular reform, suffragism has enormous contemporary relevance. It was the first independent movement of women for their own liberation. Its growth—the mobilization of women around the demand for the vote, their collective activity, their commitment to gaining increased power over their own lives— was itself a major change in the condition of those lives.[2]

Prior to the Civil War, the feminist movement was part of the abolitionist movement, sharing its bravery, its high moral tone, and its goal of equality for all human beings. When the war ended, the movement split over the strategic question of whether to try to win the franchise for both women and the newly freed slaves at the same time. Feeling that the franchise was a question of survival for Southern blacks, the New England abolitionists—

including such feminists as Lucy Stone and Henry Blackwell—
allied with the blatantly antifeminist Republican Party in order to
pass the Fifteenth Amendment. The New England group argued
that extending the vote to the freedmen was not only necessary in
itself but was a step along the gradual road to universal suffrage:
giving the vote to the blacks would make it easier for women to get
it in the long run. Seeing this position as a betrayal of women,
their one-time comrades Elizabeth Cady Stanton and Susan B.
Anthony allied with the Democrats, the openly racist party of the
former slave owners. DuBois describes their position:

> Their objections to the amendment were simultaneously feminist
> and racist. On the one hand, their commitment to an independent
> women's movement was intensifying the feminism that underlay
> their demand for woman suffrage. Although they acknowledged
> the similarities between the inferior position women held with
> respect to men and the status of other oppressed groups, they
> believed that women's grievances were part of a distinct system of
> sexual inequality, which had its own roots and required its own
> solutions. This led them to repudiate the Fifteenth Amendment,
> not only because women were omitted from its provision, but
> because they believed that its ratification would intensify sexual
> inequality. They argued that the doctrine of universal manhood
> suffrage it embodied gave constitutional authority to men's claims
> that they were women's social and political superiors. On the other
> hand, this feminism was increasingly racist and elitist. The women
> among whom it was growing were white and middle-class and
> believed themselves the social and cultural superiors of the freed-
> men. The anti-Republican suffragists chose to encourage these
> women to feel that the Fifteenth Amendment meant a loss of status
> for them, and to try to transform their outraged elitism into an
> increased demand for their enfranchisement.[3]

Despite this split and the fiery strategic debates it engendered,
by the turn of the century suffrage had become a respectable,
even boring, single-issue campaign permeated with moralism
and anti–working class attitudes. The Stanton-Anthony wing soon
became less radical in its feminism and the New England wing
more openly racist, and in 1890 both factions were again united
in the National American Women's Suffrage Association. This
quickly became a lobbying organization that mobilized huge

numbers of women to petition, speak, and campaign for the vote
in their state legislatures. Mari Jo and Paul Buhle have described
the politics of the NAWSA leadership in the 1890s:

> Many had also come to fear a lower class that refused to listen to
> their pleas. They suspected the organization of labor as a selfish
> special interest, a threat to class reconciliation based upon princi-
> ples of social harmony. Observing for themselves the votes of
> immigrants in California, North Dakota, Kansas, and elsewhere
> against woman suffrage, they made the "ignorant classes" the scape-
> goat for the limits of their movement's progress.
>
> This reaction reinforced their growing isolation from the east-
> ern, urban masses of poor and working people. The suffragists'
> alliance with the temperance movement had so alienated those
> masses that a leader estimated the linkage had set back suffrage for
> a generation. They failed to make any headway with Catholic
> opponents who feared, with some justification, that women's vote
> would be used as a weapon of nativism. Encouraged by the growth
> of women's clubs and a small suffrage movement in the South, the
> national movement publicized the claim that white votes would
> guarantee control over the Negro population. In many regions,
> and especially in the Midwest and West, where workers and farm-
> ers were mainly old-stock Protestants, the suffrage movement
> remained democratic and open. But elsewhere, and notably among
> the leaders, NAWSA became by the late 1890s a self-consciously
> elite movement.[4]

This increased conservatism was in part the result of a change
in the social makeup of the leaders of the suffrage movement:
while the early leaders were generally housewives who did most
of their own work, or self-employed women, the new leaders were
often the wives of very rich men—Mrs. Oliver Hazard Perry
Belmont, for example, whose first husband was William K. Vanderbilt and whose second was a streetcar magnate. Woman suffrage became respectable and the delegates to NAWSA conventions in Washington were even asked to tea at the White House.[5]

The political line of the suffrage movement became increasingly reactionary, even on the issue of the vote itself. The first
wave of the movement had wanted the vote as a general human
right, but as the influence of bourgeois feminist ideas increased,
this changed. The vote became a privilege to be given to women

because of their innate goodness and purity, because their mother-ing instincts made them love all humanity, and because they would consequently clean up society, stop child labor, and end war. As Julia Ward Howe (who went on to suffragism after writing "The Battle Hymn of the Republic") put it:

> Woman is the mother of the race, the guardian of its helpless infancy, its earliest teacher, its most zealous champion. Woman is also the home-maker; upon her devolve the details which bless and beautify family life. In all true civilization she wins man out of his natural savagery to share with her the love of offspring, the enjoy-ment of true and loyal companionship.[6]

This nonsense is a reflection of the Victorian ideology which put all women (except working women) on a pedestal, secluded in the home, and safely removed from the "public" world. The statement of the General Federation of Women's Clubs upon the entry of the United States into World War I, clearly demonstrates the connection between bourgeois feminism and Victorianism:

> Women are natural pacifists. Love and harmony are the factors that make the home within our gates, and so it has been our pleasure and privilege to run inside and close the gate, leaving the confusion and discord and misunderstanding on the outside to settle themselves. . . . Women realize that we are living in an ungov-erned world. At heart we are all pacifists. We should love to talk it over with the war-makers, but they would not understand.[7]

Along with its retrograde ideas about women, NAWSA took a backward position on the rights of blacks and immigrants. In 1903, it virtually adopted a program in support of white supremacy when it declared in favor of states' rights in the matter of extending the vote; it agreed that each state could decide for itself who would vote at a time when millions of black people were being disenfranchised by poll taxes and literacy tests. In the Southern states, NAWSA allied with white supremacist politicians to get the vote for women, meaning white women only, arguing that white female suffrage would assure a white majority in the South even if some black men continued to vote. NAWSA was similarly willing to act against the interests of immigrants in order to win the vote for women, as is clear from a resolution passed at its 1893 convention:

> *Resolved,* That without expressing any opinion on the proper qualifi-
> cations for voting, we call attention to the significant facts that in
> every State there are more women who can read and write than the
> whole number of illiterate male voters; more white women who can
> read and write than all negro voters; more American women who
> can read and write than all foreign voters; so that the enfranchise-
> ment of such women would settle the vexed question of rule by
> illiteracy, whether of home-grown or foreignborn production.[8]

In later years, NAWSA made overtures to immigrant voters
and in some states (like New York) won the vote because of them.
But this change was based on policy, not principle, and it never
extended to allying with black women. NAWSA made every
effort to keep black women out of the suffrage movement in
order to preserve its white Southern membership and keep its
alliance with Southern legislators. As Aileen Kraditor put it, "They
were perfectly content to secure the vote without enfranchising
any Negroes at the same time, or on terms which disfranchised
the Negroes, if that proved necessary or feasible."[9] Instead of
allying the millions of disenfranchised women with other oppressed groups—blacks, immigrants, workers—the NAWSA leadership united with white supremacist and anti-immigrant politicians. In the process it became so compromised that it could not
even lead the struggle for woman suffrage effectively. When
Elizabeth Cady Stanton's daughter, Harriot Stanton Blatch, returned to New York from England, where she had been inspired
by the militance of the British suffragists, she was appalled at the
state of the movement in the United States:

> The suffrage movement was completely in a rut in New York State
> at the opening of the twentieth century. It bored its adherents and
> repelled its opponents. Most of the ammunition was being wasted
> on its supporters in private drawing rooms and in public halls
> where friends, drummed up and harried by the ardent, listlessly
> heard the same old arguments. . . . The only method suggested for
> furthering the cause was the slow process of education. We were
> told to organize, organize, organize, to the end of educating, edu-
> cating, educating public opinion.[10]

Blatch believed that favorable conditions existed in New York
City for a more energetic and broadly based type of suffrage

agitation that could link up with the labor movement: there were the women of the Socialist Party, there was the Women's Trade Union League. In 1907 she and about forty other militants organized a new suffrage group, the Equality League of Self-Supporting Women (later called the Women's Political Union):

> We all believed that suffrage propaganda must be made dramatic, that suffrage workers must be politically minded. We saw the need of drawing industrial women into the suffrage campaign and recognized that these women needed to be brought in contact, not with women of leisure, but with business and professional women who were also out in the world earning their living.[11]

By 1908 the Equality League had nineteen thousand women members, including such leading New York radicals as Charlotte Perkins Gilman, Florence Kelley, Lavinia Dock of the Henry Street Settlement, Gertrude Barnum, Leonora O'Reilly, Rose Schneiderman, Jessie Ashley, and Inez Milholland. These women left NAWSA's tea-party style of organizing behind: they canvassed union officers, did soapboxing on the streets, campaigned at factory gates, and held the first open-air suffrage meetings in thirty years. They organized their work on a precinct basis—an innovation at the time for anybody but the Democratic Party machine. And they pioneered in organizing huge Fifth Avenue suffrage parades that became the trademark of the new spirit: thousands of women marched with their organizational banners led by Inez Milholland and other beauties in Grecian drapery on white horses.[12]

Because of the moribund character of its top leadership, NAWSA took years to respond to this new energy nationally. But its New York State organization was headed by Carrie Chapman Catt, and she immediately saw the importance of the new style of work. In 1908 she welded most of the city's suffrage groups (except the Equality League, which retained its independence) into one NAWSA affiliate, the Woman Suffrage Party. Emulating the tactics introduced by Blatch, the WSP organized on a precinct basis and, with the help of the Women's Trade Union League, tried to reach union members. They printed literature in languages other than English, a real breakthrough in the feminist movement, saying: "We must reach our friends of all nations in their own language whenever possible. It is our aim to make the Woman Suffrage Party the most democratic organization in the whole suffrage movement."[13] Their efforts were at times condescending or embarrassing—as when they dressed in Chinese costumes for a Mott Street rally or took an organ grinder's monkey along to an open-air meeting in Little Italy[14]—but at least they tried to reach immigrants in a period when much of the suffrage movement was attacking them as unfit to vote.

While this new spirit increased the interest of working women in suffrage, and while the aid given by prominent suffragists to the 1909–1910 shirtwaist makers' strike showed that their efforts at unity could be of genuine use to labor, the atmosphere of NAWSA remained uncongenial to working women: the disparities in wealth, lifestyle, and politics were too great. In 1910, with the help of Mary Beard of the WSP,[15] a number of working women withdrew to form a separate organization, which they called the Wage Earners' Suffrage League. It was headed by Leonora O'Reilly, and Clara Lemlich, famed as the organizer of the shirtwaist makers' strike, was vice-president.

The new organization saw itself as the labor wing of the suffrage movement and did not break from NAWSA; in fact, it turned over all the names of the workers it had organized to the Woman Suffrage Party. Its voting membership was restricted to workers, however, though "allies" were permitted to attend meetings and help with the work. The wisdom of keeping organizational control firmly in the hands of workers was demonstrated when, in November 1911, at the height of a strike of public maintenance workers, two of the allies went off to the Mayor without consulting anyone and offered to clean the streets: "After all, the life of the average woman is used up in moving dirt from one place to another. And to move the garbage from the sidewalks to the dumping places is only taking the usual work of the voteless women one step further."[16] Although they backed these allies publicly, the working-class leaders of the Wage Earners' Suffrage League were infuriated and made sure it would never happen again. As Leonora O'Reilly noted in her diary: "While this was an inane act—it will very likely bring sense into our body. It will make them see the wisdom of going slowly but wisely in taking in new members."[17] The Wage Earners' Suffrage League confined its agitation to the working class, going to union meetings and factory gates to carry the gospel. In a 1914 letter, Leonora O'Reilly described their work:

> Thus far we have done little more than carry the message of suffrage from the wage earners' point of view into every meeting where we get a chance to speak. By this I mean a wage earning woman tells her own reasons in her own way why working women need the vote. We do not say that all working women want the vote—we maintain she should have the vote and we the Wage Earners who believe in votes for women must keep at our uninterested sisters until they are aroused to the good they can accomplish with the ballot and to the good it will do them personally to take part in government. We go to any group of people who ask us for a speaker and give them plain facts about the conditions of employment today and how the ballot might be used to relieve these conditions. We recognize that our principal work is to go before Trade Unions of either men and women to persuade them to let us send a speaker.[18]

Perhaps the group's most effective effort was a large rally at Cooper Union in 1912. Mary Beard had noted during the suffrage debate in the state legislature that none of the antisuffrage politicians had taken any notice of the conditions of working women but had talked only of "ladies" and of wanting "to relieve women of all burdens and responsibilities." She suggested that Leonora O'Reilly get a number of her fellow workers to answer these fatuous statements at a rally that would build a working-class contingent for the suffrage parade to be held the next week.[19] The idea was a great success. Mollie Schepps, a shirtwaist maker, spoke in answer to a senator who had said, "Now there is no one to whom I yield in respect and admiration and devotion to the sex":

> We working women cannot play the simple idiot and worship man as a hero. We are not angels, nor are they gods. We are simply in business together and as such we refuse to play the silent partner any longer. . . . Some of the objections that men have to woman suffrage are the following: the first is that it would be too hard work for women to go out and cast her vote once a year, because she has too much work to do—too hard work to do. To me it seems much

harder when we have to live under laws which are made for us than it would be to go out once a year and help make laws for ourselves. [Applause] Putting a piece of paper into a ballot box won't break our backs. . . . Another reason is given against woman suffrage; it is said that equal say will enable the women to get equal pay, and equal pay is dangerous. Why? Because it would keep the women from getting married. Well, then, if long miserable hours and starvation wages are the only means men can find to encourage marriage it is a very poor compliment to themselves.[20]

This was the sort of thing O'Reilly described as a "straight labor suffrage talk," very different from most suffrage propaganda.[21] At the same meeting, Rose Schneiderman responded to a senator who had said, "Get women into the arena of politics with its alliances and distressing contests—the delicacy is gone, the charm is gone, and you emasculize women":

All this talk about women's charm does not mean working women. Working women are expected to work and produce their kind so that they, too, may work until they die of some industrial disease. We hear our anti-suffragettes saying, "Why, when you get the vote it will hinder you from doing welfare work, doing uplift work." Who are they going to uplift? . . . I think if they would uplift themselves off our shoulders they would be doing a better bit of useful work. I think you know by now that if the workers got what they earn there would be no need of uplift work and welfare work or anything of that kind.[22]

The leaflets passed out by the Wage Earners' Suffrage League spoke to working women with a directness unusual in suffrage propaganda although, like other suffragist literature, they proposed the vote as a panacea for all the evils of industrial life:

Why?

Why are you paid less than a man?
Why do you work in a fire-trap?
Why are your hours so long?
Why are you all strap hangers when you
pay for a seat?
Why do you pay the most rent for the
worst houses?
Why does the cost of living go up while
wages go down?

Why do your children go into factories?
Why don't you get a square deal in the
   courts?
BECAUSE YOU ARE A WOMAN AND HAVE NO VOTE.
   VOTES MAKE THE LAW.
   VOTES ENFORCE THE LAW.
   THE LAW CONTROLS CONDITIONS.
   WOMEN WHO WANT BETTER CONDITIONS MUST VOTE.[23]

While the Wage Earners' Suffrage League may have won working-class adherents to the suffrage movement, it was not strong enough to change the character of that movement as a whole. Some of the problems faced by the working-class suffragist are illustrated by the cases of Maggie Hinchey and Clara Lemlich, neither of whom was able to find a permanent home in the suffrage movement, dominated as it was by liberal women of leisure. Their stories say much about the limitations of the feminist movement of their period.

The Women's Trade Union League discovered Maggie Hinchey during the laundry workers' strike of 1912, when she threw up her position as a forewoman—saying "Good God, no one could be so mean as to go to work in a laundry now!"—and was blacklisted. She went to the League and said, "Use me in any way you can for the good of the cause: I am yours to the finish."[24] In 1913 NAWSA's New York affiliate, the Woman Suffrage Party, gave her a year's job as an organizer. She toured New York's ethnic neighborhoods, carrying an Italian flag in Little Italy, a Greek flag further downtown. According to the *New York Times,* she met with great success even among the derelicts on the Bowery:

> There were half a dozen of the women, among them . . . the Billy Sunday of the suffragists—Maggie Hinchey, who represents working women—Maggie is big and sisterly and, above all, human in a good, strong way. When Maggie got up to speak the Bowery succumbed to a man.
>
> "Brothers," began Maggie, rolling her r's with a good Irish brogue. As she went on her audience alternately wiped its tears and shook with laughter, and when she said at the close, "And now you know what you are going to do on Nov. 2," every hand went up to say yes, they would vote for the women.

She talked of the war and the English and the Irish, the Germans
and the Russians all "fighting like mad dogs, and don't know what
they're fighting about, and there's them that calls themselves Kings
and Kaisers that puts them up to it."

She talked religion, "and the father says come this way or you'll
go to hell, and the Protestant says come with me or you'll go to hell,
but we are all alike and we are all brothers together."[25]

The Woman Suffrage Party sent her to Rochester, where she
got up a delegation of six hundred working women to call on
President Wilson in February 1914 to ask him for the vote, and
where she did more street corner speaking. As she wrote Leonora
O'Reilly:

I have a Catholic meeting to night and I am goying to knock at the
door for the first time. I spoke outside of 3 factories at noon hour
and when I got through the men took of there hats and hurray
votes for women   Miss Climmons wanted me to rest and not
speak but I thought it would be a crime to miss a good thing in the
right Place Lenora . . . I left a Pretty good feeling by all the fighting
and drops of water falling from my forehead asking the men to
think for themselves . . . we will send you the names of other unions
I visited if you will write a letter to the firemen and explain the
received me with a cold Peice of ice but when I got speaking one
looked at the other in assaisment and when I was wishing them
good by at last they got friendly and clapped. . . . I did not ask for
any action but I asked the chairman to give some Irish leaflets to
any Irishman and he said his name was Costigan—they told me
they would notify W.T.U.L. what stand they would take. Please
write him and I think he will be fair all our men needs to let them
know we will work as one. . . . We had a street meeting last night
when we got there 2 People and 4 corners for audence I got up
upon a chare and started in hollin and in 10 minutes we had 150
people all mothers and men Mrs Climmons and myself laughed at
the way I collected People she said I could be heard 1/2 mile away
we got 14 signatures all voters.[26]

But if Maggie Hinchey was heard on the streets, she did less
well inside the conventions of the suffrage movement. To quote
another letter to O'Reilly:

I feel as if I have butted in wher I was not wanted. Miss Hay gave me a badge was very nice to me but you know they had a school teacher to represent the Industrial workers if you ever herd her it was like trying to fill a barrell with water that had no bottom not a word of labor spoken here at this convention so far. You would have to be a real politician now to be a suffrage. this convention is a verry quite serious affair after the hole thing was over some people came to me and said I had a right to speak for labor but they kept away until it was over.[27]

When the New York suffrage referendum was passed in 1917, the Woman Suffrage Party had no more need for Maggie Hinchey. She hoped for an organizing job with the Women's Trade Union League, but found no home there either. The League was under the control of Rose Schneiderman, whom she found unsympathetic. She also disagreed with the League's advocacy of protective legislation, holding the radical feminist view that this restricted opportunities for women workers. With no other job available Maggie Hinchey had to go back to work in a laundry, from which she wrote Leonora O'Reilly a last bitter letter in 1918:

I lost my bread and also lost the light or sunshine when I lost my work now I have to work long hours in darkness and take my rest in a cellor and work until 9 oclock at night for 18 a week in my last job and no work I received 32 a week we will see If Rose and the rest will resign now and save the Womens Trade League I bet she will try to hold on to her 35 or 40 job she never made a weeks wages until she got it on the workers I see it is not a League for the Working women only a Political Org so we will have to find an org that will stand by the working women that we can trust wont sell us out while our nose is to the grinding stone. I would never let them get away with it onely I believed you and I always thought you said the best thing Rember you told me the League was our friend and it would look out for our Interests. . . .

Dear Lenora

I guess this is the last letter as we are two different opinions I stand for the right of freedoms of the working women to kick themselves when and whare the[y] want work—8 or 9 hours day or night just the same as men they have no club over then why should we I will always think of you   M Hinchy[28]

Maggie Hinchey's career offers a bitter illustration of how little the organized feminist movement or the women's part of the labor movement had to offer on the individual level. Very few of the working women who were drawn into political work were able to continue in it: Leonora O'Reilly was supported by Mary Dreier, Rose Schneiderman got union and WTUL jobs, but the rest had no place to go, particularly if their politics, like Maggie Hinchey's, were different from those of the League. Maggie Hinchey's co-workers in the suffrage movement, insulated as they were by their own wealth, were probably not even aware what had become of her; still less were they likely to create jobs for her. With her particular blend of working-class politics and feminism, she truly could find no home.

Clara Lemlich, whose role in the shirtwaist makers' strike is discussed in chapter 8, was similarly discarded, first by leaders of the shirtwaist makers' union that she had helped to organize, then by the League, and finally by the suffragists. The difference here was that since she was a socialist, she was able to find political work on the left, even though she could not make a living doing it. A leader in the shirtwaist makers' strike, Clara Lemlich was blacklisted afterward and could not get a job on her union's staff because such jobs almost always went to men. Mary Beard hired her for a time to organize for the industrial section of the Woman Suffrage Party, and she toured union halls and working-class neighborhoods, speaking for suffrage outside such places as the Butterick Pattern and Uneeda Biscuit factories. At the latter, men threw rotten tomatoes out of the window and yelled, "Go home and wash your pants!"[29] Although Mary Beard was at first enthusiastic about Clara Lemlich's work—"She seems to me to be keen about it and does everything that's suggested and does it well, I think. Of course, we don't want to spoil her."[30]—by July 1912 she had changed her mind. One can speculate that Lemlich's temperament and her brand of socialism were too fiery for the suffragists, or that she found it difficult to do organizing that was so unlike union or strike work; at any rate, Mary Beard lost patience with her, as she wrote Leonora O'Reilly:

> What do you honestly think about Clara? I am anxious to be fair to the girl and do all I can for her but it seems to me that she can't swing her job. She seems to be unequal physically to the nervous

strain of organization or speaking and you know her mental make-up without my going into that. I do not see how her future is to be a success as a speaker. If she goes on hoping until November after her factory season has begun, she may be left helpless upon my hands. . . .

Clara seems much more weary physically at this kind of work than she was in the factory, even, I believe. You know all I have to tell anyway. What seems to you to be decent treatment, under the circumstances? It has been my dream to develop working women to be a help in the awakening of their class, but Clara can't make good along the line she has attempted this winter, it seems to me. She has *no* initiative.[31]

It must remembered that this same woman had sufficient "initiative" to organize the shirtwaist makers' local and lead a major strike.

A year after Clara Lemlich lost her suffrage job, she married a printer, a recent emigrant from Russia who had been active since his youth in the Bolshevik Party. She became active in a variety of community organizing activities, had three children, and worked in a succession of tie shops as well. She was part of a socialist women's group that protested food price profiteering; she organized a rent strike that got her family evicted; and she did support work for several strikes, including the great Passaic strike of 1926. According to those who would know, she was a founding member of the Communist Party.[32] Throughout the 1930s and 1940s she was active in unemployed councils, in campaigns against price fixing, in hunger marches, and in community work, especially with women. When her husband became ill and could no longer work, she went back to work as a hand finisher on cloaks and joined the ILGWU as a rank-and-file union member, unknown and unrecognized; she remained so until she retired, when she was given an honorary pension for her services to the union.[33]

Like Maggie Hinchey and Clara Lemlich, other workers in the Women's Trade Union League saw the vote as at least a partial solution to their problems on the job: with the vote they could press for legislation for an eight-hour day, a minimum wage, and better working conditions. The WTUL's suffrage work was in this way a part of its increasing tendency to emphasize legislative solutions and its discouragement over its small success in organizing. Some labor organizations, however, disagreed with this emphasis. The League's point of view was anathema to the Industrial Workers of the World: the vote was useless; any legislation was worthless without shop organization to enforce it; and the suffrage movement was therefore a dangerous diversion from the class struggle. Elizabeth Gurley Flynn developed this position in a speech she made in 1909. She gave the suffrage movement full support against the antisuffrage movement, whose members she compared to the slaves who taunted free Negroes with having no white man to take care of them. Women, she affirmed, had the right to whatever men had, including the vote. But the important question was whether the working-class movement should mobilize to help them get this right. She thought not: the vote was useless for revolutionary purposes, the agitation around it was divisive, and workers had more important things to do.[34]

This position was reflected in many IWW publications. In 1910, for instance, in an article on "Woman and Industrial Unionism," Anna Tewksbury maintained that "working women already have the suffrage, where it will count the most for them, in the industrial union which will ultimately expand into the Industrial Republic. If they want to exercise that right all they have to do is organize in the Industrial Workers of the World where they will have full equality with man."[35] Or, as the editor of *Solidarity* wrote a few years later:

> The UNION AT THE POINT OF PRODUCTION is the training school for the "equality of the sexes" that we hear so much about just now. ECONOMIC EQUALITY precedes any other kind; and as long as woman can be made the prey of the employing class in the shop, her possession of the "vote" will not in the least free her from bondage. On the other hand it might tend to delude her with the idea—by no means exclusively feminine—that some power outside herself (for example, "lawmakers") can save her and her class.[36]

It was not only their view of the triviality of the vote that led the Wobblies to see suffrage as irrelevant to, and destructive of, the interests of the working class. Their class analysis led some of them to conclude that suffrage was only in the interests of middle-class women. As Charles Ashleigh argued in the *Industrial Union Bulletin* in 1908, middle-class women needed the vote to catch up

with their men, but working-class women and men were already
on the same level:

> The middle class woman holds all the bourgeois faith in the State as a
> means for remedying all and every evil; political ballot-box equality,
> in her estimation, is synonymous with economic equality. Hence all
> this rampage about the vote. . . .
>
> The woman wage-worker and the wife of the wage-worker are
> the victims of industrial exploitation, not of suffrage inequality.
> They are robbed in the mill, factory or shop, where they, or their
> breadwinners, work. The woman worker lives by the same method
> as the male worker; by the sale of her labor-power to the boss. She is
> robbed, as the male worker is robbed, by the master appropriating
> the large portion of the product of her labor. She is robbed WHERE
> the male worker is robbed: on the INDUSTRIAL FIELD. She should
> fight for better conditions WHERE the most enlightened of the male
> workers, in ever increasing number, are fighting: on the INDUS-
> TRIAL FIELD.
>
> The woman wage-worker is not concerned in a sex war; she is
> concerned in a CLASS war. The boss enslaves men, women and
> children in the same way: by the exploitation of their labor-power.
> On the industrial field, the woman worker has the same power as
> the man: she has the power of WITHDRAWING HER LABOR-POWER
> FROM INDUSTRY.[37]

The one-sidedness of this analysis is evident. Women workers
were not in fact exploited as men were: they were superexploited,
paid an even smaller percentage of the value of what they produced, in the belief that they could depend on their husbands to
make up the difference. Working-class women did not get equal
pay for equal work any more than middle-class women did.
Moreover, their traditional position in the home—however little
reality this tradition had for increasing numbers of women—
without childcare facilities, without birth control, without any
expectation of social equality, made the demands of the feminist
movement much more relevant to them than male Wobblies such
as Ashleigh cared to believe.

The tendency of IWW theoreticians to ignore the material
inequalities between the sexes can be seen in an essay by Justus
Ebert in a special women's edition of *Solidarity* in 1916, in which he
attacks the idea of separate organizations for women as inherently

divisive. But even though he recognizes the sex prejudice inside the AFL, his only solution is, as usual, for women to join the IWW:

> In trades unionism, sex discrimination and division exist in forms that are very little modified. . . . Women are discriminated against, even where they appear to be most welcome.
>
> But a more obvious reflection and form of sex discrimination in trades unionism is the woman's trade union league. Why "a woman's trade union league?" Are women in industry hired for sex or economic reasons? Do they work as a separate sex or in co-operation with men? And since they are only one of the many cogs in the industrial machine, why organize them independently of the other cogs?
>
> It is often said that men don't understand women and consequently cannot persuade them to organize labor unions of both sexes. This argument is overdone. Besides it is not altogether a fact. Men don't want to organize women, because of sex prejudices born of a misunderstood competition. Women's trade union leagues, by their sex divisions, help to keep this prejudice alive.
>
> Besides, industrial unionism, as represented by the I.W.W., has organized through male agencies [i.e. organizers], labor unions of both sexes, with equal voices, rights and privileges. There is no sex discrimination in the I.W.W.[38]

Apart from their feeling that the vote was irrelevant and a feminist movement divisive, the IWW had a deep distrust of the bourgeois women who led the suffrage campaign, and at times saw the whole issue as a ruling-class conspiracy. Elizabeth Gurley Flynn, for instance, denied that there was any basis for a united front of women against sex inequality:

> To us, society moves in grooves of class, not sex. Sex distinctions affect us insignificantly and would less, but for economic differences. It is to those women who are wage earners, or wives of workers, that the I.W.W. appeals. We see no basis for feminist mutual interest, no evidence of natural "sex conflict," nor any possibility—or present desirability—of solidarity between women alone. . . . The "queen in the parlor" has no interest in common with "the maid in the kitchen"; the wife of a department store owner shows no sisterly concern for the seventeen year old girl who finds prostitution the only door [open] to a $5 a week clerk. The sisterhood of women, like the brotherhood of man, is a hollow sham

to labor. Behind all its smug hypocrisy and sickly sentimentality loom the sinister outlines of the class war.[39]

Working class women had no interest whatsoever in gaining the vote, which could only be used against them:

There would be but one reason for giving women the suffrage—to exploit their conservatism and use it against the overwhelming forces of radicalism, otherwise her vote would be useless to "the powers that be" and would not be granted. The cry of the woman suffragists "Taxation without representation" may be heeded, votes given to women with property and their class interests would line them up with Capitalism, but this suffragist slogan has no appeal to class-conscious working women, who have no interest in taxes on property until they have property. Further, if she received the vote, it would mean only another form of *political enslavement,* for her economic security would make her have no opinion but some man's opinion, no party but his party, no mind but his mind to guide her to the ultimatum, no vote but his kind of vote.[40]

At the same time Flynn's attitude toward the suffrage movement—and that of many of her male comrades—included a large dose of sympathy and even admiration for its work, however misguided she thought its goal. As she said on one occasion:

The early suffragists were mobbed and occupied the same place in popular opinion allotted to the I.W.W. now, yet slowly the changing economic status of woman has made suffrage respectable, even fashionable. While women were merely instruments of passion or household drudges, so long as "the ideal woman was she of whom neither good nor evil was heard outside her own home" and education stopped with reading the catechism—there was no soil in which the roots of new ideals could cling or be nourished. Today we see calm, clear-eyed women deliberating in conventions, marching in parades, and enthusiastic militant ones in long and bitter strikes. It thrills us as mighty cosmic upheavals, when the static of centuries moves, rises and is changed.[41]

Despite such recognition of the historical importance of the suffrage movement, the IWW at times opposed it in practice. In one instance, at least, IWW street corner agitators even heckled suffrage speakers, though this was over electoral politics and therefore unusual. In the 1916 presidential campaign the new radical feminist wing of the women's movement, now organized in the Women's Party, campaigned against the incumbent Woodrow Wilson on the basis that he had not used the power of his office to help pass the woman suffrage amendment. Most of the labor movement supported Wilson, a Democrat, against Charles Evans Hughes. The suffragists raised enough money to hire a private train, the "Golden Special," in which to tour the country making anti-Wilson speeches. Margaret Dreier Robins, national president of the Women's Trade Union League, was one of those who climbed on board.

When the train hit Portland, Oregon, its passengers ran into trouble in the person of Dr. Marie Equi, who was waiting at the station with a banner reading "Which Goose Laid the Golden Egg?" The suffragists had her arrested, and she wrote an account of the skirmish to her friend Margaret Sanger:

> We sure did have a strenuous time. Put the Hughesites entirely out of business. I was arrested in the afternoon. Detained one hour. Bail $100—an attempt made to lodge an Insanity complaint. . . . We had over 5000 people at 6th and Alder. Those poor weak sisters from the East! With their little N.Y. village ideas. . . . I put out their lamps those poor silly weak women! . . .
>
> They policed the Theatre here so the poor Dears from the Far East could give their little set Speeches. My God! If I had to repeat the same talk all the time—I'd take a doe [dose of] cyanide. I may be crazy! but deliver me from a simp. . . .
>
> The Reception that group of Wall Streets got they will remember to their last days. Advising us how to Vote—say, they better get their own men to give them the Ballot and then use it and see how silly and useless it is. Deliver a body of women over Lock, Stock, and Barrel to the Republican Party!
>
> Solidarity of Women! Having me arrested was an example of it.[42]

The IWW's disdain for electoral politics could easily shade, as in this instance, into an attitude of contempt for the women in the suffrage movement; such contempt was inappropriate, however accurate their perception of the class differences involved may have been since they did nothing to change the suffrage movement or to take up the issue themselves.

Unlike the IWW, the Socialist Party stood for woman suffrage, and even placed much of its emphasis on electoral work. It was, at least before World War I, a large, broad-based, and influential reform organization that had had substantial successes at the polls—winning a number of mayoral offices, several congressional seats, and garnering almost seven hundred thousand votes in Eugene V. Debs's presidential campaign in 1912. The party had an active press—in 1912 there were 323 party newspapers and magazines, including 13 dailies[43]—and was able to popularize such key Marxist ideas as class conflict and the labor theory of value. Party members led serious challenges to Gomper's policies within the AFL and were influential in the WTUL. Most important, the party held out, if even in a muddled and contradictory way, the goal of revolution, of fundamental social transformation; it was this that constituted its main appeal. It attracted many active and dedicated women: working-class women who wanted more than the trade union movement and middle-class women who wanted to go beyond the narrowness and class bias of the suffrage movement.

Yet the women within the Socialist Party who wanted to work actively for suffrage had only halfhearted and token support from their own party and were themselves divided about whether they should work in alliance with the mainstream suffrage movement or on a purely working-class basis. The following poem by Charlotte Perkins Gilman explains their dilemma, laying out the mechanical materialism that passed for Marxism at the time, and counterposing to it the idealism of the suffragists:

> Said the Socialist to the Suffragist:
>   "My cause is greater than yours!
>   You only work for a Special Class,
>   We for the gain of the General Mass,
> Which every good ensures!"
>
> Said the Suffragist to the Socialist:
>   "You underrate my Cause!
>   While women remain a Subject Class,
>   You never can move the General Mass,
> With your Economic Laws!"

Said the Socialist to the Suffragist:
   "You misinterpret facts!
   There is no room for doubt or schism
   In Economic Determinism—
It governs all our acts!"

Said the Suffragist to the Socialist:
   "You men will always find
   That this old world will never move
   More swiftly in its ancient groove
While women stay behind!"

"A lifted world lifts women up!"
   The Socialist explained.
   "You cannot lift the world at all
   While half of it is kept so small,"
The Suffragist maintained.

The world awoke and tartly spoke:
   "Your work is all the same;
   Work together or work apart,
   Work, each of you, with all your heart—
Just get into the game!"[44]

The Socialist Party's founding convention in 1901 put a demand for "equal civil and political rights for men and women" into the party's program.[45] Six years later at the 1907 convention of the Second International (the federation of socialist parties from around the world), a women's caucus under the leadership of German socialist Clara Zetkin finally got the International to call for special campaigns against the oppression of women and for woman suffrage.[46] This gave party members in the United States the ammunition to put the party program into effect. Prior to the party's 1908 convention, a large conference of women socialists met to make plans and discuss a resolution calling for a Women's National Committee. The women who came had years of experience in socialist agitation; more importantly, they had already organized socialist women's groups in Los Angeles, Chicago, New York, San Francisco, and a number of smaller cities.

These groups had grown up outside the party for three reasons: the lack of interest in, and neglect of, women's special needs by men in the party; the women's desire to concentrate on work with their own sex, which they could not do in the party; and their belief that, since they had less political experience and education than the men, they could develop their abilities better in an all-female situation where they would feel less intimidated. Activist Meta Stern spoke eloquently of the reasons they had organized separately.

> The main reason is that under present-day conditions women's interests are not and cannot be identified with those of men. . . . They have much to fight for that men obtained long ago, and they have much to learn that men, owing to the schooling of their broader, more socialized lives, have long since learned. Women are just beginning to learn the lessons of organization and solidarity and concerted action, and not until they have learned that lesson thoroughly can the sometimes dry routine work of party locals have any meaning for them. . . .
>
> And this brings us to the vital point, the suffrage question . . . an ever-increasing number of American working women is becoming profoundly and actively interested in the suffrage movement . . . it depends on the attitude of the Socialist Party towards the woman's movement whether a formidable number of these intelligent women workers will rally around the banner of Socialism, or whether they will drift away from us and ally themselves with the bourgeois suffrage movement. . . . The fact is that we do not care to wait for the realization of Socialism for the abolition of our political dependence.[47]

The scattered socialist women's groups had no organizational relationship, but in 1907 the founding of *Socialist Women* (later renamed *Progressive Woman*), edited by Josephine Conger Kaneko, provided this loose network with a center. The magazine was intended to raise the level of theory on the oppression of women, to coordinate information and activities among the socialist women's groups, and to provide a vehicle for outreach to new members. It was designed as a popular magazine, however, and even after it was taken over by the party, it restricted itself to watered down versions of Engels and Bebel on the woman question, exposures of bad conditions affecting working women, fiction of an inspirational sort, and reports on the activities of socialist women. It did not take part in party debates and consequently did not train its readers to become equal fighting members within the party in the way that Clara Zetkin's magazine, *Equality,* did in Germany;[48] it was more like the *Ladies' Home Journal* with a dose of socialism. Despite these limitations, it played an important role in developing socialist work with women.

Most of the women at the preconvention meeting in 1908 agreed that they would prefer to do their socialist work within the party rather than outside of it, if some way could be found to give this work support and if they could do it their own way. They had not wished to build a sex-segregated revolutionary movement, but had done so out of necessity because of the lack of concern of the men in the party for work with women. Josephine Conger Kaneko used the example of meeting places, always a telling one:

> It has never been very likely that we [the Socialist Party] could reach the workingman in his wife's kitchen or nursery, or her little parlor, and as it has seemed more expedient to work with him than with her, we have followed him to his lair—to the street corner, to the trade union hall, to the saloon. We have opened our locals in localities where he could most easily be reached . . . in the rear room of saloons, and frequently in other dreary, comfortless halls which are always obnoxious to women.
>
> We have said, half-heartedly, that women could come to our locals in these dreary places. But they haven't cared to come to any great extent, any more than the men would have cared to meet in the women's parlors. It has been plainly a discrimination in favor of one sex over another. . . . As we have chosen our meeting places in the favor of men, we have also directed our speeches and our published matter to mankind.[49]

The women submitted two resolutions to the Socialist Party convention: one called for setting up a Women's National Committee to coordinate work with women, and the other proposed an active campaign for woman suffrage. The convention agreed to both, although a minority resolution warning against taking "any steps which would result in a waste of energy and perhaps in a separate women's movement" got a third of the votes, signaling trouble to come. It set up a five-member committee, with funds for one full-time speaker and organizer. The committee was to do investigative and educational work among women and children, especially working women; to do propaganda work; and to "assist the Socialist women of the party in explaining and stimulating the growing interest in Socialism among women." It was to be responsible to the National Executive Committee, the regularly elected party leadership.[50]

The women set to work enthusiastically, and appear to have abandoned their early separate organizations with no reservations. They saw their main business as recruiting, with suffrage agitation and youth work (the socialist Sunday schools) as close seconds.[51] Female membership in the party began to increase dramatically: in 1909 the number of women members of both Chicago and Kansas was ten times what it had been in 1908,[52] and by 1912, the National Women's Committee estimated that 10 percent of all party members were women—great progress in only four years.[53] In 1909 the party inaugurated International Women's Day, a special day for women across the country, and demonstrations and rallies concentrated on the suffrage issue. This national campaign gave a boost to all the party's work with women, and by 1910 there were women's committees in 135 party locals (there had been none in 1908). The party also produced and distributed an enormous quantity of literature directed mainly at working-class women, ranging from *Progressive Woman* (which had a circulation of twelve thousand in 1912)[54] to books on sex relations, like Kate Richards O'Hare's *The Sorrows of Cupid,* to special suffrage leaflets addressed to different groups of women— factory workers, professional women, teachers, wives of working men, and even club women. There were also pamphlets on alcoholism, white slavery, and the evils of the Boy Scout movement.

Inevitably, once there were significant numbers of women in the party, a major debate broke out on their relationship to the mainstream suffrage movement, partly in response to a position taken by the Socialist International. In 1910 a special international convention of women socialists met in Copenhagen; Lena Morrow Lewis was the U.S. delegate. Led by Clara Zetkin and the other German women, the convention took the position that socialist women should work for suffrage as socialists, not as part of the middle-class suffrage movement. The reasons for this were related to conditions in a number of European countries, where a bitter struggle was going on between the bourgeois women's organizations, which were opposed to protective legislation for women factory workers on the grounds that such protection was patronizing and restrictive, and the socialist parties, which favored such laws. Furthermore, in many European countries the right to vote was restricted to property owners, and woman suffragists were working to extend the vote to women "on the same terms as men," that is, to women property owners, rather than campaigning for universal suffrage. Zetkin and other socialists condemned this policy sharply:

> It is easy to be understood that in England the bourgeois woman suffragists fight with the greatest energy for the limited woman suffrage. In doing so, they only act according to their class interests. They have no concern for the complete democratisation of the suffrage which is demanded in the interests of the proletarian women. The ladies have already shown on other occasions their incapacity for understanding the interests of working women. We would remind you of the doggedness with which a great and very influential portion of the English Women's Righters have opposed . . . legal protection of female labor. Here, too, the ladies have always appealed to the principle of the equality of the sexes, whereas in reality they were defending nothing else than the unlimited freedom of exploitation of the propertied over the non-propertied. They thus remained true to their character as champions of the interests of the propertied classes by sacrificing in the question of woman suffrage, too, the right of the great majority of their sex to the privilege of a small minority of their class; by demanding, instead of equal political rights for all, only a privilege for a comparatively few. Under these circumstances it must astonish us to see the Socialist women and men come foward, together with the bourgeois ladies, as champions of the political monopoly of the purse.[55]

The situation in the United States in 1908 was strikingly different: here the main opposition to protective legislation came from the AFL, rather than the suffragists, and, despite NAWSA's white supremacist alliances, no one was openly supporting a limited franchise. How, then, were U.S. socialists to apply the international resolution to their own situation? Should they defy it and work within NAWSA? Should they ally with NAWSA, speaking from the same platform but with their own message? Or should they try to organize a purely working-class suffrage movement?

The debate on these questions came to a head at the 1910 Socialist Party convention, but the controversy began in New York City, where about two hundred socialists met on December 19, 1909, to consider their relationship to the suffrage movement. They had had a month's experience of working with suffragists in support of the shirtwaist makers' strike, which began in November and already felt they were getting the worst of it. They saw the "world-wide class conscious labor movement and the world-wide sex conscious woman movement" as being fundamentally opposed; the question was, which would win the allegiance of the working women? Anita Block, woman's editor of the *New York Call,* argued in favor of a resolution that "the work of Socialist women for the suffrage must be carried on along separate and independent lines, by and through the political and economic organizations of the working class." As she saw it, this was the only way to get to the working girls with socialist-suffrage ideas, and not get swamped by the bourgeois ladies who were then swooping down on the Lower East Side looking for suffrage recruits:

> The danger in cooperation is for the workingwoman who knows nothing of either sex consciousness or class consciousness. Far better for such a woman if she comes squarely into the hands of avowed Socialist women, who proceed at once to instill in her the feeling of class solidarity and then show her how, if she wants publicly to register her class consciousness, she must get the ballot and vote for her class, than if at the same time, she is besieged by the suffragists, who teach her to get the ballot and vote for her sex. Now, can there be any doubt that the inculcation of both these ideas at the same time would tend to obscure the one that was less popular, less noised abroad, and presented by a small minority?[56]

Although Block's resolution passed by a large majority, it is interesting that it was assumed—by both sides—that the ballot would make women equal to men, ending female oppression and sex antagonism and leaving only class conflict. That was why they saw such an urgent need for suffrage work on a separate, socialist basis—without it, they would have nothing left, once women got the vote.

> The important thing is to save the working woman from the fallacious argument that political equality will right her wrongs; to convince her that freedom from sex slavery does not mean freedom from wage slavery; to show her how her enfranchised working brother is practically no better off than his disenfranchised working sister; to make her realize that, while she is entitled to the vote and must have it, it will avail her nothing till she learns to cast it on the side of the working class, against the capitalist class, and for a new and radically different social order.[57]

Between the New York City conference in December and the party convention in May, further events fueled the socialist women's anger against the suffrage movement. Not only did the enormous amount of hard work they had put into the shirtwaist makers' strike go unrecognized, but they were not allowed to speak from certain public platforms, and when they were red-baited by J. P. Morgan's daughter, no suffragists came to their defense.[58] They helped draft a strong resolution that was presented to the convention delegates which clearly subordinated suffrage work to trade union work as a method of reaching working-class women:

> As a means of coming in closer touch with the economic movement, we urge that our women comrades join the various woman's trade union leagues wherever same are in existence. In every industrial centre we urge the election of a strike committee to be in readiness whenever any occasion for action appears, as the surest means of gaining the ear of the women in the trades lies in helping them during an economic struggle.
>
> We also urge upon our women comrades the organization of women into unions wherever the opportunity presents itself, for the working girl at large is very often incapable of grasping the principles of Socialism at the first attempt, where she would be willing to do so were she used to the economic organization, which is really the first step of her awakening.
>
> Woman's disenfranchisement being a great factor in aggravating her economic dependence, we urge the Party to take more direct action in the matter of woman suffrage, which should, however, be

carried on under Party supervision and advocated from Party platforms.[59]

The drive behind the last paragraph was incomprehensible to most of the socialist women outside New York and particularly to those in the Midwest and West, where the suffrage movement was more democratic and less controlled by the rich than in New York. The resolution was taken to mean that there should be no cooperation at all with NAWSA and was seen as wildly sectarian. Ella Reeve Bloor, a delegate from Connecticut who frequently spoke from suffrage platforms, proposed an amendment that was clearly in a different spirit:

> Whether it be a legislative hearing, a public demonstration or discussion, the Socialists should range themselves on all occasions with the advocates of woman suffrage.
>
> In this country there is practically no movement for a qualified suffrage. The American woman suffrage movement as a whole stands for full political rights for women, regardless of class and property qualifications. There is, therefore, less reason for us to conduct a separate campaign upon this issue than there is for our comrades in Europe, where the suffrage movement is to some extent conducted on class lines. While the Socialist Party should never merge its identity in any other movement, we should not place ourselves in a voluntary position of isolation, where the principles and aims of our party fully coincide with those of other organizations. We should heartily support the general movement of the women of America for their enfranchisement. In this case, as in many similar cases, Socialism must break through the narrow circle of our own organization and must penetrate into the masses of the people as a living and vivifying social force.[60]

A sharp debate followed. Theresa Malkiel of New York, one of the members of the Women's National Committee, felt allying with the suffrage movement amounted to fusion with a bourgeois organization: "We should not lose our identity in working for suffrage, which would surely be the case if we should co-operate with the middle-class suffragists."[61] Kate Richards O'Hare answered that in the West and Southwest she had had no trouble in working for the vote as an open socialist, making socialist speeches from suffrage platforms; she was always asked to speak and, no matter what the subject, could bring it back to "the Socialistic basis. I don't care whether they talk on the marriage question or on the comet, I will bring the comet back to the Socialistic proposition."[62]

Algie Simons, a conservative party leader, made an impassioned speech warning the convention against

> the meanest, shrewdest, sharpest, cleverest capitalist class the world had ever known. They know what they are doing when they organize the Woman's Suffrage organization, . . . that it is better that they should seem to hand it to them as a favor; and if in so handing them this favor they can absorb the organization of the proletariat, and substitute for that organization an organization that cuts across the class lines, they will make the revolution we are seeking infinitely more difficult.[63]

He was answered by Lena Morrow Lewis, the one woman on the party's National Executive Committee at the time:

> I insist that working women will accept the Socialist philosophy in about the same proportions as the working men. And that Mrs. Belmont and Mrs. Morgan [two millionaire suffragists active in support of the shirtwaist makers' strike] can no more control the women of the working class when once they get the ballot, any more than the same Belmont-Morgan crowd can control the men of the working class. If there is anything lacking, it is possibly in our not having good propaganda among the women . . . it is up to us to present such a superior kind of propaganda that the Belmonts can have absolutely no effect upon it.[64]

Each side caricatured the other's position, presenting the only alternatives as either fusion with NAWSA or total isolation from it. No coherent proposal was put forward for working independently in coalition with NAWSA, or for varying the party's tactics according to regional circumstances, since clearly the suffrage movement differed widely from place to place. The socialist women were neither experienced enough nor theoretically developed enough to be able to formulate such possibilities in a way that could have won over the majority of delegates.

The resolution of the Women's National Committee was therefore passed, and the socialist women proceeded to set up Socialist Suffrage Societies, which did propaganda work, and, at least in New York in the 1917 referendum, heroic organizing. But the party as a whole still had a weak grasp of the importance of the suffrage issue and its relationship to the class struggle. There was an undercurrent of opposition to work with women, particularly among party conservatives, who tended to see suffrage not as something women of all classes needed and were fighting for, but as a plot to buy off working-class women, or to use them against the electoral interests of the party. As Victor Berger, who represented the most conservative elements in the party, put it in 1910:

> The question has been raised by some thinking Socialists whether the great mass of women today have the qualities that their vote would contribute to the welfare of the working class, and especially whether the women's vote would help humanity in the coming time of transition.
>
> This is a question of fact on which Socialists may honestly differ. . . . Now it is clear, and no one will deny that the great majority of women of the present day—and that is the only point we can view now—are illiberal, unprogressive and reactionary to a greater extent than the men of the same strata of society. . . . Now if all of this is correct, female suffrage, for generations to come, will simply mean the deliberate doubling of a certain church—will mean an addition to the forces of ignorance and reaction.
>
> However, we have woman suffrage in our platform, and we should stand by it. . . . Nevertheless, it is asking a great deal of the proletariat when we are requested to delay the efficiency of our movement for generations on that account. And we surely ought not to lay such stress on this one point as to injure the progress of the general political and economic movement—the success of which is bound to help the women as much as the men.[65]

In 1912 the Socialist Party split, and its most radical element, sympathetic to the IWW, left the organization as a result of a successful power play by the conservatives. When Caroline Lowe resigned as head of the Women's National Committee, the party leaders appointed Winnie Branstetter, a woman of few feminist sympathies, to her place. The literature she sent out to the party locals showed how far the capitalist-conspiracy line of thinking had gone.

> Dear Comrade: Suffrage has been granted to the women of four states during the past year. DO YOU KNOW WHY?

Organized capital wishes to use the conservatism of woman to off-set the advance of labor on the political field. For this purpose suffrage will soon be given the women of every state in the Union. . . .

Skillfully, adroitly, they have planned their nation-wide campaign for the woman vote. By their advocacy of woman suffrage they have enlisted the active support of thousands of earnest women. These women do not know that they are becoming the political serfs of a corrupt and retrogressive organization whose sole purpose is to check the forward march of labor, . . .

While the old parties are tossing bouquets of remedial messages and subtle flattery to the potential voter, we will carry her the message of real liberty and freedom—freedom from the sordidness and drudgery of endless toil— . . .

WE MUST CARRY THIS MESSAGE TO EVERY WOMAN IN AMERICA. Can we depend upon your local to do its share?[66]

When the conservative wing gained full control of the national party machinery, the Socialist Party became increasingly oriented to narrow reformist activity and electioneering: Victor Berger's "Milwaukee socialism" or, as it was called by its detractors, "sewer socialism." This transition was devastating to the party's work with women. In 1914 the party ceased to support *Progressive Woman,* which had to stop publication, leaving no English language socialist paper for women. The next year the party leadership held a referendum and abolished the Women's National Committee, using the excuse that it cost too much and that special work with women was unnecessary and incorrect. Even Winnie Branstetter and Janet Korngold, both wives of high party functionaries and members of the committee, endorsed the vote:

Working class women, if they be wage-earners, are concerned with the working conditions, the regulation of wages, and all manner of legislation that affects their labor. If they be housewives, they are concerned with the "growing grocery bill" and with the limited advantages of their children . . . these are exactly the avenues of interest by which working class men are approached in the interests of Socialism. . . .

I favor the abolition of all special machinery having for its object the execution of so-called "work for women." All the Party's work is for women.[67]

To the charges that they wasted money, committee members retorted that they had been told earlier that they would not be getting any money, so the financial objection was hardly valid: "Now that the Committee has, thus hampered, been able to do little, it is described as an 'expensive ornament' of the party."[68] Theresa Malkiel went further, and pointed to the role the Executive Committee itself had played in undermining their work:

> Is it not a fact that since the creation of the Woman's National Committee its activity, or lack of it, depended absolutely on the good will of the N.E.C.? When this latter body chanced to be of a radical trend of mind in so far as work among women is concerned, the committee succeeded in publishing a number of special leaflets, in having one or more organizers in the field, in originating and promoting the celebration of woman's day in almost every local of the Socialist Party? All this, we must bear in mind, had to be approved by the N.E.C. before it could be carried out.
>
> Unfortunately, the N.E.C. now in office did not think the woman's work of any consequence to the movement and continually practised its policy of retrenchment on the woman's work. We all know the consequences.[69]

Josephine Conger Kaneko harked back to the autonomy of the socialist women's groups before 1908 to draw the lesson of how an unsympathetic party apparatus could undermine work with women:

> Up to 1908, Socialist women were very active in study clubs for women, from New York to Los Angeles. It was the party convention which gave to the Socialist women the "Committee" form of organization, officially discrediting all other forms, and thus destroying to a large degree the work already accomplished by the women.
>
> At that time an active woman comrade cynically remarked, "This is a move to kill the women's activity in the Socialist party."
>
> Was she right?
>
> At the meeting of the Woman's Committee in May, 1914, the National Correspondent [Winnie Branstetter] triumphantly reported that all separate women's organizations—study clubs, etc.—had gone out of existence.
>
> At the National Committee meeting of May, 1915, we have the members voting the Woman's Committee out of existence, in which

action they are supported by the staunchest supporters of the
Committee form in 1908.

Thus we find every avenue of woman's work within the party
officially shut off—killed.[70]

The Executive Committee's dissolution of the Women's National Committee led to a wave of bitterness among women activists. Some, like Josephine Conger Kaneko, subsequently became inactive; some left the party to do other kinds of feminist
organizing such as work on the issue of birth control. Still others,
like Kate Richards O'Hare, one of the few women to serve on the
National Executive Committee, remained in the party but were
very clear about what they were up against:

> Personally, I have run the whole gamut of masculine jealousy,
> resentment and hindrance. As long as I did nothing that some man
> wanted to do himself, everything was lovely—but when I chanced
> to encroach on what some man felt was his job—well it was not
> lovely to say the least.
>
> My experience on the N.E.C. gave me an excellent chance to
> study the antics of the male who feels that his domain has been
> treacherously invaded by a female. Only Shaw could do justice to
> the humor of the paternalistic patronage, the lofty scorn, the fatherly
> solicitude I enjoyed lest my weak and faltering footsteps be led
> astray in the dangerous quagmires of party service. I am happy to
> say that I managed to extract enough fun from the situation to
> make the annoyance bearable, though I was totally unable to be of
> any service to the party. I am absolutely sure that my experience has
> also been the experience of every woman in the party who has ever
> held a position or accomplished a piece of party work that some man
> felt it would have been an advantage for him to have held or done.[71]

Because it suppressed the work of its own women members, the
party became increasingly unable to give any leadership to the
masses of women who were eager to organize—at a time when, as
the Women's National Committee had pointed out, there was a
great upsurge among women:

> The work of the suffrage forces has during the past year added two
> states to the list of equal suffrage states, bringing the total number
> up to twelve. Nor does the work lag. During the next two years
> suffrage campaigns will be carried on in seven states. . . .

Nor is the need for work among women less urgent in those sections where the suffrage cause remains less popular. The working women of the South, oppressed by poverty, strong social conditions, and legal sex discrimination, afford tremendous opportunities for educational work. The working women of the industrial centers, already awakening to a sense of the economic injustices done them, are ready for organization. The need for special work among women of the rural districts is likewise apparent.

The Women's National Committee recognizes the fact that economic oppression coupled with the gradual granting of political rights to women, has awakened in women a social conscience heretofore unknown. Their restlessness and dissatisfaction afford us an opportunity to direct them to the Socialist program as the only possible remedy for existing economic evils. This Committee urges upon the national organization the necessity for more extensive propaganda and organization among working class women.[72]

In May 1915 Agnes Downing noted: "Just at the time when the whole world is reaching for women's help, the Socialist party seems to be letting go. . . . In this country, Socialist women, as a body, have no influence in the social mass. They are doing nothing aggressive or positive. Individuals among them excel in various lines, but the party as an organization is benefitted little by their splendid work."[73]

Although the party as an organization abandoned special work with women, a number of individuals and some locals continued to work for woman suffrage, particularly in New York. Notable among them were the Greenwich Village socialist feminists, including Inez Milholland, Crystal Eastman, Florence Rauh, and Jessie Ashley, who were also interested in such questions as birth control and experimental living arrangements. These women became increasingly resistant to the demands of the party apparatus; on one occasion they broke party discipline to march in the great Fifth Avenue suffrage parade,[74] and the records of the New York Socialist Party contain acrimonious correspondence about $500 given Anita Block and Jessie Ashley in trust for some feminist purpose to be decided by them, which they refused to hand over to the local party women's committee.[75]

If socialist feminists became frustrated in the Socialist Party, they were equally irritated with NAWSA, especially after the

British suffrage movement began to employ terrorist tactics. When British feminists broke department store windows, chained themselves to lamp posts, bombed mailboxes, and endured forced feedings in their prison hunger strikes, U.S. feminists began to feel that their struggle too demanded something more militant than petitions and protest meetings. In 1913 the most radical elements of NAWSA seceded under Alice Paul's leadership to form a separate organization, the Congressional Union, soon renamed the National Woman's Party. Many socialist feminists were among them.

The National Woman's Party's differences with NAWSA were largely tactical. They thought the suffrage movement should go all out to get a suffrage amendment to the Constitution through Congress, rather than patiently try to get it adopted state by state. They also favored shock tactics, such as open opposition to President Wilson for not giving them enough help even though he said he was prosuffrage. In their class composition and their single-issue mentality, however, most members of the National Woman's Party had little to differentiate them from NAWSA.

With the onset of World War I tensions between the two wings of the suffrage movement became severe. In 1917, three years after fighting began in Europe, the United States entered the war and the mainstream of the feminist movement went with a great surge into the arms of the government. Hoping that if women proved their worth in this moment of national crisis a grateful government would reward them with the vote, both NAWSA and the Women's Trade Union League eagerly cooperated with the war effort. Many of their leaders took government posts. The AFL was equally enthusiastic: its leadership formed the American Alliance for Labor and Democracy and pledged not to strike for the duration of the war.

The IWW and the majority of the Socialist Party, on the other hand, were firmly opposed to the war as an imperialist one. They were persecuted, blacklisted, and jailed, and some IWW members were even killed for their beliefs. A number of feminists were also opposed to the war: Jane Addams, Leonora O'Reilly, and others were pacifists and spoke out on that basis, while the militant suffragists of the National Woman's Party thought that Woodrow

Wilson had no business making the "world safe for democracy" when there wasn't any at home. Referring to him as "Kaiser Wilson," they picketed the White House with signs denouncing the war, and were attacked by patriotic mobs of servicemen. Arrested on the flimsiest of pretexts, many of them were sent to the workhouse, where they went on hunger strikes and were forcibly fed like their British sisters.

The repression suffered by the National Woman's Party was but one part of a general wartime campaign against dissent of all kinds, culminating in the postwar "Red Scare" with its massive deportations of Russian-born immigrants and its Palmer raids against left-wing organizations. The labor movement also came under heavy attack, demobilized as it had been by its wartime collaboration. A union-busting campaign wiped out union organizations in steel, meatpacking, lumber, and on the docks, and severely weakened other unions; the AFL lost more than a million members after the war.[76] Reeling from these attacks, the socialist movement was further disrupted by its own splits over revolutionary strategy following the Russian Revolution.

Meanwhile women won the vote; the federal amendment passed both houses of Congress in 1919 and was ratified by enough states to be written into the Constitution in 1920. Historians are still debating whether the credit for this victory should go to the steady infantry work of NAWSA or the kamikaze actions of the National Woman's Party. Ultimately the vote was won by a united front of women of disparate political views working for the same end by various means—bourgeois feminists, radical feminists, socialists, and trade unionists. The wartime splits between these forces did not augur well for united action after the suffrage victory, however, and in the end even the state repression which the socialists and radical feminists had shared was not enough to bring them together.

One obstacle was their diametrically opposed ideas of program. Despite its militance, the National Woman's Party was single-issue in its approach to suffrage and remained single-issue after it reached its goal, merely substituting the Equal Rights Amendment for the suffrage amendment. The socialists within it were unable to challenge this approach successfully: a group of them, led by Crystal Eastman, prepared a program covering a wide spectrum of issues ranging from equal job opportunity to birth control to family allowances, but this program was steamrollered without even being discussed at the National Woman's Party's convention celebrating the suffrage victory. As Crystal Eastman summarized the situation: "If some such program could have been exhaustively discussed at that convention we might be congratulating ourselves that the feminist movement had begun in America. As it is all we can say is that the suffrage movement is ended."[77]

When the National Woman's Party put all its single-minded energy behind the Equal Rights Amendment, the result was more divisive to the united front of women than even the war had been, for the feminist movement was split over the issue of protective legislation for women and children—the same issue that had earlier split the Illinois Woman's Alliance. In a period where the labor movement was being dismembered and most women remained unorganized, the Women's Trade Union League, the settlement women, and even the AFL saw protective legislation as the only defense women workers had against total exploitation. The National Woman's Party saw it as discriminatory, preventing women from working at many jobs that men held, and therefore institutionalizing the occupational segregation of women into low-paid slots. When the courts struck down protective laws, the National Woman's Party openly rejoiced—therefore, according to its opponents, proving its fundamental identity with the National Association of Manufacturers.

In these circumstances the feminist movement began to look utterly reactionary to radical women of the next generation. Seeing the National Woman's Party as morally bankrupt, they ceased to identify with feminism at all and it became, as Sherna Gluck has pointed out, a "dirty word" on the left, describing "a stance inimical to their committment to destroy capitalism."[78] The fragile basis of unity that women workers, socialists, and feminists had found in the woman suffrage issue could not be maintained when the ERA seemed to counterpose the interests of middle-class women to the interests of women and child workers.[79] The remnants of the united front of women were shattered and the beginnings of a new basis of unity were not to develop for almost fifty years.

Part IV
Two Strikes

The following chapters consider two key strikes in detail: the New York shirtwaist makers' strike of 1909–1910, and the Lawrence textile workers strike of 1912. The shirtwaist makers' strike was the first massive uprising of women workers in the United States, and was a breakthrough in organizing the garment industry. It was known as the "women's movement strike" because of the unusual extent to which women of all classes participated. It is an important place to look at a broad united front of women in action, and the contradictions within it.

The Lawrence strike was a great, militant, even (it was thought at the time) revolutionary uprising of the U.S. working class. Because of the radicalism of the Industrial Workers of the World who led it, and their encouragement of the participation of women, the strike is a good place to look at the way women came to the fore when they had the chance to do so, and the way housewives were encouraged to participate in an industrial struggle.

8
The Uprising of the Thirty Thousand

A lull in the struggle,
A truce in the fight,
The whirr of machines
And the dearly bought right,
Just to labor for bread,
Just to work and be fed.

For this we have marched
Through the snow-covered street,
Have borne our dead comrades
While muffled drums beat.
For this we have fought,
For this boon dearly-bought.

We measure our gain
By the price we have paid.
Call the victory great
As the struggle we made;
For we struggled to grow,
And we won. And we know.

Ah, we know, as we hear
Once again the loud hum
Of machines all in motion,
Commanding we come
In our newly-won powers,
To this labor of ours.

Together we suffered
The weary weeks past,
Together we won and
Together at last
As we learn our own might,
We will win the great fight.

Mary O'Reilly
"After the Strike"[1]

On November 22, 1909, the tiny waistmakers' local of the International Ladies Garment Workers Union called a general strike of all the shirtwaist makers in New York. The strike became known as the Uprising of the Thirty Thousand (or, depending on the source, the Twenty Thousand) because that was the approximate number of strikers who rose spontaneously in answer to the union's call. The strike also came to be thought of as the "woman's movement strike," because, under the leadership of the Women's Trade Union League, the whole of the women's movement, from the society matrons of the Colony Club to the socialists of the Lower East Side, joined with the strikers, most of whom were teenage girls.

Local 25 of the ILGWU, the shirtwaist makers' local, had rented Cooper Union for the November 22 meeting. Three shirtwaist shops were already on strike—Leiserson's, Rosen Brothers, and the Triangle Waist Company—but union leaders had no idea how many workers outside those three shops would come to the meeting. The crowd began to pour into the hall hours early. People waited patiently, talking mainly in Yiddish. Most of them were teenage girls, nervous and excited at being at their first union meeting. The *Jewish Daily Forward,* a Yiddish socialist paper, reported some of their conversations: "What if a general strike is decided upon? Who knows how many will join in it? Who can tell how long it may last? And what if a motion for a strike will be voted down? When will there be another chance to improve the conditions? Are we to suffer forever?"[2] Soon there was not even standing room in the hall, and the union officers began to scurry around, renting other halls in the neighborhood for the overflow, until Beethoven Hall, the Manhattan Lyceum, and Astoria Hall were full and people were still lining up in the street.

In Cooper Union, the speakers arranged themselves on the platform. Unlike the audience, they were well dressed, prosperous, respectable looking, and almost all men. Chief among them was Samuel Gompers of the AFL; it was considered a coup to have gotten him to come. Then there were other union officials, socialist lawyers, and Mary Dreier of the Women's Trade Union League—an endless series of speakers, none of whom worked in the shirtwaist shops. The speeches went on for two hours. Finally, as the union has described the events in its *Souvenir History of the Strike:*

Then came the dramatic climax of the evening. At Cooper Union, down in the body of the hall, arose a working girl, a striker, an unknown, who asked the chairman for the privilege of the floor. Many grumbling dissensions came her way, some excitement was visible on the platform, but the chairman held that as she was a striker she had as good a right there as himself, so Clara Lemlich made her way to the platform. She was a striker from the Leiserson shop; she had been assaulted while picketing; she knew from actual experience what her sisters were up against, and that they were tired of oratory; she knew they had come there for business; she knew they were seething with discontent and hatred of their bondage; that they were pulsing with sympathy for their fellow workers and that each was ready, aye, anxious, for the charge into the camp of the common oppressor, and, as has been well said, after an impromptu phillipic in Yiddish, eloquent even to American ears, she put the motion for a general strike, and was unanimously endorsed.

The chairman then cried, "Do you mean faith? Will you take the old Jewish oath?" and up came two thousand right hands, with the prayer, "If I turn traitor to the cause I now pledge, may this hand wither from the arm I now raise," and thus started this historic general strike, probably the greatest struggle for unionism among women the world has ever seen.[3]

Clara Lemlich may have been an "unknown" to the public, but to the Lower East Side labor movement she was already a heroine: she was a founder of the shirtwaist local, had led the walkout in Leiserson's shop, and had been beaten by hired thugs while picketing. During the two weeks she was laid up, her health was the subject of almost daily comment in the *New York Call.*

Clara Lemlich had had to fight since the day she was born in the Ukraine in 1888, so she had become good at it. Her father was an Orthodox Jewish scholar, and as tradition dictated, he did not permit his daughter to learn to read; in particular the study of Russian (as opposed to Yiddish) was forbidden. Clara Lemlich would sneak down to the village to make buttonholes for the little tailor shops, and use the money she earned to pay students to teach her to read Russian. Although her father burned her Russian books, she had already become literate by the time her family fled Russia in 1903—she had even read revolutionary literature.[4]

Clara Lemlich wanted to go to school in New York, but instead she had to go to work to help support her family. She got work in a shirtwaist shop, making the elaborate blouses that were virtually the uniform of working women in this period. She continued to study, however, and hoped to become a doctor. She would work for eleven hours, then walk to the public library, stopping only for a glass of milk, and study until it closed. She would not get home for supper until late at night. She recalled later: "All week long I wouldn't see the daylight. I remember once, when things were slow, they let us out in the middle of the day. 'What!' I said, 'Are all the people on strike?' I had never realized that there were so many out during the daytime."[5]

In 1906 Clara Lemlich joined a group of shirtwaist makers who went to the office of the *Jewish Daily Forward* to find out how to form a union. She was one of seven young women and six young men who formed Local 25, at a time when the ILGWU was small and its members mainly comprised of male cloakmakers. She was by then a skilled draper, still saving money to go to school, but she seemed unable to work in a shop without trying to organize it. Even when she vowed to be a "good girl," she found herself talking union two days later. She began to look for work in the smaller shops where she could have more influence. The oppressive conditions in the trade kept her at the boiling point: the forewoman following a girl to the toilet, nagging her to hurry; the new girls being cheated of their pay; the fines; the charges for electricity and needles and thread; the "mistakes" in the pay envelopes that were so difficult to get fixed; the time clock that was fixed so that lunch was twenty minutes short, or was set back an hour so the workers didn't know that they were working overtime.[6]

In 1907 she took part in her first strike, a ten-week strike against speedup in the small shop where she worked at the time. At one of the union meetings she heard strikers arguing about Gompers and his "pure-and-simple trade unionism." She asked one of them what that meant. He asked her to go for a walk, and they walked forty blocks while he gave her her first lesson in Marxism:

> He started with a bottle of milk—how it was made, who made the money from it at every stage of its production. Not only did the boss take the profits, he said, but not a drop of milk did you drink unless

he allowed you to. It was funny, you know, because I'd been saying
things like that to the girls before. But now I understood it better
and I began to use it more often—only with shirtwaists.[7]

She also began taking classes in Marxist theory at the Socialist
Party's school, the Rand School.

In 1908 the young women at the Gotham shop, where Clara
Lemlich was then working, struck in sympathy when the boss
fired men to make room for women, because he could pay them
less. The strike failed and the other girls went back to work, but
Clara Lemlich stayed outside the shop, distributing boycott leaflets
until the boss finally had her arrested for disorderly conduct.
This was the first of many such arrests.

She then went to work at Leiserson's. The male operators, who
were in a different ILGWU local than the shirtwaist makers,
planned a strike without even informing the other workers, many
of whom were women. When Clara Lemlich found out about it,
she went to their strike meeting and, asking for the floor, gave
them a piece of her mind, telling them that if they went out on
strike alone they would surely lose, but if they organized, they
could take the whole shop with them. They followed her advice
and the whole factory struck. Clara Lemlich's leadership was
decisive in keeping the Leiserson strike together—certainly the
boss thought so, for during the eleven weeks the picket line was
outside the shop she was singled out numerous times by his hired
thugs. In one battle six of her ribs were broken. In later years she
recalled her fearlessness: "Ah—then I had fire in my mouth. . . .
What did I know about trade unionism? Audacity—that was all I
had—audacity!"[8]

Her militance was an appropriate response to conditions in the
shirtwaist industry, which was notorious for irregularity, ineffi-
ciency, and severe exploitation. The industry was divided into
hundreds of tiny shops, each employing between five and twenty
girls and each competing with the others to drive down labor costs
and sell more cheaply, but it was dominated by a group of larger
shops, each employing between two hundred and three hundred
workers. The work was seasonal; all of the workers toiled long
hours during the busy season—fifty-six a week with overtime—
but were laid off when things were slow. Wages varied greatly,

depending on whether the workers were paid on a time or a piecework basis, and whether they were skilled or not. All workers were charged for the equipment they used, and many firms made a 20 percent profit on electricity for sewing machines, and 25 percent on needles and thread. Workers were docked an hour's pay for being five minutes late, and were made to pay for a whole length of cloth if they spoiled a corner.[9]

Within the work force there were further inequities, the greatest of which was between women and men. Most of the men were either skilled workers (cutters and pressers)[10] or subcontractors who were given orders by larger bosses and hired female assistants to do the work. The union believed that the subcontracting system had grown up as a result of the disorganization and lack of management skills that characterized the entire garment industry:

> It must first be understood that an overwhelming majority of the proprietors in this trade were laborers themselves but a few years ago, and not being endowed with a superabundance of executive ability or knowledge of modern business methods, especially those belonging to organization, they soon found the details of their business growing too numerous to be handled by personal attention.
>
> Therefore, instead of dividing their factory into departments and employing a foreman to supervise the same, they called in a workman and made a contract with him for a period of three or four months, agreeing to pay him so much a week for so much work turned out. They rented or loaned him the machines and encouraged him to get as much work out of a young girl for as little money as he could, and actually classified it as the speeding up system. By this means the girls' bosses were doubled, the inspection and criticism of her work was doubled, the incessant supervision of her every move was doubled, and two profits to one were taken out of her labor.[11]

In the shirtwaist industry, subcontracting went on inside large factories, where the subcontractors were responsible to a foreman. A subcontractor could pay his female employees what he pleased and usually paid them as little as possible. He had two categories of employees; women who had two or three years of experience and "learners" or apprentices. The union estimated that 37 percent of the workers in the shirtwaist trade were learners, young girls who made from $2.50 to $4.00 a week, while about 50 percent were more experienced young women, who made an average of $9.00 a week. The skilled male workers, on the other hand, who made up the remaining 15 percent of the workforce, made $15.00 to $23.00 a week.[12]

It was the skilled male workers and the subcontractors who led the ILGWU and Local 25, and who negotiated for it during the strike. The women workers, the most exploited section of the work force, had their bosses as their union leaders.[13] It is only in the light of this basic structural fact that developments in the union, which became increasingly clear in the years after the strike, can be understood: the absence of women from leadership or even staff positions; the leadership's tendency to look at the women workers as so many cattle who needed a strong leader to look up to, and their desire to run the union like a business. This view of the world stemmed from the leadership's position as employers of the other workers, privileged, skilled, and upwardly mobile. Needless to say, their attitude also rose from the male supremacy of the society as a whole, for they held their positions because of their sex—women did not become subcontractors, cutters, or paid union officials.[14]

If the sexual contradiction was built into the structure of the industry, ethnic differences also made uniting the work force difficult. Russian Jews, Italians, and native-born Americans formed 55 percent, 35 percent, and 7 percent respectively of the women in the trade. The men in the industry were mainly Russian Jews. Of those who actually went out on strike, however, 70 percent were Russian Jewish women, 20 percent were Russian Jewish men, 6 percent were Italian women, and 3 percent native-born women. The strikers were thus 90 percent Russian Jewish.[15] The Italians were particularly underrepresented among the strikers, partly, no doubt, because very few of them spoke English and none of the union leaders spoke their language. In fact, they mainly spoke Yiddish.Not only were the Italians and Jews separated by language and cultural barriers, but the Italians were also newcomers to the industry, brought in to undercut the wages of the Jews. The employers consciously used national differences to divide the work force; according to the union, "they placed an Italian girl beside a Jewess, so that they might not understand

each other, and then started stories to arouse race prejudice."[16]
There were also problems with the native-born American women,
who considered themselves superior to the others. They usually
earned more, they worked in different shops, further uptown
and they were unwilling to accept the leadership of "foreigners."

Local 25 did not attempt to deal with these ethnic differences.
Overwhelmingly Russian Jewish in membership, it made few
efforts to reach the Italians and the "American girls." It was small
and weak, and its organizing techniques were primitive. Its usual
strategy was to wait until there was a spontaneous movement such
as a walkout in a shop. The union would quickly go there and try
to sign the workers up, and then negotiate with the boss for union
recognition. As described by B. Witashkin, secretary of the local
in its early days, this method seldom worked:

> Our organizing work we generally carried on in a stereotyped way.
> We would issue a circular reading somewhat as follows: "Murder!
> The exploiters, the blood-suckers, the manufacturers. . . . Pay your
> dues. . . . Down with the capitalists! Hurrah!" The employers would
> be somewhat frightened and concede the demands of the union.
> After the demands would be granted, the workers would drop out
> of the organization. We would thus gain "recognition" and lose
> the workers.[17]

By 1909 the number of spontaneous actions indicated that
conditions were changing and that it might be possible to use
different methods. More workers started to seek out and join the
union, and then a small strike wave began in the East Side shops.
The first of these was a walkout at the Triangle Waist Company in
the fall of 1908. Just before the Jewish holidays, a protesting
subcontractor announced that he was sick of being a slave driver
and was going to quit. As the foreman began to drag him out, he
appealed to his fellow workers: "Brothers and sisters, are you
going to sit by your machines and see a fellow workman used this
way?" That was all it took; they laid down their work and walked
out. The strike lasted only three days, for without an organization
or benefits, the workers were quickly driven back.[18] The Triangle
management then organized a company union or benefit society
whose officers were all relatives of the owners. After a few months
some of the workers began to realize what a travesty this "union"

was and went to Local 25 for advice. They began to hold small meetings in secret.

Another strike at about this time, also initiated by male sub-contractors, was at Rosen Brothers. Two hundred workers went out when the boss refused to pay the price the subcontractors demanded. This strike lasted five weeks; the union was called in to negotiate, and the subcontractors won.

A third strike began in September 1909 at Leiserson's, where Clara Lemlich worked. Leiserson had begun to lay off his ex-perienced workers on the pretext that he had no work to give them. They learned that he was sending their work to a cheaper shop he had started downtown and even giving it on the sly to the learners in their own shop. Outraged, one hundred workers walked out. After the walkout Leiserson immediately advertised for scabs. He also hired thugs—"sluggers," as they were called, led by the "notorious Dominick"—to beat up the picketers.

At this time mass picketing, involving large numbers of workers, was not yet common. Instead, a handful of strikers would walk up and down in front of their shops, wearing placards or carry-ing signs and trying to persuade the scabs not to go in. The union bent over backwards not to be offensive. It issued rules for the picketers, which it hoped would save them from arrest—a vain hope:

Rules for Pickets

Don't walk in groups of more than two or three.

Don't stand in front of the shop; walk up and down the block.

Don't stop the person you wish to talk to; walk alongside of him.

Don't get excited and shout when you are talking.

Don't put your hand on the person you are speaking to. Don't touch his sleeve or button. This may be construed as a "technical assault."

Don't call anyone "scab" or use abusive language of any kind.

Plead, persuade, appeal, but do not threaten.

If a policeman arrests you and you are sure that you have com-mitted no offense, take down his number and give it to your union officers.[19]

These ladylike instructions did not prevent strikers from being enthusiastically set upon by hired thugs, beaten, and then arrested by the police. If a picketer spoke to a scab, she was arrested and charged with assault or intimidation; the scab was then bribed to swear in court that the striker had grabbed or threatened her. Such daily dramas in front of the Leiserson shop had an unforeseen effect, however: increasingly distressed by this treatment of their fellow workers, a second group of workers walked out, including some Italians. This was the first sign of the labor solidarity that was to become such a remarkable element in the general strike; it certainly amazed the employers, who had succeeded in pitting Italians against Jew for so long.

Three days later, on September 28, 1909, the workers at the nearby Triangle Waist Company, a number of whom had secretly joined Local 25, also went on strike. Management called a meeting of the company union, and one boss quoted the company union's bylaws, which said "no member of this society shall belong to any other organization." He went on to say that those who had joined Local 25 had broken this rule and unless they immediately left the union they would lose their jobs. After the workers held a union meeting and decided to fight back, the company locked them out and advertised for scabs.[20]

The Triangle management went one better on Louis Leiserson's tactic of hiring local gangsters: they hired Broadway prostitutes and their pimps, guessing that the strikers would feel more intimidated that way. The prostitutes beat up ten women in one day.[21] After a striker was beaten, she was charged with assault and fined. On October 14, for instance, twenty-eight strikers were arrested and fined $3 each—a week's wage for a learner. The drain on the union treasury began to be insupportable, while the male workers lost heart and stopped picketing, not wanting to be beaten up. The women carried on, suffering assault and arrest day after day.[22] Clara Lemlich was arrested seventeen times.

On October 19, a group of policemen broke into the union hall during a meeting. They stared at those present, so they would be able to recognize them on the picket line, then left. Such open intimidation was the last straw: some of the women strikers went to the Women's Trade Union League and appealed for protection against false arrest. The League "allies" began to come down to the picket line to observe and then act as witnesses in court.

Union officials were meanwhile trying to work out a strategy for dealing with the police repression and the unwillingness of the companies to negotiate. The strikers were getting no publicity, except in the Jewish and radical press, and the manufacturers found it easy to subcontract their work to other shops. The union still had few members, little money for strike benefits, and no influence. Nevertheless, it seemed to the officers of Local 25 that the industry was beginning to move and that it might pay to take a chance, particularly since they had neither a treasury nor prestige to risk. So they decided to call a general strike of the whole shirtwaist industry and hope it would catch on. The ILGWU, their own International, thought the plan had no chance of working. Most trade unionists agreed.

Once the members of the Local 25's executive board had decided to call the strike, they had to convince the rest of the union's one hundred members. They called a general meeting on October 21, and used a "strategic ruse": various executive board members and Leiserson strikers sat scattered around the hall and described the dreadful conditions in the trade as if they were representing different shops. They then called for a general strike.[23] They swung the meeting, and the next day the *New York Call* carried the banner headline "25,000 Waist Makers Declare for Strike!" By the day after, the *Call* had realized this joyful news did not correspond to reality and printed a bewildered retraction: "For reasons which the union leaders refuse to divulge, the time for calling the big strike will be kept secret until the blow is ready to fall upon the bosses who are backing up Louis Leiserson . . . and the Triangle Waist Company."[24]

The executive board waited to see how the workers would respond to their call. In the next four weeks, before the general strike was finally declared, about two thousand workers joined the union. Meanwhile, on November 4 the strike got the necessary publicity boost. Mary Dreier, president of the New York Women's Trade Union League, socialite, and resident of Beekman Place, was arrested while observing police brutality on the picket line. As the *New York Call* reported the incident:

> Mary Dreier . . . was covered with insults and arrested without cause yesterday while doing picket duty in the strike of the Ladies'

Waistmakers against the Triangle Waist Company. . . . A member of the Triangle firm heard her speak to one of the girls as she came from work and in the presence of an officer he turned on Miss Dreier and shouted: "You are a liar. You are a dirty liar." Miss Dreier turned to the officer and said, "You heard the language that man addressed to me. Am I not entitled to your protection." The officer replied, "How do I know you are not a dirty liar?"[25]

She was arrested, then discharged by the judge, who apologized for having mistaken her for a working girl. But the publicity given the arrest was crucial in arousing the interest of the press and the public in both the strike and police brutality, and the union used the occasion to intensify its shop propaganda. When it called a mass meeting for November 22 at Cooper Union, the response was overwhelming. Fifteen thousand workers, mostly young girls, walked out on their jobs the morning after the Cooper Union meeting. By nightfall there were twenty-five thousand on strike, and more joined in the next few days. Only a handful had been union members before the strike, and no one had expected such a huge response—75 percent of the workers in the trade were out on strike.

Most of the women who had been at the meeting and voted to strike went to work the next morning excited but uncertain what they were supposed to do. What happened in Natalya Urosova's shop is typical of the kind of chain reaction that took place:

"But I did not know how many workers in my shop had taken that oath at the meeting. I could not tell how many would go on strike in our factory the next day," said Natalya afterward. "When we came back the next morning to the factory, though, no one went to the dressing-room. We all sat at the machines with our hats and coats beside us, ready to leave. The foreman had no work for us when we got there. But, just as always, he did not tell when there would be any, or if there would be any at all that day. And there was whispering and talking softly all around the room among the machines: 'Shall we wait like this?' 'There is a general strike.' 'Who will get up first?' 'It would be better to be the last to get up, and then the company might remember it of you afterward, and do well for you.' But I told them," observed Natalya with a little shrug, "'What difference does it make which one is first and which one is last?' Well, so we stayed whispering, and no one knowing what the other

would do, not making up our minds for two hours. Then I started
to get up." Her lips trembled. "And just at the same minute all—we
all got up together, in one second. No one after the other; no one
before. And when I saw it—that time—oh, it excites me so yet. I can
hardly talk about it. So we all stood up, and all walked out together.
And already out on the sidewalk in front, the policemen stood with
the clubs. One of them said, 'If you don't behave, you'll get this on
your head.' And he shook his club at me.

"We hardly knew where to go—what to do next. But one of the
American girls, who knew how to telephone, called up the Women's
Trade Union League, and they told us all to come to a big hall a few
blocks away."[26]

All through the day the girls streamed out of their shops
toward Clinton Hall, the union headquarters. The situation was
chaotic. The officers of Local 25 were virtually prisoners in their
tiny office, hemmed in by hordes of young women trying to join
the union. Thousands of strikers milled about in the streets,
unable to find their shop meetings—about twenty different halls
were in use—or unable to get into them because of the crowds.
Some people wandered around without help for a day or two and
then went back to work, demoralized.

It was the WTUL that brought order out of this chaos, though
the women of the Socialist Party were of notable service as well.
WTUL women did secretarial and organizational work and were
responsible for most of the publicity. The strike was run out of
twenty halls, each of which had a woman in charge, sometimes a
League member, usually a rank-and-file striker. The male staff of
Local 25 was not large enough to do this and to give interviews
and conduct negotiations as well, and it was due to this weakness
that the women were able to run their own strike and to gain
experience doing so. It was they who arranged picketing schedules, made reports on scab and police brutality, wrote leaflets,
spoke at other unions, visited rich women to raise money, went to
court to bail out strikers or act as witnesses, kept track of the shops
that settled, gave out strike benefits to needy workers, organized
new women into the union, kept up spirits, and persuaded people
not to go back to work.

Local 25 had called a general strike in order to organize the whole industry at one time. This approach put it somewhere between the traditional AFL unions, with their narrow craft orientation and methods, and the IWW's revolutionary industrial unionism. The ILGWU attempted to combine the spirit of industrial unionism with the tactics of craft organization. Had the union been organized on a purely craft basis, for instance, the cutters and the dressmakers might have struck at different times, thus setting up divisions between the workers in the same shop. It was this approach that Clara Lemlich had had to combat when she organized the strike at Leiserson's. In a normal AFL situation, the cutters would have crossed the dressmakers' picket lines and kept on working, even if the company brought in scabs.

The strikers were thus generally grouped by shop, instead of craft, though there were a few language groupings, and each shop formulated its own particular list of demands. The main issue was "union recognition"—which meant a union shop, where a worker would have to join the union to get a job—but the strikers also demanded the abolition of subcontracting, payment every week instead of every two, a fifty-two hour week, no more than two hours a day overtime, and an end to making the workers pay for materials and electricity.[27]

The workers felt the demand for the union shop was critical. In an industry where most work was paid by the piece, and the piece-rate varied wildly from season to season and shop to shop, the only way to set uniform wages and standards was to have the union do so—the employers would always try to undercut each other by cheating the workers. The union would not have the power to standardize the industry unless it could control the supply of labor through the union shop. Needless to say, this demand was extremely controversial. Despite the fact that an arbitration board was established, made up of two representatives of the manufacturers and two of labor (Morris Hillquit, a socialist lawyer, and John Mitchell of the United Mine Workers, then a vice-president of the AFL), the employers would not even discuss the issue of recognition.

Meanwhile the picketing continued through a bitter winter. As before, the pickets were almost entirely women, because it was assumed that they would be handled less roughly than the men.[28]

In many cases the women voluntarily gave up their strike benefits so that the married men could get more. The heroism of these shirtwaist strikers was remarked by all observers:

> In spite of being underfed and often thinly clad, the girls took upon themselves the duty of picketing, believing that the men would be more severely handled. Picketing is a physical and nervous strain under the best conditions, but it is the spirit of martyrdom that sends young girls of their own volition, often insufficiently clad and fed, to patrol the streets in midwinter with the temperature low and with snow on the ground, some days freezing and some days melting. After two or three hours of such exposure, often ill from the cold, they returned to headquarters, which were held for the majority in rooms dark and unheated, to await further orders.
>
> It takes uncommon courage to endure such physical exposure, but these striking girls underwent as well the nervous strain of imminent arrest, the harsh treatment of the police, insults, threats and even actual assaults from the rough men who stood around the factory doors. During the thirteen weeks over six hundred girls were arrested; thirteen were sentenced to five days in the work-house and several were detained a week or ten days in the Tombs.[29]

Helen Marot thought it was the spirit of the strikers that distinguished this strike from others. She felt it came from the fact that they were women, turning all the cliches about why women couldn't be organized upside down:

> The same temper displayed in the shirtwaist strike is found in other strikes of women, until we have now a trade-union truism, that "women make the best strikers." Women's economic position furnishes two reasons for their being the best strikers; one is their less permanent attitude toward their trade, and the other their lighter financial burdens. While these economic factors help to make women good strikers, the genius for sacrifice and the ability to sustain, over prolonged periods, response to emotional appeals are also important causes. Working women have been less ready than men to make the initial sacrifice that trade-union membership calls for, but when they reach the point of striking they give themselves as fully and instinctively to the cause as they give themselves in their personal relationships. It is important, therefore, in following the action of the shirtwaist makers, to remember that eighty per cent were women.[30]

The judges who sentenced the women showed extreme prejudice against the union, strikers, and women who stepped out of their assigned position in the scheme of things. Judge Cornell sentenced strikers to the workhouse—for the offense of picketing— with the words, "I find the girls guilty. It would be perfectly futile for me to fine them. Some charitable woman would pay their fines or they could get a bond. I am going to commit them to the workhouse under the Cumulative Sentence Act, and there they will have an opportunity of thinking over what they have done."[31] Magistrate Olmstead sentenced another girl with the message: "You are on strike against God and Nature, whose firm law is that man shall earn his bread in the sweat of his brow. You are on strike against God."[32] Those who were sent to the workhouse were often only fifteen or sixteen years old. Two WTUL women went to remonstrate with a judge who had sentenced a sixteen-year-old to thirty days, and "tried to make him understand that she had done nothing wrong. We asked if he realized what it would mean to a girl her age to be locked up with prostitutes, theives, and narcotics addicts. 'Oh,' he said, 'It will be good for her. It will be a vacation.'"[33]

The police and courts went out of their way to classify the strikers as prostitutes as an attempt to break their spirit. Prostitution was never very far from the lives of working women who tried to live on $6 a week; they had seen women they had grown up with fall into the life of the streets, and the thin barrier between themselves and that life meant a great deal to them. The memoirs of jailed women strikers and radicals in the early part of the century focus rather obsessively on the prostitutes they met. The police and employers called the strikers whores because they were walking the streets shamelessly; they tried to insult them sexually, as if the way to stop them from rebelling as workers was to put them back in their places as sexual objects. At a meeting protesting police butality, Yetta Ruth, a seventeen-year-old, described her treatment:

> "I acted as spokesman for my shop and when the boss, Beekman, told me that he would not accept the terms of the union, walked out and others followed. He then had me arrested for taking out his workers.

"While I was at the station house, on 20th street, the officers treated me in such a manner that a girl is ashamed to talk about. I am only seventeen and many of the insinuations escaped me. But what I did understand was bad enough. . . .

"The policeman asked me with how many men I was living. One officer told me that I was a dirty Socialist and Anarchist. One man said, 'Here is a nice fellow, Yetta, hook onto him.' One policeman showed me a torn pair of pants and asked me to mend them."

The little girl stopped abruptly and her voice failed her. She was urged again to continue and after some hesitation, said "One man went to some place and winking to me, said: 'Come along, Yetta!'"[34]

The WTUL and socialist women made police repression one of their main issues. On December 3, the League organized a parade down to the mayor's office, led by three League members and three girls who had been arrested. Ten thousand women strikers marched behind. The mayor received their petition politely and promised to read it, and things went on as before.

Despite the forces arrayed against them, these young strikers fought on in an extraordinary fashion. One sixteen-year-old girl came into the union office covered with bruises from head to foot: her father and brothers had beaten her to try to make her go back to work, but she had refused. She begged Helen Marot to find her another place to stay. Another striker swore she'd go to the workhouse the next time she was arrested rather than have the union use its funds to pay her fine.[35] There were women who were arrested time and time again, who seemed able to do without food or sleep, and who spent all their time at meetings or on the picket line. Several observers noted that the most militant strikers were often the most highly paid and skilled workers, though it would seem that they had least to gain from the strike. These were often the women who, as pacesetters or forewomen, organized the work process in the shop; it was a natural transition for them to become leaders in the strike:

"It's because there are so many girls who can't make decent living wages that we had to strike," said one. "I can work unusually fast, and I make $12 a week during the busy season; but there are many who make only $4." All the strikers take it as a matter of course that they shall feel for each other, and act unselfishly on that feeling, too.[36]

The solidarity the strikers built was their greatest achievement, and it is this that makes their strike memorable. They showed the world that the slow entry of millions of women into the U.S. industrial work force had set new conditions for woman's struggle and had liberated women from the privacy of household drudgery in sufficient numbers for them to be able to act together. A number of observers saw them as a working-class analogue to the suffragists, showing what the women's movement could be like when the issues included survival. With the shirtwaist makers' strike, the U.S. working woman showed what she was made of, and even Samuel Gompers had to acknowledge that here was a force to be reckoned with:

> The strike . . . brought to the consciousness of the nation a recognition of certain features looming up in its social development. These are the extent to which women are taking up with industrial life, their consequent tendency to stand together in the struggle to protect their common interests as wage earners, the readiness of people of all classes to approve of trade-union methods in behalf of working women, and the capacity of women as strikers to suffer, to do, and to dare in support of their rights.[37]

Looking back on the strike, Helen Marot of the League thought the general-strike gamble had succeeded only because of the unusual history and temperament of the Russian Jewish workers: "The Russian workers who filled New York factories are ever ready to rebel against the suggestion of oppression and are of all people the most responsive to an idea to which is attached an ideal. The union officers understood this and . . . answered, 'Wait and see,' when their friends urged caution before calling a general strike in an unorganized industry."[38]

The Italian and the native-born American women played a less forceful role in the strike than did their Russian Jewish sisters. Although the Americans came out on strike initially, they went back to work after a few weeks. According to Marot, their working conditions and pay were so much better than the Russians' that they did not strike on their own behalf, but because they felt sorry for the rest:

> They acknowledged no interest in common with the others, but if necessary they were prepared to sacrifice a week or two of work.

Unfortunately the sacrifice required of them was greater than they had counted on . . . the Russians failed to be grateful, took for granted a common cause and demanded that all shirtwaist makers, regardless of race or creed, continue the strike until they were recognized by the employers as a part of the union. This difference in attitude and understanding was a heavy strain on the generosity of the American girls. It is believed, however, that the latter would have been equal to what their fellow workers expected, if their meetings had been left to the guidance of American men and women who understood their prejudices. . . . It was the daily, almost hourly, tutelage which the Russian men insisted on the American girls' accepting, rather than the prolongation of the strike beyond the time they had expected, that sent the American girls back as "scabs."[39]

Marot and the other women of the League believed that they could have handled the American-born women better than the union did. Their broadmindedness did not extend to the Italian workers. The patronizing tone of the League's analysis of the Italians is common to reform and even labor descriptions of them during a period when they were the most recent immigrants:

The Italian girls and women . . . are the oppressed of the race, absolutely under the dominance of the men of their family and heavily shackled by old customs and traditions. They are very much afraid of trade unions and everything that involves danger to their job either through strikers or discharge. In the shirtwaist strike they joined the strike, but failed to hold out, and were used successfully as strike breakers, following the instructions of their priest. This was, however, largely due to the fact that they were mostly Sicilians. . . . They have no collective vision. They follow willingly and devotedly a leader whom they trust and the all-important thing therefore is to get the right kind of leader.[40]

Two years later the Italian women of Lawrence proved that they could be as militant as any other strikers, provided they were organized by people who spoke their language and understood their culture and their special needs as women.

If the American-born and Italian women had an ambiguous relationship to the union during the strike, the black women in the shirtwaist industry had none at all. They were few in number—the 1900 census put the total number of black working women in New York at 16,114, and 90 percent of these were domestic workers.[41] Black women were by and large kept out of the factories, and only 803 were listed as dressmakers in New York. Mary White Ovington, a founder of the National Association for the Advancement of Colored People, described the situation of black women in the garment industry in 1903:

> Colored women have always been known as good sewers, and recently they have studied at their trade in some of the best schools. From 1904 to 1910, the Manhattan Trade School [where Leonora O'Reilly, a member of the NAACP as well as the League, taught sewing] graduated thirty-four girls in dress-making, hand sewing, and novelty making. The public night school on West Forty-Sixth Street . . . has educated hundreds of women in sewing, dress-making, millinery, and artificial flower-making. . . . Occasionally an employer objects to colored girls, but the Manhattan Trade School repeatedly, in trying to place its graduates, has found that opposition to the Negro has come largely from working girls. Race prejudice has even gone so far as to prevent a colored woman from receiving home work when it entailed her waiting in the same sitting-room with white women. Of course, this is not a universal attitude. In friendly talks with hundreds of New York's white women workers, I have found the majority ready to accept the colored worker. Jewish girls are especially tolerant. They believe that good character and decent manners should count, not color; but an aggressive, combative minority is quite sure that no matter how well-educated or virtuous she may be, no black woman is as good as a white one.[42]

As in many other strike situations, the garment manufacturers made a special effort to keep their few black workers on during the strike and to recruit other black women as scabs. This led to a full-scale debate within the black community: should black women take jobs as scabs if this was the only way they could break into the industry? or should they put pressure on the union to enroll them as members, knowing that in the long run their future as workers lay on the side of the labor movement and not the employers?

On January 10, 1910, the *New York Age*, a black weekly, editorialized on the subject: "Why should Negro working girls pull white working girls' chestnuts out of the fire?" The *Age* had been asked to refuse to print advertisements for strikebreakers and to "help induce these colored girls to join the union"; it had not only refused this request but had recruited black women as ironers for firms that were on strike. The reason: before the strike "Negro girls were not asked to join the union," and it was safe to assume that the union would discriminate against them after the strike, whether they scabbed or not.[43]

The day after the editorial was published, a crisis meeting was called by the Cosmopolitan Club, an organization of black and white progressives and radicals which Mary White Ovington had helped pull together during her seven years' sociological investigation of the conditions of Afro-American people in New York. The club met in various homes, usually those of black society leaders in Brooklyn (the Petersons, Mars, Wilbecans) to discuss "various phases of the race question."[44] The meeting was held at the black community church in Brooklyn on January 21 and passed a historic if little known resolution, which was reprinted in the *New York Call:*

> *Resolved,* That the citizens of Brooklyn in mass meeting assembled, protest and urge the women of color to refrain from acting in the capacity of strikebreakers in the shirtwaist making concerns of New York, because we regard their action as antagonistic to the best interests of labor.
>
> We further urge that, in the event of the successful termination of the strike, organized labor exercise a proper consideration of the claims and demands of the men and women of color who desire to enter the various trades in the way of employment and the protection of the various labor unions. . . .
>
> Those familiar with negro opinion will feel the significance of this appeal from the leaders of the race. The colored girl is urged, not to enter the market and underbid, accepting any chance to learn a trade, but to refrain from injuring other working women, and whenever possible, to ally herself with the cause of union labor.[45]

If the shirtwaist strikers won their demand for a closed shop, the future of black workers in the industry would depend on the union's willingness to recruit them. A Brooklyn reader of the *Survey,* a social work magazine, argued that black women were already excluded from Local 25: "I happened to read your editorial just after I had been talking with a social worker who is much interested in work among the colored people. . . . She told me that colored shirtwaist makers could not get into the union and were likewise not permitted by the union to work in the shops."[46] The Women's Trade Union League attempted to rebut these accusations of racism within the union, but the numbers cited in their defense are so small as to cast doubt upon the question. Margaret Dreier Robins wrote the *Survey* to say that the union did have black members—*one* in New York and *two* in Philadelphia.[47] And Elizabeth Dutcher, an officer of the New York League, wrote in W. E. B. DuBois's magazine, the *Horizon:*

> In New York, colored girls are not only members of the union, but they have been prominent in the union. One colored girl has been secretary of her shop organization all through the strike and has been very frequently at union headquarters doing responsible work. The editor should also know that meetings were held during the strike at the Fleet Street Methodist Memorial Church (colored) in Brooklyn and the St. Marks Methodist Church in Manhattan and that in both, members of the Ladies' Waist Makers' Union said definitely and publicly that colored girls were not only eligible but welcome to membership.[48]

The Cosmopolitan Club urged that the union make an effort to organize black workers after the strike, "both for their own protection against the rapacity of their employers, and that they may not be used to take the place of other strikers,"[49] and at its poststrike executive board meeting, the Women's Trade Union League passed a resolution to "offer its services to the National Association for the Protection of Colored Women stating the very great desire of the League to cooperate with them in their efforts to protect the colored women workers through organization."[50] There is no indication that either the League or the union made any further effort.[51] The League does not seem to have actively organized black women workers until 1919, when their Southern organizer, Mildred Rankin, organized unions of black teachers and service workers in Virginia, and their first black organizer, Irene Goins, worked with some success in the Chicago stockyards.[52]

The weaknesses in the work of the ILGWU and the WTUL with black and Italian workers were only one of the problems they had to confront as the strike wore on. Equally important was the contradiction between those strikers whose shops settled in the early days of the strike and those whose shops held out until the end or never settled at all. Local 25 allowed its member shops to settle and go back to work one by one, like a craft union, rather than holding out for a single settlment, like an industrial one. The shops that settled then took work on a subcontract basis from companies that were still on strike. By November 27, one-third of the strikers had gone back to work. This drastically weakened the economic base of the strike and undermined its collective strength, even though the union treasury benefited from the dues of those who had gone back to work.[53]

Early in the strike, the biggest employers joined together in an Association of Waist and Dress Manufacturers which negotiated with the union at the same time as they pledged never to officially recognize it. On December 27, the arbitrators came out with a proposed compromise. The employers said they would "welcome conferences" about contract violations; they would only reinstate former employees "as far as practicable"; and they would not hire new workers until the strikers were back at work. (This clearly left loopholes for blacklisting union militants.) The agreement also stipulated a fifty-two hour week, no discrimination against union members, equal division of work between workers in the slack season, four paid holidays a year, shop negotiations for wages and prices, and an end to making employees pay for equipment.[54] These were substantial concessions, considering conditions in the trade prior to the strike, but they avoided the key question of union recognition. The Association was obdurate in its refusal to agree to this, and the strikers were furious that the union leadership had offered to compromise on this question. When the proposal was explained, " 'Send it back, we will not consider it!' 'We refuse to vote on it!' 'We want recognition of the union!' 'We will go to jail again and win!' and similar exclamations uttered in the highest pitch by 2,000 men and women made further reading impossible."[55]

At this point the united front of workers, AFL, League, suffragists, and women of the Socialist Party that had come together to support the strike began to disintegrate. As Helen Marot noted, the AFL and many of the suffragists deserted the strike because it was becoming too radical.

An uncompromising attitude is good trade-union tactics up to a certain point, but the shirtwaist makers were violating all traditions. Their refusal to accept anything short of the closed shop indicated to many a state of mind which was as irresponsible as it was reckless. Their position may have been reckless, but it was not irresponsible. Their sometime sympathizers did not realize the endurance of the women or the force of their enthusiasm, but insisted on the twenty to thirty thousand raw recruits becoming sophisticated unionists in thirteen short weeks.[56]

The League and the Socialist Party stuck by the strikers, despite their intransigence. A closer look at the strike support work of the League, the Socialist Party, and the wealthy suffragist "allies" shows how diverse were the elements in this united front, and how unstable was their unity.

The WTUL's list of their activities during the strike shows what an enormous contribution they made:

(1) We organized a volunteer picket force of allies of 75 League members. This is the first time in our knowledge in the history of trade unions where a volunteer picket corps was organized.

(2) Organized volunteer legal services, 9 lawyers.

(3) Furnished bail amounting to $29,000.

(4) Protested against illegal action on part of police, and interceded for strikers with the City authorities.

(5) Organized shops.

(6) Organized parade of 10,000 strikers over night.

(7) Took part in Arbitration Confererence.

(8) Arranged large meetings where arbitrators representing the Union explained situation to strikers.

(9) Took active part in shop meetings and paid benefits to those meeting at League headquarters.

(10) Made publicity for strike through the press, through meetings of all descriptions, edited two special strike editions of the *New York Call* and *New York Evening Journal.*

(11) Appealed for funds.[57]

They also sent organizers to help a related strike in Philadelphia, and to raise funds by touring New York State and New England.

Despite all this work, League members did not attempt either to claim credit for more than their due, or to impose caution on the workers who resisted the arbitrated agreement. Although privately they recognized that Local 25 could never have managed to organize such a vast strike without their help, in their public report on the strike they were unequivocal about the union's role: "It is untrue to state, as has been stated, that the League financed and led the strike. The strike was organized and led by the union. Perhaps it is more correct to say that it was organized by the union and led up to a certain point: the point of compromise. When that point was reached the strikers themselves turned leaders, continuing the strike to one of the most remarkable victories in the history of trade unions."[58]

The League emphasized those aspects of the strike that linked the labor and suffrage movements. One of their aims was to help feminists understand the struggles of working-class women, and they felt the strike was a major advance in that respect, even though some of the forms this female solidarity took were slightly bizarre. Borrowing a tactic from the suffragists, the League organized a car caravan to publicize the strike. The cars, lent by various millionaire women, honked their way through the narrow streets of the Lower East Side, "taking on and leaving off pickets. . . . Within the autos rich, fashionable women and poor frail striking girls . . . were making merry over this exceptional affair. It was amusing to see rich women carrying cards on which was proclaimed the need for organization for labor and which demanded shorter hours and increased pay."[59] The cars were no doubt chauffered.

No aspect of the strike attracted as much attention in the press as the support given it by certain wealthy women, notably Alva Belmont and Anne Morgan. Alva Belmont was the daughter of an Alabama plantation owner and one of New York's most prominent society matrons. She married William K. Vanderbilt and embarked on a lavish campaign to break into New York society's "Four Hundred." After building a $3 million chateau on Fifth Avenue and a $2 million mansion in Newport, she finally achieved her goal, after which she divorced Vanderbilt and married Oliver Hazard Perry Belmont, heir to the New York subway system. She became an ardent suffragist, active first in NAWSA and then in the National Woman's Party.[60]

During the strike she personally financed a mass meeting that was sponsored by the suffragist Political Equality Association and held at the Hippodrome on December 5. Speakers included Dr. Anna Howard Shaw for NAWSA, Leonora O'Reilly for the Women's Trade Union League, and Rose Pastor Stokes for the Socialist Party. Alva Belmont never lost an opportunity to note that the strike showed the need for woman suffrage. After observing at the trials of some of the strikers, she told the press:

> During the six hours I spent in that police court I saw enough to convince me and all who were with me beyond the smallest doubt of the absolute necessity for woman's suffrage—for the direct influence of women over judges, jury and policemen, over everything and everybody connected with the so-called course of justice. . . . Every woman who sits complacently amid the comforts of her home, or who moves with perfect ease and independence in her own protected social circle, and says, "I have all the rights I want," should spend one night at the Jefferson Market Court. She would then know that there are other women who have no rights which man or law or society recognizes.[61]

The press was almost as enthralled by Alva Belmont's strike support work as they were with that of Anne Morgan, daughter of robber baron J. P. Morgan ("Mr. Morgan," said a very intimate friend of the family, "naturally has very different views from Anne, but he is a broad-minded man and respects his daughter for thinking and acting for herself. . . . The story that he had angrily sworn to disinherit her for her avowed sympathy with the strikers is absolutely false.").[62] The Morgan financial interests were not involved in the garment industry.

The support of the "millionaire women" climaxed in a fund-raising meeting at the exclusive Colony Club on December 15, when a group of strikers, including Clara Lemlich, told their life stories to the women of the "Four Hundred." Theresa Malkiel, a socialist activist who wrote a fictionalized first-person account of the strike, drew the moral for her readers:

> They've brought me to their fashionable clubhouse to hear about our misery. To tell the truth, I've no appetite to tell it to them, for I've almost come to the conclusion that the gulf between us girls and these rich ladies is too deep to be smoothed over by a few paltry dollars; the girls would probably be the better off in the long run if

they did not take their money. They would the sooner realize the great contrast and division of classes; this would teach them to stick to their own. . . . The women gave us a thousand dollars, but what does this amount to? Not even a quarter apiece for each striker.[63]

And in fact, when the strikers voted down the arbitrated agreement, some of their rich supporters began to change their minds. On January 3, the Socialist Party and the League, together with various other organizations, called a meeting at Carnegie Hall to protest police brutality. The 370 arrested strikers sat on the stage, and speakers included Leonora O'Reilly and Morris Hillquit, the Socialist Party lawyer who was one of the arbitrators. At a special press conference the next morning, Anne Morgan deplored the undue influence of the socialists who, she said, were taking advantage of the strike situation to stir up trouble:

> I attended the meeting at Carnegie Hall last night. There was no doubt that some of the girls have been badly treated, both by some of the manufacturers, some of the police, and some of the magistrates. But I deplore the fanatical statements of Morris Hillquit, Leonora O'Reilly and others at such times as these. . . . In these times of stress such meetings should be an appeal to reason and sound judgement, and it is extremely dangerous to allow these Socialist appeals to emotionalism. It is very reprehensible for Socialists to take advantage of these poor girls in these times, and when the working people are in such dire straits, to teach their fanatical doctrines.[64]

Anne Morgan was joined in her attack by her friend Eva McDonald Valesh, a close associate of Samuel Gompers, who had left her job as managing editor of the *American Federationist* to come to New York. When she became involved in the shirtwaist makers' strike, most people were under the impression that she was acting as Gompers' emissary, and she even referred to herself as "general organizer of the AFL."[65] In fact, she was on her own.

Eva McDonald Valesh was peripherally involved in the arbitration agreement that had been rejected by the strikers on December 27, and, like Anne Morgan, she thought it had been voted down because of excessive Socialist Party influence. In a speech at the Woman's Civic Forum a few weeks later she attacked the Socialist Party and included the Women's Trade Union League in

her offensive, on the theory that it was a socialist "front" organization. She tried to use the contradiction between men and women
in the union as a basis for undermining the strike, telling the *New
York Daily Tribune:*

> "The strikers' committee refused to consider any overture but
> one agreeing to the closed shop. What is that strikers' committee?
> Eighteen men and two girls were present the day I saw them—the
> men all socialists, connected with the trade perhaps, but ignorant of
> what the girls want. And to show you the feminine viewpoint, those
> girl strikers are actually grateful to the men who are using them for
> their own purposes. 'It's so nice of the men, who know so much
> more than we, to serve on our committees,' they say.
>
> "I propose," Mrs. Valesh went on, "to start a campaign against
> socialism. This strike may be used to pave the way for forming
> clean, sensible labor unions, and I want to enroll every woman of
> leisure, every clubwoman, in the movement. The existing unions
> aren't doing what they ought to stem the tide of socialism in this
> country. The Women's Trade Union League is dominated by so-
> cialists, though I won't deny that they have helped the shirtwaist
> strikers some.
>
> "Socialism is a menace, and it is alarming to some one who has
> been, as I have, away from New York for some years, to come back
> and see how socialism has grown here. I've been down to Clinton
> Hall [the union office], and I am terrified at the spirit that fills the
> people who congregate there. There's nothing constructive about
> socialism. It just makes those ignorant foreigners discontented, sets
> them against the government, makes them want to tear down. And
> the socialists are using the strikers."
>
> "How about the suffragists?" demanded Mrs. William H.
> McCartney.
>
> "That's different," said Mrs. Valesh. "The suffragists have used
> the strikers, but they've helped them, given them spiritual vision,
> and, besides, the suffragists say frankly to the strikers, 'We want
> votes for women,' while the socialists veil their purposes under all
> sorts of pretences."[66]

The papers printed Eva McDonald Valesh's comments with
great enthusiasm, announcing that she and Anne Morgan were
starting a rival organization to the Women's Trade Union League,
of which both happened to be members. The League feared that
Gompers was behind the attack, and a controversy erupted over

whether to expel Eva McDonald Valesh. The socialists in the New York League wanted a public denunciation. Margaret Dreier Robins, the national president, rushed to New York to try to dampen the fire before it got out of control; she and her husband Raymond felt that Eva McDonald Valesh wanted publicity and that if she were openly expelled she would "herald forth how the 'reds' could not stand her great arguments and her mighty influence and had to expel her."[67] Meanwhile Eva McDonald Valesh kept sending in resignations, and the League had to table each one in order to go on with expulsion proceedings. In the end, the New York League—as usual—yielded to Margaret Dreier Robins' persuasion, and kept the expulsion a confidential matter. Reflecting upon this episode, Raymond Robins wrote to his wife, "What an old Pup the Hon. Samuel Gompers really is. It seems that Gompers is worthy of all the Socialists say about him and that the Socialists are worthy of all that Gompers says about them. We shall let these ill tempered and low natured people scrap among themselves. Each knows the smut of the other and they can wash their dirty linen to their souls delight."[68]

In fact, the women of the Socialist Party had played an important role in the united front that supported the strike but had received no public recognition for it. They had come from all over the New York area and, according to their own reports, had been "clerks, organizers, speakers, pickets, watchers, newsies, human sandwiches, solicitors for relief funds, took an active part in the Hippodrome meeting, for which Mrs. Belmont alone received the credit, and helped arrange the demonstration and parade to City Hall."[69] They had initiated the Carnegie Hall meeting, and, once the strikers rejected the arbitrated agreement and other support began to fall away, they collected most of the strike funds.[70] Bitter and hurt by the attacks on them and by the League's unwillingness to defend them publicly, several of the most active socialist women made their own defense:

> If large advertising in the capitalist dailies, so generously given the "society" ladies during the strike, helped, the well-to-do women certainly did everything for them; for the Socialist women's activity was never mentioned by the newspapers until Mr. Gompers and his assistant, Mrs. Valesh, chose to open war on the Socialists.

There has never been a more humiliating position in the history of the labor movement than that occupied by the Socialist women in the shirtwaist strike. So long as they did the work of the black man "Friday" they were tolerated and permitted to go on; but no sooner did they attempt to do anything that would count officially then they were put in the background.

The result was, however, well worth the price; the Socialist women have become a power with the girls themselves.

No wonder Mr. Gompers raises his hands in alarm. The girls have found out by experience who their friends are. They will not allow themselves to be fooled, as did the workingmen.[71]

The strike dragged on through January with less and less hope of a finale as splendid as its opening chords. After December 27, the employers' association refused to arbitrate further; support fell away; some large shops were allowed to settle without mentioning the issues of union shop and recognition, and the union began to settle on whatever basis it could with the remaining firms. On February 15, 1910, the strike was declared over despite the fact that thirteen shops were still on strike and between one thousand and three thousand workers went back with no gains and no guarantee against blacklisting.[72]

The Triangle Waist Company was one of those in which there was only a partial settlement. One demand that was not met was for adequate fire escapes and open doors—the foremen used to lock the doors for fear the girls might sneak out for a minute's break or steal a few needles or a little thread.[73] Shortly before closing time a year later, on March 25, 1911, the fire alarms began to shrill. Like most garment factories, Triangle was a firetrap, with piles of material lying about, and so much lint that the air itself could catch fire. The factory went up in minutes. There was no sprinkler system. One exit was blocked by fire, the other door was locked, and the workers could not get out. The fire escape let down onto an iron spike fence, impaling the girls trying to jump to the ground. It was a holocaust. Of the 500 people who worked there, 146 died in the fire and many more were injured. A League member who was passing by described the scene:

> I was coming down Fifth Avenue on the Saturday afternoon when a great, swirling, billowing cloud of smoke swept like a giant

streamer out of Washington Square and down upon the beautiful houses in Lower Fifth Avenue. Just as I was turning into the Square two young girls whom I knew to be working in the vicinity came rushing toward me, tears were running from their eyes and they were white and shaking as they caught me by the arm.

"Oh," shrieked one of them, "they are jumping."

"Jumping from ten stories up! They are going through the air like bundles of clothes, and the firemen can't stop them and the policemen can't stop them and nobody can help them at all."

"Fifty of them's jumped already and just think how many there must be left inside yet"—and the girls started crying afresh and rushed away up Fifth Avenue.

A little old tailor whom I knew came shrieking across the Square, tossing his arms and crying, "Horrible, horrible." He did not recognize me, nor know where he was; he had gone mad with the sight.[74]

Rose Schneiderman of the WTUL made a bitter speech at the memorial meeting held a week later at the Metropolitan Opera House, rented for the occasion by Anne Morgan. She threw out a challenge to the liberal public:

I would be a traitor to those poor burned bodies if I came here to talk good fellowship. We have tried you good people of the public and we have found you wanting. The old Inquisition had its rack and its thumbscrews and its instruments of torture with iron teeth. We know what these things are today: the iron teeth are our necessities, the thumbscrews the high-powered and swift machinery close to which we must work, and the rack is here in the "fire-proof" structures that will destroy us the minute they catch on fire.

This is not the first time girls have been burned alive in this city. Every week I must learn of the untimely death of one of my sister workers. Every year thousands of us are maimed. The life of men and women is so cheap and property is so sacred. There are so many of us for one job it matters little if 143 of us are burned to death.

We have tried you, citizens; we are trying you now, and you have a couple of dollars for the sorrowing mothers and daughters and sisters by way of a charity gift. But every time the workers come out in the only way they know to protest against conditions which are unbearable, the strong hand of the law is allowed to press down heavily upon us. . . . I can't talk fellowship to you who are gathered here. Too much blood has been spilled. I know from my experience it is up to the working people to save themselves.... by a strong working-class movement.[75]

The owners of the Triangle firm were tried for negligence but not convicted. The press blamed the fire on a worker who had been smoking. The League embarked on a crusade for stronger legislation for fire protection and better enforcement of existing laws. They printed leaflets informing the workers of the laws and their rights, and did soapboxing on fire protection; Clara Lemlich, blacklisted after the strike, was one of the speakers. League members also helped organize relief and legal aid for the families of the victims. The IWW, which was beginning to be active in the Lower East Side garment industry, sneered at this palliative approach:

> A stirring commentary upon the policy of the league is to be found in the conduct of the Triangle Company. Compelled to seek new quarters, what did they do in the face of "public opinion" and the "vigorous action" of the unions? Go and seek out, with scrupulous care, a real fire-proof building? Not these butchers for profit. THEY RENTED A CONDEMNED BUILDING AND PROCEEDED TO AGAIN DEFY THE LAW TO WHICH THE WOMEN'S TRADE UNION LEAGUE APPEALS TO REMEDY THESE CONDITIONS. The capitalists know that the law is on their side every time, hence they have no fear of it.[76]

Everyone in the labor movement knew that the best way to protect the Lower East Side workers was to have a union strong enough on the shop level to enforce the law and to agitate around safety issues. But although Local 25 had gained enormously from the strike, enrolling twenty thousand members, it quickly went into a decline and by the fall of 1911 it had only thirty-eight hundred members and little influence.[77] The women of the New York League became increasingly critical of its general strike approach, unless it could be followed up by "effective leadership which instructs the rank and file in the principles of trade unionism and the best method of getting practical results, so that a permanent advance may be established after such a magnificent struggle."[78] The League felt that its responsibility was to the women in the trade, whose interests were not being served by male leadership of Local 25. Helen Marot became disturbed when the idea began to circulate after the fire that another general strike would be necessary to recoup the union's membership. She recommended that the League oppose this and instead endorse candidates for union office who had "constructive" ideas. The League, however, refused to interfere in the union's internal policies, and Marot then wrote a letter to the *Jewish Daily Forward* about the inadequacies of the union's leadership: "It is becoming clear to the League that it is a betrayal of the faith and fine spirit of the girls to encourage them to organize into trade unions if their union is to be dominated by men without business sense or executive ability and by men competent to talk but not to act."[79]

The lack of democracy inherent in an all-male leadership over a female rank and file was exacerbated by a new movement for "protocols"—pacts signed with the garment manufacturers to set up compulsory arbitration boards that would settle conflicts between labor and management as they arose, without strikes. In other words, the ILGWU leadership was prepared to bargain away the power to strike (the only real power the workers had) in order to consolidate its control over the trade. When the idea met with initial success among the male cloakmakers, the ILGWU wanted to extend it to the female waistmakers. The conservatives in Local 25 were strongly in favor of the experiment, as was the AFL leadership; Gompers himself came to the 1912 negotiations that set up the shirtwaist protocol. Some radicals opposed the idea. The rank and file of the union was divided, as was the Women's Trade Union League, which did not publicly endorse the campaign.[80]

The manipulative attitude of the union leadership toward the women workers became clear in these contract negotiations. The protocol was based on the union's ability to keep its members in line; it ruled out any displays of spontaneous militance such as the rejection of the arbitrated agreement in the shirtwaist strike. The manufacturers' association made it clear that they expected the union to "control" the workers.[81] Since there was widespread unrest in the industry, the union decided to stage a theatrical event in January 1913 to give the workers a sense that there was more of a struggle with management than was in fact the case. The workers would vote for another general strike, only this time everything would have been settled beforehand, the strike would last only a few days, and the industry would not be disrupted. As the union's historian described the events:

> Such a strike would give the workers a chance to express "their protest against the bad conditions in the trade" and also create in them a sense that each and all had helped to "uplift the trade." The plan was to issue a call for a general strike; then at the very inception of the strike call a mass meeting of the workers and inform them of the standards agreed upon between the manufacturers' association and the union, and then direct the workers in the shops of the association to return to work . . . the union promised not to sign individual agreements with individual firms, but to refer all employers to the association, which they would be asked to join. It was also understood that the agreement between the association and the union would become effective only if the union succeeded in bringing into its membership the majority of the workers in the trade. . . . The manufacturers agreed to give the union a list of their workers in order to facilitate the work of organization. . . .
>
> The course of the strike was smooth and peaceful. The "girls" accepted the protocol as a *fait accompli*, with some surprise but without much animation. A few thousand Italian "girls" under the leadership of Nicholas Lauretano and other I.W.W.'s expressed some dissatisfaction, but were easily pacified.[82]

Under this happy arrangement the membership of Local 25 quickly rose to about twenty-five thousand.[83] But although in theory union and management would now meet to settle the problems of the trade without any disruption from below, in practice it soon became clear that the protocol's machinery didn't work. It took forever to settle grievances, and although the "impartial" arbitration board was supposed to give the workers wage increases and other awards, its decisions never seemed to lead to improvements in wages or working conditions.[84] The employers soon began to introduce speedup measures to gain an edge on competitors, and they refused to give the arbitrators the information necessary to set wages in advance, because that would have entailed releasing information about the next season's styles and they were afraid rival firms would steal their ideas. They acted in general like benign dictators and refused to meet with the union officials on an equal footing.[85]

So the protocol broke down. One of its early casualties was the employers' promise to hire union members first. The membership of Local 25 began to decline as a result, until by November 1913, eight months after the protocol was initiated, it was down to about sixteen thousand; it lost three thousand by the end of 1915.[86]

At this point both the manufacturers and union officials agreed that a new protocol was necessary, and in January 1916 they announced an agreement. But when the union called another "general strike" for February 9, 1916—meant to be merely a "demonstration of unity"—they got more than they had bargained for.[87] Rank-and-file women, dissatisfied both with protocolism and with the undemocratic way the union was run, led an open revolt. The ILGWU had made no progress in integrating women into the leadership since the first criticisms made by the Women's Trade Union League, and as a result relations between them had become strained. Late in 1912, Helen Marot informed an ILGWU official in her usual forthright manner that

> the business of the League was to bring women into places of responsibility in the organization of their trade; that we know and he knew if we should now work even with representatives in a general strike that the union would be carried on and controlled by the men, and the women would have no place and power, and probably mostly no voice.[88]

And she summarized the situation in her book *American Labor Unions* published in 1914:

> It was the strike of the Shirt Waist Makers which gave the first great impetus to the organization of the workers making women's clothing and which placed at last the International Ladies' Garment Workers' Union in its present position—the third largest union affiliated with the American Federation. This union has jurisdiction over one of the largest fields in which women work. It is officered by men who believe that women make good strikers, but who have no confidence in their ability to handle union affairs. They have gone further than any other union in building up organization by protocol agreements with manufacturers without a conscious sentiment or understanding among the workers. They claim that the workers as a whole have no real conception of organization.[89]

In 1916 some of these women not only found a voice but found fists as well:

A meeting of shop chairmen at No. 175 East Broadway, ended last night in a general fight. Women became hysterical, and Charles Jacobson, a union official, was injured. The fight began because Jacobson, who had charge of the door, refused admission to a crowd who were without tickets.

It was announced that 5,000 of the strikers would return to work this morning. Miss Ida Grabinski, who has been named chairman of one of the dozen committees of women in the new "equal voice" movement, said today that she intends to lay the whole matter before Saumel Gompers, President of the Federation. She and her followers are not satisfied with the way mere man had conducted the affairs of the union until now.

"The officers of the union boss us worse than the bosses," she said. "Now they tell us to go to work. The next minute they withdraw that order. The women workers comprise more than 65 per cent of the union members throughout the country. The association shops have a woman general manager. Why shouldn't we have something to say about what concerns us most?"[90]

Although a large number of dissident workers refused to go back to work at the union's command, they did not succeed in staying out for long, and the strike was over by the end of February.[91]

The ILGWU leadership in this period initiated policies that were to become its general practice: it put stability in the industry first, followed by good fringe benefits and services to its members, who were expected to show their desire for a job and their appreciation of their union benefits by remaining in their place. The separation of men from women in the trade, and the more privileged position of the men—reinforced by the social inequality of women in general—created a strike situation in which the generals were men and the soldiers were women. Only certain kinds of wars can be won by such an army, and a war for women's liberation is not among them. When women fill all the most exploited categories in an industry, a fight for economic justice is inseparable from a struggle for women's liberation. This struggle has yet to take place in the U.S. garment industry.[92] Yet, despite its limitations, the Uprising of the Thirty Thousand brought great gains to women garment workers, gains in self-respect as well as wages. As Clara Lemlich summed it up: "They used to say that you couldn't even organize women. They wouldn't come to union meetings. They were 'temporary' workers. Well, we showed them!"[93]

9
Lawrence, 1912

As we come marching, marching in the beauty of the day,
A million darkened kitchens, a thousand mill lofts gray,
Are touched with all the radiance that a sudden sun discloses,
For the people hear us singing: "Bread and roses! Bread and roses!"

As we come marching, marching, we battle too for men,
For they are women's children, and we mother them again.
Our lives shall not be sweated from birth until life closes;
Hearts starve as well as bodies; give us bread, but give us roses!

As we come marching, marching, unnumbered women dead
Go crying through our singing their ancient cry for bread.
Small art and love and beauty their drudging spirits knew.
Yes, it is bread we fight for—but we fight for roses, too!

As we come marching, marching, we bring the greater days.
The rising of the women means the rising of the race.
No more the drudge and idler—ten that toil where one reposes,
But a sharing of life's glories: Bread and roses! Bread and roses!

James Oppenheim
"Bread and Roses"
written for the women of the Lawrence strike[1]

The Lawrence strike was fought over a pay cut of thirty cents a week, the cost of five loaves of bread.[2] Massachusetts textile workers lived so close to the bone that thirty cents was the difference between bare survival and starvation for them and their children. "Better to starve fighting than to starve working," they cried, and twenty thousand of them struck in the second week of January 1912.

To the newspapers and the mill owners, their outrage seemed to explode from nowhere. There were not even any unions to speak of in Lawrence: the AFL had a couple of hundred men and the IWW a few hundred more.[3] Where did twenty thousand strikers come from?

In fact, there had been minor ripples for years, showing that the water was beginning to boil underneath the surface. As James P. Thompson, the IWW's agitator in Lawrence, wrote in his report:

> It is absolutely foolish to say "it happened without any apparent cause," "that it was lightning out of clear sky," etc.
>
> As a matter of fact, it was a harvest; it was a result of seeds sown before; it was the ripened fruit of propaganda. The strike and the remarkable solidarity shown between the many nationalities and different crafts was simply the carrying out of ideas drilled into them before the strike began.[4]

Lawrence became an important textile center after the Civil War. At first the mills ran on the labor of native sons and farm girls, all skilled workers, but in the 1880s technical innovations made it possible for the Wool Trust (the alliance of large firms that monopolized the industry) to mechanize and turn what had once been skilled jobs for local workers into jobs anyone could do—even immigrants. The Wool Trust began to import its labor from Europe, first concentrating on English-speaking workers, then in the 1890s turning to workers from southern and eastern Europe. The employers made an effort to get workers from as many different language groups as possible in order to prevent them from uniting to make trouble; if they competed rather than combined, wages would be kept down. By 1912 there were twenty-five different ethnic groups in the Lawrence mills, although most of the workers were Italians, Poles, Russians, Syrians, or Lithuanians.[5] More people came than the companies could use, but a surplus labor pool was part of the Wool Trust's general plan.

The policy worked well. Wages and conditions in the mills declined steadily until a family could survive only if every member who was old enough worked. Although Massachusetts law stated that children could not work until they were fourteen, the companies had agents who could provide forged birth certificates from as far away as Italy.[6] Ten-year-olds were often pulled out of school to help pay the rent. Sometimes they weren't in school to begin with, since their parents couldn't afford to buy them enough clothes to go. The employers even went so far as to declare this "family system" helped keep the family together, since they all worked at the same looms.

Immigrants were drawn to Lawrence by posters placed in towns throughout the Balkans and the Mediterranean showing happy workers carrying bags full of money from the factory gate to the bank. In many of the workers' tenement rooms, these posters were the only decoration. Their dead hopes stared down from the wall. Elizabeth Gurley Flynn and the other IWW organizers drove this point home to the workers:

> They had hopes of a new life in a new world, free from tyranny and oppression, from landlordism, from compulsory military service. They had hopes to educate their children, to be able to work, to save, to send for others to come to freedom. What freedom? Had they expected to be herded into great prison-like mills in New England, into slums in the big cities, into tenements in these mill-towns? Was it to be called "Greenhorns" and "Hunkies" and treated as inferiors and intruders? Heads nodded and tears shone in the eyes of the women. . . .
>
> "What freedom?" we asked again. To be wage-slaves, hired and fired at the will of a soulless corporation, paid low wages for long hours, driven by the speed of a machine? What freedom? To be clubbed, jailed, shot down—and while we spoke, the hoofs of the troopers' horses clattered by on the street. . . . We spoke of their power as workers, as the producers of all wealth, as the creators of profit. . . . We talked Marxism as we understood it—the class struggle, the exploitation of labor, the use of the state and armed forces of government against the workers. It was all there in Lawrence before our eyes. We did not need to go far for the lessons.[7]

About half of the Lawrence mill workers were women and children. Unable to take time out to give birth (occasionally a baby would be born between the looms)[8] or take care of their children, the workers labored hard and died young. The average spinner died at the age of thirty-six—twenty-nine years less than the average lawyer or clergyman.[9] Their children suffered as well: the infant mortality rate in Lawrence was 172 out of 1,000.[10] When the strikers' children were sent to New York to be cared for, they were all found to be suffering from malnutrition. As Bill Haywood noted, "It was a chronic condition. These children had been starving from birth. They had been starved in their mother's wombs. And their mothers had been starving before the children were born."[11]

The IWW first came to Lawrence in September 1905 and organized a small mixed local, drawing from all occupations and language groups. It was shortlived: when J. P. Thompson went to Lawrence in 1907, he found it had not met in months. He contacted two activists, Gilbert Smith and Camille Detollonaire, and they put together a French-speaking branch which began slowly and systematically to agitate and distribute literature. By March 1911 they had formed both English and Italian branches.[12]

The previous year three small, independent craft unions had formed a coalition, the Alliance of Textile Workers Unions, and had invited the IWW local to affiliate with them. The IWW was opposed to craft unionism, but after some soul-searching it agreed to join, as long as it could continue to work at convincing the craft unionists to join the IWW. As the IWW paper noted: "The idea of meeting with the unions, even the conservatives, can only result in good, because through our contact with them we can lead them first of all in a more progressive direction, and finally to the revolutionary conception."[13] The IWW's willingness to unite bore fruit: within a month it had convinced the craft unionists to join its national agitation for the eight-hour day and to cosponsor a mass meeting.

In April 1911 the workers at one of Lawrence's largest mills, the Atlantic Cotton Mill, struck against the speedup system. The mill had announced that each weaver was to tend twelve looms at a piece rate of forty-nine cents rather than seven looms at seventy-nine cents. Forty percent of the weavers would become unnecessary.[14] The weavers' strike was small, but it lasted for months, and because of the IWW's vigorous support campaign it came to the notice of a large number of workers in Lawrence. The union issued frequent leaflets and brought in some of their best speakers, like J. P. Thompson and Elizabeth Gurley Flynn, to do street-speaking.

William Yates, national organizer for the IWW's textile union and an experienced textile worker who had gone into the New Bedford mills at the age of ten, became excited about the spirit developing in Lawrence. He asked J. P. Thompson to come as soon as he could:

> I am writing you to find out if you can come East for six weeks or two months, to start in Lawrence as soon as possible. I was over

there yesterday and find conditions such that some one is wanted in that city at once. Conditions are rotten ripe for reaping the harvest that we have so diligently sown. There is a strike in the Atlantic Mills, . . . also one in the Arlington Mills. . . . The worm (textile workers) has turned at last. He has been stepped on in such a way that there was nothing left for him to do but kick over the traces. The IWW is to the front in Lawrence.[15]

J. P. Thompson arrived in Lawrence on November 2, 1911, and the IWW local stepped up its campaign. It printed stickers and ten thousand leaflets telling the workers that speedup was "murder on the installment plan" and that "overwork for some means out of work for others."[16] It held mass indoor meetings and open-air meetings at the mill gates every noon for three weeks. Enormous crowds came to these meetings, and the union's membership grew. Even before J. P. Thompson arrived, the local had about three hundred members organized in English, Polish, Italian, and French language branches.[17] The workers of Lawrence were clearly getting ready to move. William Yates and J. P. Thompson agreed that when the lid blew, the local would wire Joe Ettor, the IWW general organizer for the Northeast, who spoke six languages. Ettor got a telegram on January 11, 1912 and left for Lawrence the next morning.

On January 1 a reform law had gone into effect in Massachusetts making it illegal for women and children to work more than fifty-four hours a week (they had been working fifty-six in Lawrence). The reformers who fought for the law did not realize that the workers' wages would be cut by two hours' pay, and the law contained no defense against this. The mill owners first tried to replace women and children with men, but there weren't nearly enough men.[18] So they cut everyone's work and pay by two hours.

Although none of the workers knew for sure that their pay would be cut until they got their pay envelopes on January 12, they feared the worst. Local 20, the Italian branch of the IWW, called a mass meeting for January 10 and a thousand workers showed up. They voted to call all the Italians out on strike on payday if there was a cut, and the next day a number of them circulated a petition asking people to pledge to strike if their envelopes were short. Two thousand weavers and spinners in a couple of the smaller mills were so excited, they jumped the gun and went out a day early; but most waited, like Fred Beal, who was fifteen at the time and worked in the Pacific Mills:

> Just like any other Friday, the paymaster, with the usual armed guard, wheeled a truck containing hundreds of pay envelopes to the head of a long line of anxiously awaiting people. . . . The first ones nervously opened their envelopes and found that the company had deducted two hours' pay. They looked silly, embarrassed and uncertain what to do. Milling around, they waited for someone to start something. They didn't have long to wait, for one lively young Italian had his mind thoroughly made up and swung into action without even looking into his pay envelope.
>
> "Strike! Strike!" he yelled. To lend strength to his words, he threw his hands in the air like a cheer-leader.
>
> "Strike! Strike! Strike!"
>
> He yelled these words as he ran, past our line, then down the room between spinning frames. The shop was alive with cries of "Strike!" after the paymaster left. . . . A tall Syrian worker pulled the switch and the powerful speed belts that gave life to the bobbins slackened to a stop.
>
> There were cries: "All out!"
>
> And hell broke loose in the spinning room. The silent, muted frames became an object of intense hatred, something against which to vent our stored-up feelings. Gears were smashed and belts cut. The Italians had long, sharp knives and with one zip the belts dangled helplessly on the pulleys.[19]

The strike began in subzero weather. It was snowing. The strikers poured out of the mills and roamed the streets in large, unorganized groups. Some formed a flying squad to go into other factories and bring the workers out. The mill owners had set up a group of men with hoses to guard the bridge over the canal leading to some of the factories. They turned streams of icy water on the strikers. Infuriated, the strikers took sticks from a nearby boxcar and went into one of the mills where they broke the machinery and windows and tore the fabric out of the looms.

In response to this violence—which Bill Haywood later estimated as a few hundred dollars' worth of property damage[20]—the mill owners demanded that the mayor call out the troops. The mayor in turn called the governor, who called out the National

Guard—popularly known as the "gray wolves." Soon the town was crowded with police and soldiers. A number of the guardsmen were Harvard students who had been given time off to "have their fling at these people."[21]

The soldiers were prepared to crush the strikers at the slightest provocation, and the workers needed organization. The IWW leaders helped them restrain their anger and militance and form themselves into an organized mass rather than small, desperate groups. The strikers were "violent" (they damaged property) before the IWW took charge, but after that the violence was almost entirely on the side of the state. As Joe Ettor told them: "You can hope for no success on any policy of violence. . . . Remember the property of the bosses is protected first by the police, then the militia. If these are not sufficient, by an entire army. Remember, you are also armed . . . with your labor power which you can withold and stop production."[22] Or, as the IWW leaders pointed out continually, "Can they weave cloth with bayonets?"[23]

The IWW emphasized both organization and Marxist political education, thus enabling the workers to put Lawrence in the context of a broader struggle between classes. The Wobblies also had experience in dealing with the press, in speaking, and in fundraising. They had a network of sympathizers, especially in the Socialist Party, who gave publicity to the strike and raised money. They knew how to bring people together, fill them with enthusiasm, and stir their emotions with the songs that were part of their fighting equipment. And they had a genius for tactical leadership.

But it was the strikers themselves who were responsible for the spirit of struggle, which came from their desperation and existed before the IWW came and after it left, and it was the rank-and-file strikers who were the source of most of the strike's tactical innovations. It was they who thought of sending their children to comrades in other cities.[24] Historians say the IWW "invented" mass picketing, but they merely regularized what the strikers had begun spontaneously. The IWW summed up and popularized the best ideas of the rank and file, and then took them from Lawrence to other strike centers.

Mass picketing was the most important tactic developed in Lawrence. The strikers had been forbidden to picket in front of the mills because the sidewalk was declared private property, but they had to form some kind of barrier to keep out scabs, and because of the guardsmen they had to do this in a way that was both forceful and nonprovocative. They decided to use the full force of their numbers (at least twenty thousand) to form a moving belt of people who walked the public sidewalks surrounding the entire mill district. It was a dramatic contrast to the method of picketing used in the shirtwaist makers' strike, in which isolated handfuls of strikers were easily picked off by the police. The mass picket line prevented scabs from getting anywhere near the plants, and at the same time became a political demonstration. In this "endless chain" the strikers, singing as they marched, affirmed their solidarity and demonstrated their collective power every day.

On Monday, January 29, the mill owners announced that they would make a special effort to keep the mills open. That day the strikers all turned out to picket, wearing IWW buttons and pieces of red cloth saying "I am not a scab." They had virtual control of the streets. The police grew desperate and tried to halt the parade by firing into the crowd. One of their shots killed a young girl striker named Anna Lopezza. Two IWW leaders, Joe Ettor and Arturo Giovannitti, were later arrested, along with a striker named Joseph Caruso, and charged with this murder, although they were two miles away when it took place; they spent the next nine months in jail awaiting trial. The police argued that they had incited a mob to riot, thus causing Anna Lopezza's death.

Many people, from congressmen to the Boston press to the local police force, were convinced that the strike was the work of outside agitators and could be broken by identifying and arresting a few leaders. After Joe Ettor and Arturo Giovannitti were jailed, the Boston paper announced—in an anti-Italian spirit typical of the time— that violence would thenceforth cease and the struggle would become a routine craft union strike, because "the passing out of Ettor means the ascendancy of the white-skinned races at Lawrence."[25] Similarly, members of the congressional committee that investigated the strike held to a conspiracy theory of the struggle; they repeatedly asked the workers who had told them to go out on strike and seemed unable to understand when strikers said "the stomach" had told them to go, or that they had decided it "all together."[26]

After Joe Ettor and Arturo Giovannitti were arrested, the strikers gave the police no opportunity to pick off the rest of the IWW leadership. Bill Haywood, Elizabeth Gurley Flynn, and the rest were accompanied by anxious bodyguards wherever they went. The police were unable to figure out who was giving tactical leadership in street demonstrations, as the police chief, Captain Sullivan, confessed to the congressional committee:

> I will tell you—there were no leaders in the streets. . . . The crowds on the street were usually led by women and children. The women and children were usually in the front rank, but when they came to the scene of the action they were brushed aside and the men did the work. . . . There were no recognized leaders except on that Monday morning when the cars were stoned. On that morning Ettor was going from place to place. He was the leader, and he was here, there, and at the other place. Wherever he was there was sure to be trouble to follow but at the time when the trouble actually occurred he was gone somewhere else.[27]

The police continually harassed the strikers. Hundreds were arrested and fined or jailed. Many were held for a while, then released without being charged. Others were charged with obstructing the sidewalk, and a number were given a year in jail for that.

The IWW sent all its top leaders to Lawrence: Joe Ettor came from a year of organizing in New York; Bill Trautman, an IWW founder, had just led a militant steel strike at McKees Rock, Pennsylvania; William Yates and Francis Miller were both active in the New England textile mills. J. P. Thompson, the IWW's star educator, famous for his simple and direct exposition of Marxist economics, was almost killed in Lawrence when hired thugs broke into his bedroom, fired three shots at him, and blackjacked him so hard he got a concussion. But the acknowledged strike leader was "Big Bill" Haywood, a miner from the West, a labor hero who had become famous after being framed in a Colorado bombing,[28] and a member of the Socialist Party's executive board. When he came to Lawrence after Joe Ettor's arrest, he was welcomed by a huge demonstration. Elizabeth Gurley Flynn recalls:

Wherever Bill Haywood went, the workers followed him with glad greetings. They roared with laughter and applause when he said: "The A.F.L. organizes like this!"—separating his fingers as far apart as they would go, and naming them—"Weavers, loom-fixers, dyers, spinners." Then he would say: "The I.W.W. organizes like this!"—tightly, clenching his big fist, shaking it at the bosses.[29]

Haywood was particularly idolized by the children, who saw him as a cowboy, with his ten-gallon hat and big boots. Mary Heaton Vorse tells about his sensitivity and openness to other workers. He was giving a press conference in the relief hall when an Italian woman came in and said, "I want to see Bigga Bill." One of the other IWW officers told her that Haywood was busy, but he interrupted his press conference and said, "Brother, I'm never too busy to see any workers that want to see me. They come before reporters." As Mary Heaton Vorse recalled him years later:

> He was always accessible. He always felt the labor movement in terms of the individual worker—a little boy, shucking oysters and getting sores on his hands; the woman picking vegetables and cricking up her back. He knew how they lived. He felt what they needed. He knew their hunger. He saw the people dying of pellagra. He saw his own boy shunted around—these migratory workers. I've known very few labor leaders to feel continuously the actual human thing, especially in relation to women and children. He could hardly bear it.[30]

Elizabeth Gurley Flynn was amazed at Bill Haywood's ability to communicate with the many different nationalities and at his grasp of the problems of the women and children, since before this he had worked mainly with English-speaking men. Many of the foreign-born workers had learned what little English they knew from their children. Haywood's language was down-to-earth and unrhetorical, so that everyone could understand him. Elizabeth Gurley Flynn, who was twenty-one at the time, said later that she had learned how to speak to workers from Bill Haywood in Lawrence: "To use short words and short sentences, to repeat the same thought in different words if I saw that the audience did not understand. I learned never to reach for a three-syllable word if a one or two could do. This is not vulgarising. Words are tools and everybody doesn't have access to a whole tool chest."[31]

Besides working with the women and children, Elizabeth Gurley Flynn was responsible for fundraising and support work outside of Lawrence. She traveled endlessly, going to Milwaukee, to West Virginia, to Pittsburg, raising money at workers' meetings and at Socialist Party locals. Off the platform, she was quiet and calm; she reserved her tremendous energy for speaking. Mary Heaton Vorse, who became her lifelong friend during the Lawrence strike, remembers:

> When Elizabeth Gurley Flynn spoke, the excitement of the crowd became a visible thing. She stood there, young, with her Irish blue eyes, her face magnolia white and her cloud of black hair, the picture of a youthful revolutionary girl leader. She stirred them, lifted them up in her appeal for solidarity. Then, at the end of the meeting, they sang. It was as though a spurt of flame had gone through the audience, something stirring and powerful, a feeling which has made the liberation of people possible; something beautiful and strong had swept through the people and welded them together, singing.[32]

Every weekend there were mass meetings where the strikers could come together in all their numbers to hear speeches, vote on the decisions of their strike committee, and feel their own strength. They concluded every meeting with "The Internationale," the song of the Paris Commune and of workers around the world: "Arise, ye prisoners of starvation, Arise, ye wretched of the earth . . ."

Mass meetings were the ultimate vehicles of decision making during the strike. Day-to-day decisions were made by the strike committee, which had been set up by Joe Ettor and Arturo Giovannitti when they first came to Lawrence. Observing that the strikers lived and socialized according to their language groups, the IWW decided to make this informal and practical division the basis of the strike organization. Each language group elected four representatives to the Central Strike Committee; very few of those elected belonged to the IWW at the beginning of the strike, although they accepted IWW advice and leadership. Since Ettor realized that strike committee members might well be arrested, each language group elected alternates as well. When Ettor himself was arrested, Haywood replaced him as leader of the commit-

tee, Elizabeth Gurley Flynn was in charge of subcommittees for
relief, finances, publicity, welfare of strikers, and children.

One of the first actions of the committee was to make public the
demands of the strike. These were

1. A fifteen percent increase in wages on the fifty-four hour basis.
2. Double pay for overtime work.
3. The abolition of all bonus and premium systems (the basis
   of speedup).
4. No discrimination against workers who were active during
   the strike.[33]

After Joe Ettor and Arturo Giovannitti were arrested, a demand
was added for their release on bail.

The language groups, under the supervision of the strike committee, were responsible for organizing picketing and for keeping track of morale. Active strikers were assigned to keep tabs
on certain people to see that they did their picket duty and went
to meetings, and that they "were kept as quiet and sober and
orderly as possible, which was due to the fact that there were
over 1,200 militiamen in the city, and we were very much afraid
of any kind of riot, knowing that the strikers would be worsted
in it."[34] The language groups were also responsible for keeping
people from scabbing. Each nationality would get the names and
addresses of its scabs and then use various forms of persuasion,
ranging from informal visits to serenading them with calls of
"scab" under their windows all night, to publishing their names
in their home country. If persuasion failed, their houses would
be splashed with red paint or pictures of the black hand; and a
scab's wife might be told she had better keep her husband home if
she didn't want him to get his throat cut. Not only were these
methods extremely effective, but the strikers' security was so
good that the police were never able to convict anyone on charges
of intimidation.

The business of running the strike was for the most part handled
not by IWW leaders but by the strikers. They did the book-
keeping—and their books were open, one of many departures
from AFL practice. They ran six commissaries and eleven soup
kitchens. They formed a committee to investigate cases for relief.
And, as Haywood stressed, all this organizational work was car-

ried on by "material that in the mill was regarded as worth no more than $6 or $7 a week."[35]

The democratic character of the strike, its bottom-up structure, were based on IWW theory. The union believed that this was the way workers would learn how to run the society they would assuredly take over. Both they and the men who led the ILGWU were socialists, but their ideas about democracy and participation were strikingly different. The Central Strike Committee's last statement, after the strike was won, shows that they had learned the IWW's lesson thoroughly:

> Until the workers themselves in the mass are sufficiently educated to demand and progressively secure these immediate advantages for themselves and to understand the necessity for control by ownership of the means of production and distribution as the only solution of the class struggle, their miserable condition is incapable of betterment. When the workers, or any number of them, do understand these principles, control of the organization is essentially democratic, each individual having an equal voice and vote with any other.[36]

The IWW felt that the political education of strikers was one of its main accomplishments. It knew that a strike is like a school for workers, a space of time where they can develop their understanding and abilities in practice. Mary Heaton Vorse observed this process in Lawrence:

> People who have never seen an industrial struggle think of a strike as a time of tumult, disorder and riot. Nothing could be less true. A good strike is a college for the workers. When the workers listen to the speeches they are going to school. Their minds are being opened. They are learning history and economics translated into the terms of their own lives. Many of them suddenly find hitherto unsuspected powers. Men and women, until now dumb, get up on platforms and speak with fire and with the eloquence of sincerity to their fellow workers. Others write articles and leaflets. New forms of demonstrations are invented, and the workers set off singing the songs they themselves have made up under the pressure of the strike. Like new blood these new talents flow through the masses of the workers.[37]

No one developed more during the Lawrence strike or came

forward faster than those who had been most underdeveloped, most in the background—the women of Lawrence. About half of the Lawrence strikers were women and, along with the wives and children of male strikers, their role in street actions was noticeable from the beginning. One of the first instances of striker "violence" occurred when a group of Italian women caught a policeman alone on the bridge. They took his gun, club, and star, and were beginning to remove his pants before throwing him into the river, when the cavalry charged and rescued him. Many of these women were arrested and sentenced to jail by Judge Mahoney, who explained to them in awful tones that the body of a policeman was sacred.[38]

In the course of the strike women became increasingly active; from February on clashes between the women and the police and militia grew more frequent. The police, mill owners, and press raised loud objections to the role women played in the street. The Lawrence district attorney said in court that the strike committee was made up of cowards who sent their women onto the picket line; he thought they should put men there instead, since "one policeman can handle ten men, while it takes ten policemen to handle one woman."[39] The women spontaneously began to take leadership in street confrontations. Fred Beal describes one such occasion:

> One day, after the militia was called, thousands of us strikers marched to Union Street again. In the front ranks a girl carried a large American flag. When we arrived at the junction of Canal and Union Streets, we were met by a formidable line of militia boys, with rifles and attached bayonets. They would not let us proceed.
>
> An officer on horseback gave orders: "Port Arms! Disperse the crowd!"
>
> Whereupon the militia, boys between the ages seventeen to twenty, guns leveled waist-high, moved toward the crowd. Their bayonets glistened in the sunlight. On and on they moved. The strikers in front could not move because of the pressing of the crowd behind them. It looked as if the murder of Anna LoPezza would be multiplied many times. And then the girl with the American flag stepped forward. With a quick motion she wrapped the Stars and Stripes around her body and defied the militia to make a hole in Old Glory.

The officer on horseback permitted us to proceed and there was no further trouble.[40]

The IWW did special work with women to ensure that they were able to play a strong role in strike activities. Wobbly leaders struggled with the attitudes of husbands and priests, who wanted to hold women back. Elizabeth Gurley Flynn describes the way the IWW dealt with this problem:

> We held special meetings for the women, at which Haywood and I spoke. The women worked in the mills for lower pay and in addition had all the housework and care of the children. The old-world attitude of man as the "lord and master" was strong. At the end of the day's work—or, now, of strike duty—the man went home and sat at ease while his wife did all the work preparing the meal, cleaning the house, etc. There was considerable male opposition to women going to meetings and marching on the picket line. We resolutely set out to combat these notions. The women wanted to picket. We knew that to leave them at home alone, isolated from the strike activity, a prey to worry, affected by the complaints of tradespeople, landlords, priests and ministers, was dangerous to the strike.[41]

Flynn also told the women how to deal with shopkeepers' complaints: they should try to get credit by pointing out that the people who used their stores were workers, not mill owners, and that when they got more pay they would spend more.

Organizing housewives was basic to the IWW's strike strategy, just as using the opportunities generated by an intense struggle was the IWW's fundamental method of organizing women. While AFL strikes often forced husbands and wives apart, IWW strikes united them. As Elizabeth Gurley Flynn described it:

> The I.W.W. appeals to women to organize side by side with their men folks, in the union that shall increasingly determine its own rules of work and wages—until its solidarity and power shall the world command. It points out to the young girl that marriage is no escape from the labor problem, and to the mother, that the interest of herself and her children are woven in with the interests of the class. . . .
>
> Where a secluded home environment has produced a psychological attitude of "me and mine"—how is the I.W.W. to overcome

conservatism and selfishness? By driving women into an active participation in union affairs, especially strikes, where the mass meetings, mass picketing, women's meetings and children's gatherings are a tremendous emotional stimulant. The old unions never have considered the women as part of the strike. They were expected to stay home and worry about the empty larder, the hungry kiddies and the growling landlord, easy prey to the agents of the company. But the strike was "a man's business." The men had the joy of the fight, the women not even an intelligent explanation of it. . . .

Women can be the most militant or most conservative element in a strike, in proportion to their comprehension of its purposes. The I.W.W. has been accused of putting the women in the front. The truth is, the I.W.W. does not keep them in the back, and they go to the front.[42]

As a result of the Wobblies' encouragement, female leaders began to develop from the rank and file, and women were elected as delegates to the strike committee. Among them were Rose Cardullo, Josephine Liss, and Annie Welsenbach, probably the most remarkable. She was a highly skilled worker who did invisible reweaving, repairing tiny holes in the cloth. Her husband was also skilled and they were well off, as Lawrence workers went. But she had begun work at the age of fourteen and knew well what conditions were like for most of the workers. She told a reporter: "I have been getting madder and madder for years at the way they talked to these poor Italians and Lithuanians."[43] She became utterly dedicated to the strike, leading the mass of strikers down Essex Street day after day, and was elected to the ten-person negotiating committee. It was said after the strike that if she lifted a finger, three of the mills would go out.

When Bill Haywood took over the leadership, the IWW began to hold special meetings not only for women but for children. The children of immigrants in Lawrence, as elsewhere, tended to become Americanized and grow away from their parents' "old-country" culture. Those who were fortunate enough to be able to stay in school were taught to despise their parents for being immigrants and workers. After the strike began, they were taught that it was "un-American." Elizabeth Gurley Flynn

describes the situation and the way the Wobblies tried to deal
with it:

> The efforts of the church and schools were directed to driving a
> wedge between the school children and their striking parents.
> Often, children in such a town became ashamed of their foreign-
> born, foreign-speaking parents, their old-country ways, their ac-
> cents, their foreign newspapers, and now it was their strike and
> mass picketing. The up-to-date, well-dressed, native-born teachers
> set a pattern. The working-class women were shabbily dressed,
> though they made the finest woolen fabrics. Only a few American-
> born women wore hats in Lawrence. The others wore shawls,
> kerchiefs, or worsted knitted caps made at home. Some teachers
> called the strikers lazy, said they should go back to work or "back
> where they came from." We attempted to counteract all this at our
> children's meetings. Big Bill, with his Western hat and stories about
> cowboys and Indians, became an ideal of the kids. The parents
> were pathetically grateful to us as their children began to show real
> respect for them and their struggles.[44]

The strikers could not make their children stay indoors when
so much was happening in the streets, but as more and more
troops poured into the city they became increasingly worried
about their children's safety. Their fears increased after a sixteen-
year-old Syrian striker named John Ramey was bayoneted in the
back. The soldiers accosted teenage girls roughly, and the younger
children were terrified and confused by the soldiers' hostility to
them and their parents. Samuel Lipson, a striker, told the congressional committee about his fears for his children:

> Many children, you know, are hurt. While going along the street, I
> have seen a soldier—a striker went along with a little dog with him,
> and the soldier wanted to start trouble and stabbed that dog with his
> bayonet. . . . I sent my child away because I did not want my child to
> see what is going on in that city; because he opened his eyes and said
> to me: "Why do they hurt those people? Why do the soldiers try to
> hurt those people and put the bayonets against them?" . . . He is
> eight years old.[45]

Fear for their children's safety, together with the desire to have
them securely fed, gave the strikers the idea of sending their

children to sympathizers in other cities. It was a common practice in Italy to send children from a town on strike to relatives and comrades in other towns, and the Italians suggested the idea to the strike committee.[46] Elizabeth Gurley Flynn communicated with various Socialist organizations, and the New York Socialist Party and Italian Socialist Federation were very enthusiastic about the idea. They made plans for a giant reception for the children at Grand Central Station, after which the children would be given dinner and then taken to the homes they were to stay in, all of which were thoroughly investigated by a committee of New York socialist women. The IWW press reported proudly that only left-wing or labor homes would have the privilege of playing host. Margaret Sanger, a trained nurse, was to go and fetch the children from Lawrence.[47]

The exodus of the Lawrence children, which began in early February, gave all the sections of the New York labor movement a chance to demonstrate their support for the strike. Hundreds of people spent most of the day in Grand Central Station, since the IWW had neglected to inform anyone what time the train was due. Mary Heaton Vorse, who had not yet gone to Lawrence, wrote her friend Arthur Bullard about the goings-on:

> The waiting part of the Grand Central was just crammed. The babies spoke between them something like forty-four languages and dialects, so there were all sorts of nationalities and people there, and every sort of a local was represented. Italians were very much in evidence. The Sergeant on duty was an Anarchist hater, and he intemperately remarked that "the red flag of anarchy shouldn't fly in New York while he was a cop." This irritated deeply the Comrades and the Brethren, and for a minute there was a curious little tenseness in the air,—that little mob growl, not the real growl yet, but the first whisper of a storm. The sergeant went out to send for more cops, and the mob got black in the brow. . . .
>
> The whole situation was charmingly saved by some humorous, wide-faced gentleman who played a joke on the cops and Anarchists both, for he went out and got a blackboard and wrote on it:
>
> "This is a free country. Harvard Students," in red letters, and he placed this lovely device beneath the red flag of Anarchy. Of course the Italians didn't know what it was all about while the cops grinned sheepishly. I think they had a lingering suspicion that there might

be a little college nonsense back of it and it is of course so tactless to run in a student when you think you have got a Black-Hander.

Of course the Anarchists wouldn't do anything they were asked to do, not feeling that they could be good Anarchists and take an order from anyone or be obliging, so the whole bunch surged up and down, and a nice, fine, heady mob feeling grew and grew until you felt that the slightest thing might touch it off. I love it. And after hours and hours of waiting the children at last came. . . .

I followed them down to the Labor Temple and you could trace their progress down the road by the little mittens that had been provided by the reception commiteee.[48]

The exodus of the children provided the Lawrence strike with its first good publicity. The press had a field day over the dreadful, starved, and sickly condition of the travelers. The radical papers pointed out that this condition was due to low wages as well as the strike, and the Lawrence authorities claimed that the strike committee had deliberately dressed the children in rags to fool the press. They even accused the strikers of deliberately exploiting the suffering of their own children.

This publicity enabled Victor Berger, the socialist congressman from Wisconsin, to arrange an inquiry by the House Rules Committee, where Margaret Sanger bore witness to the condition of the children:

All of these children were walking about apparently not noticing chicken pox or diptheria: one child had diptheria, and had been walking around, and no attention paid to it at all, and had been working up to the time of the strike. Out of the 119 children four of them had underwear on, and it was the most bitter weather; we had to run all the way from the hall to the station in order to keep warm. . . . They were very much emaciated; every child there showed the effects of malnutrition. . . . I have been brought up in a factory town where there were glassblowers and children of glassblowers, and I must say that I have never seen in any place children so ragged and so deplorable as these children were. I have never seen such children in my work in the Italian districts of New York City; in the slum districts, I must say, there are always a few of them who are fat and rugged, but these children were pale and thin.[49]

Another group of 126 children left Lawrence on February 17,

some for New York and some for Barre, Vermont. They also got considerable sympathetic publicity. The Lawrence mill owners and town fathers began to get alarmed, and the police decided that not only did they have to stop more children from leaving, but they also had to try to get back the ones who had already gone. Samuel Lipson reported to the congressional committee:

> Many women, Polish women, came up to my house. They have children in New York, and they cried. I said, "What is the matter?" They said, "Two or three times the policemen came over to my house and told me to send for my children to call them back"; I said, "What is the matter? I received letters daily from my children saying that they were happy; that they have new clothes, and they are eating there every day as they used to eat at home on Sunday; and they have so much to eat that if the parents have not enough they want them to come to New York, and they will give it to them." And they were frightened by the police, and also they sent the landlord up, and the landlord said to these women: "If you are not going to call your children back we will put you out of the house." They frightened the parents to make them call the children back; and the women said: "I received letters from my children saying that they are happy, and I don't know what to do."[50]

On February 22 seven children were arrested at the station and told that if they were hungry they should go to the city poor farm. The chief of police told the press: "There will be no more children leaving Lawrence until we are satisfied that the police cannot stop their going."[51]

A large group of children was supposed to go to Philadelphia two days later. Gertrude Marvin, a one-time reporter for a Boston daily who had quit when the editor refused to print her pro-strike stories, told the readers of the IWW paper *Solidarity* what happened at the station:

> The police closed in on them. Mothers seized their children in their arms as the police charged down on them. Fathers and other men who had been waiting outside were dragged away and thrown to the ground as they tried to interfere. Children were dragged from their mothers and knocked down and trampled. The women, infuriated, sprang at the officers to rescue their little ones, and instantly the officers drew their clubs. Scratching, kicking, scream-

ing, the mass of men and women and children vibrated back and forth across the platform. . . . Officers clubbed right and left with their heavy loaded sticks, steadily, persistently. Wails of the children as they were knocked down and kicked about, and the screams of maddened women made a terrifying noise. Details were lost. It became a confused hideous melee of brutality and suffering. Underneath was the sickening dread that some of these lives would be lost. One shot just then would have meant many more.[52]

The officers dragged the women and children to a wagon waiting at one end of the station, took the women to jail, and put the children in the city poor farm—it being against the law to keep minors in the same lockup as adults unless they were babes in arms.

The story of "cossacks" beating defenseless women and children who were merely trying to leave Lawrence made headlines across the country. The tide of public opinion began to turn in favor of the strikers. Some of the children from Lawrence later testified to great effect before the congressional committee in Washington.

The same day that the children were beaten and arrested at the railway station, the women strikers launched their first major independent offensive in the streets. It was probably their intention to draw most of the troops away from the railway station. The offensive had been organized the day before by a pregnant Italian woman, who gathered up some of her compatriots and went to the Polish meeting where Bill Haywood was to speak. He lifted her onto a table and she spoke in broken English:

> "Men, woman: I come speak to you. I been speaking to others. Just now tomorrow morning all women come see me half past four at Syrian church. Tonight no sleep. You meet me at half past four, not sleep tonight.
>
> "You all come with me. We go tell folks no go to work. Men all stay home, all men and boys stay home. Just now all woman and girl come with me. Soldier he hurt man. Soldier he no hurt woman. He no hurt me. Me got big belly. She too," pointing to one of her friends, "she got big belly too. Soldier no hurt me. . . . Soldier he got mother."
>
> As Haywood lifted her from the table a scene of the wildest enthusiasm ensued in the packed hall, containing over 1,500 strikers. Men and women were in tears. Tears were streaming down the woman's face, down Haywood's face, down the face of everybody in

the room. The woman kissed Haywood's hands while Haywood kissed hers, and had to leave the hall without giving his speech.[53]

The optimism of the pregnant woman proved unfounded. The troops attacked the picketers, beat them, and arrested them. Both Italian women miscarried.[54] When these events were described to the congressional committee, Mrs. Taft, wife of the president, is reported to have rushed from the room in distress. Chief of Police Sullivan gave his own version of events, emphasizing the "assaults" the women made on the scabs:

> There were times when we had difficulty in keeping these women from getting in the patrol wagon to be arrested; they were martyrs, heroines; they wanted to be held up, they wanted to be brought to the police station and charged with an assault and interfering with people; lots of them had money in their pockets, but they would not pay fines and would not accept bail; they wanted to be sent to jail. Now, on that Monday morning, a great many people were arrested—that is, these women, for assaulting workers who were going to the mills [i.e., talking to them]—and they were brought to the police station and locked up.[55]

The strikers presented their point of view with equal vividness, as in a letter to Massachusetts Governor Foss describing similar events on March 1:

> Since the federal investigation is on, women thought they were secure in walking on the streets and that their constitutional rights were guaranteed. Peaceful women went to a meeting on March first, on a Friday. Returning home, about 15 of them were suddenly surrounded by 50 or more Metropolitan police officers. There had been no provocation, no shouting even or any noise. These women were assaulted and clubbed, and an officer in blue, leaning out of a window of city hall, urged them on in their fiendish, savage attacks. Breaking into two divisions they would not allow the women to escape. . . . Not until one of the women, Bertha F. Carosse, 151 Elm Street, was beaten into insensibility did the thugs in uniform desist. The beaten woman was carried unconscious to a hospital and pregnant with new life; this was blown into eternity by the fiendish beating and was born dead, murdered in a mother's womb by the clubs of hired murderers of the law that you have so recklessly overridden and abridged. . . . we will remember, we will never forget and never forgive.[56]

The Lawrence strike was like a roadblock in history, stopping every person and organization involved, making them decide which way they were going and which side they were on. Mary Heaton Vorse and her future husband, Joe O'Brien, felt that way:

> Something transforming had happened to both of us. We knew now where we belonged—on the side of the workers and not with the comfortable people among whom we were born. . . . Some synthesis had taken place between my life and that of the workers, some peculiar change which would never again permit me to look with indifference on the fact that riches for the few were made by the misery of the many. . . . The sense of indignation . . . was not the whole story. . . . It was seeing of what beauty human beings are capable.[57]

After the strike had gone on for eight weeks, the mill owners began to meet with the strike committee. The pressure of public opinion was an important factor in inducing the mill owners to come to the negotiating table, as were the questions the congressmen began to raise at the inquiry about Tariff K, which had raised the price of imported woolen goods from 50 to 100 percent in order to protect the domestic manufacturers, but which, the investigators suggested, had failed to protect the workers and should therefore be reduced. The owners offered the strike committee a 5 percent increase; when this was rejected, they offered 7 percent, then 7.5 percent. Each offer was rejected. Finally, on March 12 the negotiating committee came back with an offer of 25 percent increases for the lowest-paid workers, who were making nine and a half cents an hour. The wage increases were arranged on a sliding scale, with the lowest-paid workers getting the highest increase. Everyone would get time and a quarter for overtime, and the companies promised no discrimination against strikers.[58] The strike committee advised the strikers to accept the package.

At a mass meeting on March 14 on the Lawrence Common, twenty thousand strikers voted unanimously to accept the agreement and go back to work. They vowed to keep their organization intact and concluded, as always, by singing "The Internationale": "The earth shall rise on new foundations, We have been naught, we shall be all."

As a result of the strike's success, there was a wave of strikes across New England. In Lowell, Massachussets, the mill owners rushed to offer a 5 percent raise as soon as the IWW organizers hit town. A quarter of a million textile workers in New England got wage increases as a result of the Lawrence strike.[59] The settlement was a great victory, not only for the Lawrence workers but for all U.S. textile workers.

The Lawrence strike was supported by a wide range of organizations, including the WTUL and the Socialist Party—though because of the explicitly revolutionary character of the IWW's unionism, the range was less broad than it had been in the shirtwaist makers' strike. The AFL's contribution to the strike, however, was primarily negative. The AFL's United Textile Workers had never organized more than a handful of skilled workers in the Lawrence mills, but when the strike began to show its strength, they came to town to see what they could get out of it. The UTW's leader, John Golden, was second to none in his hatred for the IWW: as soon as the strike broke out, he wired the mayor of Lawrence to offer his support for the city's efforts to suppress the strikers. He later praised the city fathers for calling out the National Guard. The AFL organizers in Lawrence repeatedly referred to the IWW as a violent bunch of anarchists, and to its immigrant members as a lawless rabble.

John Golden even went so far as to support the Lawrence police in their policy of beating up and arresting children at the Lawrence railroad station. He told the congressional committee as much:

> MR. GOLDEN: . . . these children are not being sent away for any benefit to the children or their parents. . . . The motive, as I said before, was to draw sympathy of people by the advertising or exploiting of these children so that the propaganda of the industrial workers, which means the destruction of our movement, could be preached, and not in the interest of these children or their parents.
>
> MR. STANLEY: You mean that that labor organization would absorb yours and you are kicking about that?
>
> MR. GOLDEN: We do not consider it a labor organization.[60]

Golden set up his own relief station, hoping to divert funds from the relief committee set up by the Central Strike Committee. He then attempted to negotiate not only for his few members, but for the masses of unskilled workers represented by the Committee. He failed, as the head of the Everett Mills told the press:

> In the deputation which came to see me the other day I was surprised to find not a single employee who either works or has worked at our mills. There was even one who does not live in Lawrence at all. The leader of the deputation admitted that the American Federation of Labor had not succeeded in getting enough of the Everett employes to their meetings to make up or form part of a committee.[61]

The tiny AFL craft unions negotiated as a bloc, separately from the other workers. They were offered a small increase and voted to return to work on March 5, a full two weeks before the rest of the workers settled. The AFL relief station subsequently gave food only to strikers who agreed to go back to work. This extraordinary example of AFL strikebreaking got an unusual amount of publicity and increased public sympathy for the IWW. Many AFL locals were completely disgusted with their leadership and sent their relief contributions to the IWW's Central Strike Committee instead.

Despite the outrageous character of his actions, John Golden, as leader of the UTW in New England, had considerable influence with liberals who would ordinarily support a strike, as well as with the press, the labor movement, and the Women's Trade Union League. Mary Kenney O'Sullivan, who went up to Lawrence to see what was happening for herself, spoke sharply of John Golden's adverse effect on the strike:

> There is in Boston a group of social workers who have not gone to Lawrence, who are believed to have been guided by the president of the Textile Workers of America, and who have fought the strikers from the beginning. Among them are some who have asserted that it would be better for the strike to be lost than to obtain a settlement through the general strike committee. These social workers know or should know that under the old regime, children, thousands of them, suffered from underfeeding, and that other children as old as nine years have never seen the inside of a schoolhouse because they have no clothes. . . . The influence of Mr. Golden with the power and prestige of the American Federation of Labor in the background, has proved astounding. Yet, judging

from the relief funds that have continued to pour in to the general strike committee from unions in the American Federation, the organization as a whole could not have approved his acts.[62]

Mary Kenney O'Sullivan played an important role in the strike, for she was the only one of the old-time AFL leaders who supported the "new unionism." She did so on her own, not on behalf of the Women's Trade Union League, whose support was compromised and equivocal at best. She even put up bail for Ettor and Giovannitti and on one occasion helped in negotiations. As her companion in the Boston League, Elizabeth Glendower Evans, wrote Margaret Dreier Robins, "She is the only one of us who had sense, and did anything better than muddle."[63] Although half of the Lawrence strikers were women, the Boston branch of the League did not even visit Lawrence until almost three weeks after the strike began. John Golden had told them to stay home, and many members of the League felt that their AFL affiliation prevented them from giving aid to a rival organization. The League dithered until the beginning of February, when Golden told them they could help the AFL with its relief station. But if the women had been expecting that their relief efforts would become as central to the Lawrence strikers as they had been to the shirtwaist strikers, they were disappointed. The AFL's relief work was at best a sideshow; it helped few workers and was a front for Golden's effort to sell out the strike, efforts in which the League became implicated. When Golden settled separately and ordered that anyone who came to the AFL relief station must be told to go back to work, the Boston WTUL withdrew from the situation in dismay. But since Sarah Conboy, a Boston textile worker who was working for the League but had previously been employed by Golden, stayed on at the relief station, the masses of strikers assumed the League supported the AFL's efforts to break the strike.

Like Mary Kenney O'Sullivan, Elizabeth Glendower Evans, a broad-minded rich woman who was the financial mainstay of the Boston WTUL, was outraged by Golden's conduct and the cooperation he got from the League. She wrote:

> Well, I was such a fool that I accepted Mr. Golden's and Miss Gillespie's [Mabel Gillespie, secretary of the Boston League] say-so that the strike was legitimately ended and that those who refused to

come in should be disciplined. I had not been on the spot, and I exercised no independent judgement, but accepted their say-so. It was later that I went to strike headquarters and I saw the *real* vital immense thing—the great body of many races and tongues dominated by a single purpose—and realized the absurdity of ever having thought of the tiny little C.L.U. [Central Labor Union of the AFL] headquarters as anything more than a travesty and a fake. It simply filled me with despair for our League as a live thing at all, that our secretary and Mrs. Conboy, vice-president and organizer, had been there continuously for weeks and had muddled along as remote from the real condition so it seems to me, as if they had been in Alaska—had maintained and indeed believed that "organized labor was in control" because of the petty relief work of the C.L.U. relief station and John Golden's conferences up in Boston—had accepted his say-so that the vague concessions announced in the papers and a vote of four small locals was an "honorable settlement" that should bind all strikers—it fills me with despair, I say, that such preposterous claims should be accepted and still defended by Miss Gillespie and Mrs. Conboy and by the League as a whole.[64]

There was considerable debate within the League following the debacle of their work in Lawrence. Was there any way they could retain their link to the AFL and not close off all possibility of working with this new, vital movement for industrial unionism? Sue Ainslie Clark, president of the Boston League, summarized the different opinions and added her own:

Certain members of the Boston League believe that its course was the only one open to it since it was affiliated with the A.F. of L. and aimed to propagate the principles of craft unionism endorsed by that organization. Certain others believe that we might have cooperated with the Strike Committee from the first, as individuals. . . . Still others think that our part has been a disgraceful one in this great struggle. Others regard the success of the Lawrence strike, through the I.W.W. methods, as an object lesson by which the League—and the A.F. of L.—must profit in order to play a vital part in the rapidly moving evolution of the labor movement today.

To me, many of those in power in the A.F. of L. today seem to be selfish, reactionary and remote from the struggle for bread and liberty of the unskilled workers. The danger confronted by the A.F. of L. is that immemorially confronted by organizations in church and government when creed and consideration of safety obscure the original spirit and aim. Are we, the Women's Trade Union League, to ally ourselves inflexibly with the "standpatters" of the Labor Movement or are we to hold ourselves ready to aid the "insurgents," those who are freely fighting the fight of the exploited, the oppressed and the weak among the workers?[65]

Margaret Dreier Robins did not think the League had any choice. During the Hart, Schaffner and Marx strike in Chicago the year before, when the corrupt AFL leadership of the United Garment Workers were locked in a struggle with an insurgent IWW-led rank-and-file movement, she and the Chicago Federation of Labor had been caught in the middle. The IWW's criticisms of her role in the Chicago strike probably made her even less receptive to cooperation with them than she would otherwise have been.[66] The League had a national executive board meeting in April 1912, and Lawrence was on the agenda. According to the minutes:

> Miss Dreier asked what the future action of the League would be in a situation where the I.W.W. people were in and there was need for the organization of women as in the textile trade.
> Mrs. Robins stated that owing to our affiliation we could not go into a strike where the I.W.W. was in control.[67]

As usual, Margaret Dreier Robins prevailed. After 1912 the League stayed as far away as possible from any IWW strike, completely ignoring the enormous strike of female textile workers in Paterson, New Jersey, the next year. Mary Kenney O'Sullivan and Elizabeth Glendower Evans dropped out of the Boston League as a result of the Lawrence strike and what it revealed about the AFL and the League:

> The A.F. of L. in Massachusetts, and perhaps pretty generally, is losing its hold. Its strict craft organization is not adapted to the assimilation of the unskilled foreign races. Perhaps it has got to be smashed, or purged, or reorganized. Just at present, I don't see where a person in my position can lend a hand. And I don't see how a League linked strictly to the disintegrating A.F. of L. can become real.[68]

The only outside organization that unequivocally supported the Lawrence strike was the Socialist Party, and its aid was indispensable. Socialist locals sent about $40,000 in strike funds. (IWW locals sent about $16,000, and AFL locals about $11,000, despite their leadership's opposition.) Victor Berger arranged the congressional hearing that brought the strikers their first favorable publicity, and Socialists put the real news of the strike in their own newspapers to counteract the lies of the regular press. When the Lawrence Common was barred to the strikers and they had nowhere to meet, the socialist Franco-Belge consumer cooperative gave them its hall, sold them bread at cost, and provided a soup kitchen. After the strike victory, Bill Haywood paid tribute to the help of the Socialist Party:

> The success of the Lawrence strike was largely due to the support and the influence of the socialist movement of America. (Applause.) It was you who came to our relief. When we made an appeal for financial aid it was the socialists who sent nearly three-fourths of all the funds that were raised during that strike. It was the working class of New York City, of Philadelphia, of Manchester and Barre, many of whom were socialists, who took care of the children during the long period of the industrial war. Without the support of the socialists, the strike of Lawrence could never have been won. (Applause.)[69]

Nevertheless, the Lawrence strike was the last waltz in an increasingly troubled romance between the IWW and the Socialist Party. Even as the strikers were celebrating their victory, the music ended in discord. The night before Joe Ettor went to Lawrence, two members of the party's executive committee, Morris Hillquit, a New York lawyer, who represented the party's reform elements, and Bill Haywood, who represented its left wing, held a debate on strategy at Cooper Union. So much factional feeling was in evidence that admission was restricted to party members. Haywood responded to a certain amount of baiting by waving the red flag repeatedly in Hillquit's face, especially in his talk of sabotage (a favorite slogan in the IWW). Among other things, he said:

> I am not here to waste time on the "immediate demanders" or the step-at-a-time people whose every step is just a little shorter than the preceding step. . . . I am going to speak on the class struggle, and I am going to make it so plain that even a lawyer can under-

stand it. . . . we know the class struggle in the west. And realizing, having contended with all the bitter things that we have been called upon to drink to the dregs, do you blame me when I say that *I despise the law* (tremendous applause and shouts of "No!") and I am not a law-abiding citizen. (Applause.) And more than that, no Socialist *can* be a law-abiding citizen. (Applause.) When we come together and are of a common mind, and the purpose of our minds is to overthrow the capitalist system, we become conspirators then against the United States government. And certainly it is our purpose to abolish this government (applause) and establish in its place an industrial democracy. . . .

I again want to justify direct action and sabotage. . . . I don't know of anything that can be applied that will bring as much satisfaction to you, as much anguish to the boss as a little sabotage in the right place at the proper time. Find out what it means. It won't hurt you and it will cripple the boss.[70]

This speech so infuriated the right wing of the party that some of them could not even wait until the Lawrence strike was over to attack Haywood publicly. One such was Lena Morrow Lewis, the lone female member of the party's national executive committee, who stated emphatically in an interview that

the advice of Joseph J. Ettor to put emery dust into the machines precipitates an issue between those who believe in destructive tactics as against constructive methods. . . . To advocate the destruction of property is a reversion to the brute instinct in men. Machinery is the stored-up labor of the producer, and any attempt to destroy the productive force is a menace to humanity. . . . The Lawrence strike is only a pebble. . . . The statement of some of our utopian friends that this is the beginning of the social revolution is, to say the least, evidence of their lack of knowledge as to what constitutes the social revolution. The social revolution takes place in society when a class having no political or economic power as a class organizes itself and becomes the dominant class, politically and economically. The social revolution may be accomplished without the shedding of a drop of blood, or the destruction of any property.[71]

The war between the party's left and right wings broke out in full force at the Socialist Party convention in May 1912. The right wing made a motion to amend the party's constitution to expel any member who opposed electoral work or advocated sabotage.

In the ensuing struggle, they were clearly dominant. The left wing never controlled the party machinery or convention and in any case probably accounted for no more than a third of the party's membership. During the floor debate, Victor Berger, who had served the strikers so well in Congress, distinguished himself:

> Berger then got the floor and made his regular biennial threat of quitting the party and forming a new organization. "You will have a split yet," he shouted, "and by God, I am ready to split right now! I am going back to Milwaukee and tell them to cut the cancer of anarchy from their body. There is a difference between revolution and organized murder. We, in Milwaukee, believe in revolutionary political action (laughter) but we are opposed to the bomb and the dagger. You know where sabotage leads to. It led to the Haymarket riots. . . . I can see anarchism under the cloak of the I.W.W. and it is trying to fasten itself on the Socialist party."[72]

The anti-sabotage amendment passed in a party-wide referendum. The right wing then staged another referendum to recall Haywood from the national executive committee; it passed by two to one—but only 20 percent of the party membership bothered to vote.[73] As a result of these developments, most IWW members and sympathizers left the party. The coalition of forces that had helped the Lawrence strikers win such a resounding victory no longer existed, and both the Socialist Party and the IWW were weaker for the lack of it.

Encouraged by the failure of the Paterson strike in 1913, the *New York Call* launched a campaign to criticize the IWW's strike conduct a year after the split. Its editor charged:

> Lawrence was won by the I.W.W. There are at present over 12,000 people out of work in that city. It is not a strike. It is a shutdown. . . . Would it be just to demand an accounting from the I.W.W.? Here are so many promises made. How have they been carried out? Here are so many boasts of superior tactics. Where are the goods? It is about time to get down to earth and realize there is no short cut to the industrial republic, and that a theory does not stay a starving belly. . . . The only capitalist map is still all black, and you can go to any battlefield and find out what the results have been.[74]

Ben Williams, the editor of *Solidarity,* stoutly defended his organization and the workers in it:

That they failed to end the class struggle, or to permanently improve conditions by one manifestation thereof, seems to the genius
of the *Call,* an unforgivable sin. If the *Call* were really a socialist
paper, instead of berating the workers for their folly in struggling
under the banner of the I.W.W., it would understand that only
through such constant struggles can the working class finally be
brought to sufficient unity to overthrow capitalism.[75]

William's rebuttal was correct, but so was the *Call*'s description
of the way conditions had deteriorated in Lawrence. Immediately
after the strike the mill owners began an offensive which included
not only the prosecution of Ettor and Giovannitti, but the impor-
tation of new groups of workers, especially French Canadians,
the massive use of spies, and the blacklisting of IWW militants.
Most of the IWW's national leadership left Lawrence as soon as
the strike was over, and when they were blacklisted many of its
militant workers left as well. Samuel Lipson, a member of the
Central Strike Committee who had testified at the congressional
hearings, wrote Victor Berger in April 1912:

All the people returned to work, and do pleasantly enjoy the
increased wages, but me. There is really no chance for me to earn a
living in this city. Because all are united against me, especially the
manufacturers inside the mills and good citizens, business-men,
police, clergymen, in brief all are trying to the best of their ability, to
get such a dangerous man as I am, out of their dear old home town.
. . . Therefore, I have decided to look for bread some where else.[76]

Undeterred and still riding high from the strike, the IWW in
Lawrence turned its attention to getting Ettor, Giovannitti, and
Caruso freed from their trumped-up murder charges. The case
became a national issue; there was a one-day general strike over it
in Lawrence; and finally the jury, all working men, handed down
a verdict of not guilty. It was a considerable victory.

When the demonstrations of rank-and-file militancy around
the Ettor–Giovannitti trial led to a one-day general strike, the
employers became convinced that their previous tactics had been
inadequate, and that they needed a more concerted effort to
redivide the working class along national and political lines. Using
as their pretext a "No God! No Master!" banner flaunted by some
Boston anarchists at an Ettor–Giovannitti rally in Lawrence, the

mill owners began to rally the Lawrence middle class around the flag of patriotism. A huge banner reading "For God and Country! The Red Flag Never!" was stretched across Essex Street, the main shopping area. Merchants were urged to hang the Stars and Stripes outside their shops. The Lawrence Citizens' Committee, made up of the mill owners and their friends, started a vigilante movement to terrorize foreigners, particularly Syrians, Poles, Lithuanians, and Italians, the national groups that had been most active in the strike.[77] One Polish worker was killed in a fight with vigilantes.[78]

The IWW met the God-and-country offensive in various imaginative ways. Its members began to boycott the flag-waving shops on Essex Street, and made vivid speeches inside them to tell the shopkeepers why: "You gotta da flag outa, huh? Youa greata Americano? Say Italiano no gooda. . . . Ah, me no want youa shoesa!"[79] The Polish members of the IWW drew $50,000 in deposits out of the Lawrence banks, saying they would keep the money in Boston until Lawrence financial interests learned to treat foreigners with respect.[80]

These measures had some effect on the small shopkeepers, but there can be little doubt that the God-and-country campaign disrupted the unity of the Lawrence working class. Even during the strike, some national groupings had sided with the employers. The French Canadians had almost all scabbed, and now hundreds more were being imported into the city. The Irish workers of Lawrence were almost a separate caste; they were favored over non-English speaking nationalities in the mills and had an entrée into the city's political patronage machine. Many of them participated in the vigilante attacks.[81] (The antistrike Judge Mahoney, Mayor Scanlon, Chief of Police Sullivan, and School Commissioner John Breen, who planted dynamite in an attempt to frame the IWW, were examples of the kind of reactionary leadership the Irish workers got from their politicians. Their priest, Father O'Reilly, was the major organizer of the patriotism campaign.)

The IWW responded to the vigilantes by threatening to move its workers out of Lawrence. The plan indicates how demoralized and fearful some of the IWW-led workers were becoming and how successful the mill owners' campaign was, IWW bravado notwithstanding:

Plans are being made to move the Syrian, Polish, Lithuanian and Italian members of the I.W.W. out of Lawrence, if the outrages against them continue. . . . The I.W.W. has advice from Western Pennsylvania that several thousand positions may be secured in the steel and iron mills there. The threatened migration has frightened the mill corporations. They are pushed with orders and complain of a shortage of labor.[82]

In fact, the corporations were advertising for workers—not because they were afraid the IWW members would leave, but because they wanted to replace them and create an atmosphere of fear due to an oversupply of labor. They also began to shut down their Lawrence mills, while running their mills in other cities full time, in order to create unemployment in Lawrence that could break the IWW.[83]

The IWW was aware of what was going on. The Lawrence union wrote the national in February 1913:

It is apparent on every hand that the masters are laying plans for a wholesale reduction in wages; from present indications the tariff is to be monkeyed with, and this will give the bosses a pretext for taking back what they so reluctantly gave us last winter. Are we to permit another outrage upon the workers? . . . Here in Lawrence there are over 5,000 workers, idle, laid off, no work. The American Woolen Company, who never run all their machinery at one and the same time are, at this writing, shutting down their most modern machinery in Lawrence, while keeping their other mills running full and overtime. This would seem to the casual observer a suicidal policy, but the American Woolen Company are no fools. In shutting down in Lawrence they are trying to kill two birds with one stone—to curtail production on the one hand and kill the I.W.W. on the other.[84]

Though they were aware of the problem, they could find no way to deal with the effects of the "runaway shop." The induced depression in Lawrence was deepened by a national depression that began in the summer of 1913 and lasted until war orders started to pour in from Europe in 1915. There was massive unemployment in the winter of 1914–1915, and fifteen thousand textile workers walked the streets of Lawrence looking for work.[85] IWW militants tried to organize among the unemployed but were not very effective. IWW members became increasingly isolated, and their numbers began to decline: in September 1912, half a year after the strike, Local 20 still had over ten thousand paid-up members, but a month later when the God-and-country campaign was at its height, the IWW could rally only four thousand workers to a counterdemonstration.[86] By the summer of 1913 when the depression was in full force, Local 20 was down to seven hundred members, few of whom were active. Phillips Russell, an IWW sympathizer, described a meeting of Local 20 at that time:

> There were 30 or 40 workingmen, comparative strangers to each other a short time before, more or less separated by differences in race, nationality, politics, religion and custom, who sat down in perfect amity to discuss their common interests as workers in an industry; to work out their problems as producers, to regulate as far as lay within their, as yet limited, power their conditions of toil and to provide for the good and welfare of all.
>
> The Italian sat next to the German, the Syrian next the Frenchman, the Pole next the Portuguese, the Lithuanian next the American, and an Irishman was chairman over all![87]

He was right to be impressed by such internationalism, but the numbers were small and there were apparently no women present. As far as we can tell, the women of Lawrence sank back into household obscurity, childbearing, and endless labor in the mills when the strike was over. They had been able to rise when their whole class rose: in the crisis enough pressure was lifted from the backs of working mothers to give them room to think and move. But when their class went under in defeat, they were the most submerged, for their struggle for equality within the working-class movement could only succeed when the whole class was in motion.

Part V
Practical Conclusions

Marxism emphasizes the importance of theory precisely and only because it can guide action. . . . Many theories are erroneous and it is through the test of practice that their errors are corrected.

Mao Tse-tung
"On Practice"[1]

From the 1880s to the present Marxists have asked, Can women really unite across class lines to fight their common oppression without betraying the revolution? And feminists have wondered, Why do we have to choose sides, anyway? While these questions were being posed in the realm of theory, women built united fronts that both crossed class lines and took clear political positions on the side of the working class. In the United States practice has often been more developed, flexible, complex, and rich than revolutionary theory, and nowhere is this more evident than in work with women. For this reason I have concentrated on describing practice rather than debating theory, except to draw the following conclusions.

The Relationship Between Sex and Class

The working-class struggle and the struggle for women's liberation developed simultaneously in the vortex of changing relations of production and changing family and gender patterns. How could they fail to be related? Yet the exact nature of their relationship continues to elude precise formulation, and much of the current discussion of it is curiously flat.

Is the struggle for women's liberation subordinate to working-class issues, or, as many Marxists would have it, the struggle for women's liberation is a component part of the proletarian revolution. It is certainly clear that one is *dependent* upon the other: not only does women's ultimate liberation demand socialist revolution as a precondition, but at every turn the political character

277

of the women's movement depends on the strength of the revolutionary forces in society as a whole. The release of new energies, the creation of new space to move, the sense of a common upward surge among all the oppressed give women greater strength, and the working-class parts of the united front of women have most influence when the working-class movement is powerful.

But *dependency* is not the same as *subordination*. There can be mutual dependency. The prevalent notion that the struggle for women's liberation is "secondary" to that for proletarian revolution, meaning not only dependent but also comparatively unimportant, is not Marxism but mechanical materialism. It has led to dreary, half-hearted, and unsuccessful efforts to mobilize women, and to ridiculous oversimplifications such as "When the working class rises, so will women"; "When women enter production, they become liberated"; and "Socialism inevitably brings women's liberation in its train."

The relationship between socialist revolution and women's liberation is complex and dialectical. Women, organized as women, have at times been in advance of the working class as a whole, and not only on questions of their own sectional interests. They have frequently, for instance, raised general questions of democracy. And while it is true that women cannot win liberation without a proletarian revolution, what kind of revolution can there be without significant shaping by women? Questions of quality as well as quantity are involved here, as Clara Zetkin pointed out:

> Our Programme must realise that the collaboration of the broad masses of women does not only mean the increase in the number of the revolutionary forces, but also the improvement in the quality. Woman is not only not an unsuccessful copy of man, as a female being she possesses her special characteristics and value for struggle and construction, and the free development of long chained-up energy will help in the struggle and the work of construction.[2]

On the other hand the opposing notion, common among socialist feminists, that the two struggles are separate but equal, like two sides of a scale or two wheels spinning at different rates on the same axis, is static and inadequate. It leaves out the relationship between the struggles and the way each affects the other—not to mention the fundamental fact that women are very much a part of the class struggle and their lives are entirely mediated by class relations. There is no struggle for women's liberation that is separate and independent of class. Indeed, how could such a thing be? Such a picture of the world leads to work that is detached, disoriented, floating in limbo.

The working class is at least half female; and certainly more than half of all women are working class. The struggles are not only interrelated—they are interwoven, meshed. That is the nature of a dialectical relationship and that is why it is so hard to reduce it to a simple formula without all meaning dropping out of it, as the history discussed in this book must show. At the same time, this history does lead to certain conclusions about revolutionary strategy for women in the United States, based on organizing done in a variety of conditions over a period of about forty years. I may add that these conclusions are in agreement with my own observations of more recent organizing.

The United Front of Women

Women are oppressed in ways not shared by men. Prior to 1920, for instance, we were denied the right to vote. This common oppression gives women a basis to unite across class lines, since such unity is an obvious way to address a suffering that transcends class and national differences.

But the particular form that woman's oppression takes is determined by class and national factors as well as by general cultural and economic ones. A female industrial worker is caught up in a system of class relations reproduced in family units designed to ensure the continuation of her class in its powerless and plundered state. A black female worker is, in addition, involved in a system of national oppression that makes her subject to extra exploitation at work, and that impinges on and affects her family life and the continuation of her people. Both women workers share common class experiences with their male fellow workers, such as the fear of unemployment or oppressive and unsafe conditions at work. In addition, the minority woman shares the specific experience of national oppression with minority men. But the women workers' submersion in domestic labor, their responsibility for the upbringing of children, their participation in a process of human reproduction over which they have minimal control, their vulnerability to sexual harassment and abuse, and their lack of familiarity with trade union and political organization all combine to make their experience of productive labor different from that of men and to make them subject to greater exploitation at work—exploitation based on their subordination in the society as a whole.

So while the female industrial worker can and must unite with her male fellow worker along class and national lines, she has particular needs that demand attention. These go far beyond the obvious—if seldom met—needs for childcare, educational opportunity, and a rational division of labor in the home; they include the need for control over her own sexual and reproductive being, a sense of her own dignity and worth as a person, and a way to gain experience in political work without being instantly subordinated to men. Working-class and national liberation organizations have often seemed to find it difficult to give these sorts of needs much attention under ordinary, nonrevolutionary circumstances. Consequently women have tended to develop separate, though not necessarily separatist, organizations to work for their demands and provide them with an arena in which they could fully participate as equals.

At certain points in history the labor movement and the women's liberation movement have perceived that they have common interests: birth control, woman suffrage, or the organizing of women into unions. This perception has provided the basis for an organized united front of women, bringing together women from the feminist, labor, and socialist movements around particular demands. The women from each of these movements have had their own interpretation of what is needed, their own preferred tactics, and their own politics, which they struggled for within the united front. The direction taken by the whole movement has at times depended on which group was strongest ideologically, which had the best organization, and which could mobilize the most outside support.

In the 1880s in Chicago, for instance, when the labor movement's strength was growing and it had an energetic socialist leadership, women organizers had enough backup to be able to give direction to the united front of women as a whole. Their organization, the Illinois Woman's Alliance, is an early embodiment of themes that developed later on: the need to connect workplace and community, the benefits of support from the male labor movement, and the contradictions between trade union women and their middle-class allies.

When the labor movement that sustained the Illinois Woman's Alliance split, this united front of women could no longer exist. The themes that had appeared in embryonic form within it were developed by other organizations in a more fragmented way. The Women's Trade Union League sought to organize working women, pioneering feminist methods of doing so. Swayed by the example of the AFL, however, and unable to understand how to organize working women without more help from the labor movement, the League ended up settling for legislative remedies to the class oppression of working women, combined with efforts to create a female auxiliary to the labor aristocracy. The IWW, on the other hand, successfully experimented with bringing issues of birth control into the labor movement and found ways to organize women workers and housewives in the heat of its mass strikes, but did not undertake special organizing campaigns around the oppression of women and had difficulty keeping women as active members. It also seriously underestimated the importance of the suffrage issue. Meanwhile, the suffrage movement, led by bourgeois women whose politics were often not even liberal, became detached from the working class and often hostile to it. The Socialist Party's lack of unity on the importance of organizing women resulted in a failure to give solid organizational support to its own campaigns. These problems made it hard for left-wing women to have substantial impact on the feminist movement, which remained centered on a single-issue campaign, and had no way of educating or organizing women around the many other issues related to the vote.

None of this is to assign blame. These movements were young and new, they were under increasing government pressure, and they had no examples of victorious revolutionary work to draw on. Nor is successful work dependent solely on the will and strategy of organizers: a certain level of struggle in the society as a whole, many changes in consciousness, and a ripening of conditions are clearly necessary before substantial changes can be made. The boundaries of what is possible in the meantime, in a non-revolutionary period, are not set primarily by the desires of socialists or feminists, but by the relative strength of the classes involved in the struggle and their degree of consciousness and organization within the women's movement and elsewhere. In the period before World War I, as in the present, the employers were more conscious of their class interests in regard to women workers than was the labor movement, and they were unquestionably more powerful as a class.

Within the limitations set by these general conditions, however, policies pursued by the left have made a difference. The persistently sectarian response of U.S. Marxists to class contradictions whenever these have surfaced in the united front of women is one reason socialists have failed to be more influential in the women's movement. In his discussion of the U.S. labor movement, William Z. Foster describes a purist tendency to split which he holds partly responsible for the movement's general backwardness, in contrast to the European labor movement:

> Because of this policy, thousands of the very best militants have been led to desert the mass of labor organizations and to waste their time in vain efforts to construct ideally conceived unions designed to replace the old ones. In consequence the mass labor movement has been, for many years, systematically drained of its life-giving elements.[3]

Splitting to form "pure" organizations, and the consequent abandonment of the existing mass movement, has also occurred in the united front of women. It can be seen most clearly in the work of the IWW, but also existed as a tendency in the Socialist Party's suffrage work and in the demise of the Illinois Woman's Alliance. Strategically, it is essential for both working-class and socialist women to have their own organizations, with their own programs, and to develop their own leaders—this is not the issue. The problem occurs when these women fail to see themselves as part of a united front demanding both alliance and struggle. Too often, U.S. socialist women have seen the only alternatives as either capitulation to the bourgeoisie on the one hand, or flight into political isolation on the other. They have seemed unable to envision a difficult, protracted relationship combining unity on some questions with contention over others. Unless working-class and socialist women have a strong base outside the united front, they have little hope of winning the battles inside it. Since such strength is hard to build and long in coming, the irritating, tedious, and often fruitless struggles within the united front of women can make activists despair, as did the radicals in the Illinois Woman's Alliance, and go off in a fury to work on their own. We know where it got them. The united front of women involves both a necessary sisterhood and class war: both can be unpleasant; both are unavoidable.

Women and Unions

The main obstacle to organizing women into unions is their different and conflicting work lives, one at home and the other on the job; this double burden makes it hard for them to move. When this is taken into account and unions deal with both aspects of their oppression, women can be extremely militant, as they were in strikes led by the IWW.

The way women are organized depends on the character of the labor movement at the time. When trade union men have been eager to help them organize, not only have women built unions, but they have participated fully in the labor movement, using their organizations as a base from which to build and influence the united front of women. This is most likely to happen when the labor movement is led by socialists, as in Chicago in the 1880s. The presence of socialist men, however, does not guarantee a high level of understanding of female oppression; therefore female socialist leadership is of critical importance, not only for organizing women but for the political development of the movement as a whole.

Even when the labor movement's leadership has been more conservative and indifferent to the need to organize women, it has still been possible for women to organize themselves into unions. In this situation working women often turned to the feminist movement for help. But while the assistance of middle-class feminists can be invaluable, as in the organization of the garment industry, it can also result in a dilution of the militance of women's unions. The liberal feminists who are most likely to enter such alliances seldom have had a good understanding of the potential strength of the working class and the possibility of changing male indifference to support in the context of an intense struggle. Consequently, women's union campaigns under middle-class feminist leadership have tended to rely on solutions imported from without, particularly on state intervention through lawsuits and legislation. Rather than viewing such reforms as secondary weapons in the industrial struggle or as tools which are ultimately controlled by the ruling class but which are temporarily subject to mass pressure, the feminist movement has frequently worked on the assumption that the state is neutral and can be made to act independent of the particular interests of any class. Because this is not true, the legislative machinery set up to protect women has often been turned against their interests in the absence of a strong movement that could keep the pressure up, and laws that were progressive in one period have turned into their opposite in another.

When the labor movement has been actively hostile to the organization of women, it has been extremely difficult for women's unions to survive, even with help from feminists. Unions that were heavily infiltrated by racketeers, such as the construction unions and the United Garment Workers, seem to have been particularly antagonistic to women, since their leadership was threatened by any popular upsurge that could not immediately be controlled and channeled for purposes of private graft. In a number of instances, the political conservatism and entrenched privilege of unions in the skilled trades led them to play the same role as racketeers, sabotaging efforts to organize women.

In situations where the work force was segregated by sex, where male unions were reluctant to organize women, or where the differences in the work schedules, desires, or consciousness of the sexes were marked, it was sometimes advantageous to build separate women's locals. These have obvious inherent limitations —a tendency to reinforce the segregation of women into powerless positions within the larger union, reflecting their position in the industry—but they have sometimes proved more viable than other forms of organization.

In short, the overall political character of the labor movement has strongly affected the form of women's organization within it, the degree to which these organizations were dependent on outside help from feminists, and even their ultimate survival. The organization of women proved important not only to women workers, but to organized men as well, for the labor movement seems to have a different character—more open, innovative, and militant in a mass way—when large numbers of women are part of it, as both the shirtwaist makers' strike and the Lawrence strike demonstrate.

Workplace and Community Organization

In a mass strike under radical leadership, it sometimes became possible to transcend the traditional forms of workplace organization and draw community women into the labor movement. The conflict was then transformed from an industrial battle located in the workplace to a class struggle located in both the workplace and the community as a whole. This happened in Lawrence in 1912; that strike has been called a mini-revolution because it prefigured the level of involvement characteristic of a revolutionary uprising. When a whole community was at war, working mothers and housewives, the most submerged part of their class, could rise up and find their own forms of organization and militance, and in this way change their own lives as well as the strike. They brought to the struggle a sense of overall class, family, and sometimes national oppression that can be stronger in the community than it is in the workplace, and they learned in their turn from the discipline and focus of the organized workers. While the Lawrence strike is the clearest example of this process, the work of the Illinois Woman's Alliance was a more primitive, less mass-oriented attempt to merge community and labor struggles, and to bring the strength of the organized workers to bear on the problems of school children, unorganized sweatshop workers, and even prostitutes.

Problems with the Socialist Movement's Work with Women

Since so much of the impetus for organizing working-class women has come from socialists, wrong ideas within the socialist movement have had very damaging effects. Two kinds of errors have been made: "right errors," which try to eliminate women's problems by various reforms, and "left errors," which see only the class struggle as important and negate the need for any separate work against the oppression of women.

The "right error" of thinking that the oppression of women could be eliminated under capitalism was fundamental to the suffrage movement and a strong tendency in the work of both the Women's Trade Union League and the Socialist Party. The WTUL's tendency to look to the state to solve the problems of working women was one example; another was the belief held by many socialists that suffrage would make the sexes equal, leaving only the class contradiction to worry about. The Socialist Party therefore emphasized woman suffrage agitation far and above any other form of work with women.

The IWW's work exemplifies "left errors" in this area. Seeing women only as exploited workers and denying the existence of any significant sex oppression, the IWW failed to comprehend the significance of the suffrage movement. This failure fed their economism—seeing the economic arena as the only important focus for revolutionary work—and their sectarianism. The IWW's practice was, however, often much better than their theory. In theory, the only task was to build industrial unions; in practice, they did agitation and education around birth control, a demand which no other working-class organization in this period had the vision or courage to raise, and one which directly challenged the state's interest in controlling reproduction.

Women's Work in Party Organizations

Within parties or socialist organizations, some special body to lead and focus work with women and to provide a basis for the struggle against male supremacy within the organization is essential. When the Socialist Party had a Women's National Committee, it was able to build large-scale campaigns around suffrage, put out a monthly women's magazine, and do education about the oppression of women. While the party may have had difficulty integrating this work with the rest of its program, the destruction of the WNC certainly did not mean that work with women was taken up by the party as a whole rather than being ghettoized in one committee. It meant, rather, that the oppression of women was no longer addressed in a systematic, national way. The IWW never had any special committee to develop its work with women; as a result, this work was inconsistent, sporadic, and largely dependent on one individual, Elizabeth Gurley Flynn, despite the heights it rose to during certain strikes.

It would be pure formalism, however, to think that any organizational structure offers a guarantee against chauvinism. Unless a party organization is either solidly behind the idea of special campaigns for women, or is at least engaged in study and struggle around the question, women's committees can easily become powerless "ladies' aid societies" whose appeals for support are ignored. Their efforts to develop separate campaigns may be attacked as divisive of the working class; they can even, if necessary, be put under the leadership of figureheads such as wives of party leaders who are remarkable mainly for their support of the status quo. The only "guarantees" that work with women will be kept alive seem to be a high level of commitment to it in the organization as a whole, and the presence of a number of experienced women whose understanding of their own oppression has made them determined to do the work.

While again avoiding formalism, it is easy to see the importance of special women's committees in training such women leaders and giving them experience in coordinating work on a large scale. Without such systematic training, the IWW never developed more than two or three women organizers of national caliber; the years of organizational experience that formed the women who eventually built the Illinois Woman's Alliance were simply not available to women in the IWW. The fact that Socialist Party women were, if only briefly, in a position to make decisions about their own national campaigns accounts in part for that organization's large number of outstanding female organizers and speakers.

It is a truism that every oppressed group must in the final analysis liberate itself. Freedom cannot be conferred from the outside; it must be won. Without leadership developed in the struggle for women's liberation, the best will in the world cannot enable a party organization to really understand the struggle of women, to support campaigns initiated by women around their own needs and link them with other issues, to organize masses of women. Without strong women, a revolutionary organization becomes what Joe Hill called "a kind of one-legged, freakish animal," or one that has the appearance of walking on two legs but in reality puts all its weight upon one, effectively crippling itself.

The United Front of Women and the Autonomous Women's Movement

Much of this book revolves around a central question: What can socialist women do to organize for women's liberation in a nonrevolutionary period, when socialist forces and the labor movement are weak, divided, and frequently uninterested in the oppression of women, and when the women's movement is—partly as a result—under bourgeois leadership? This situation existed in 1910; it exists in 1980.

In the late 1960s a new mass feminist movement was born. Like the earlier movement, it had bourgeois and socialist organizations.[4] Since the first few years of radical exuberance, bourgeois forces have unquestionably been in control of the movement's national organizations, publications, and image as reflected in the media. Their work has been directed toward gaining an equal place for women in the mainstream of American life, rather than at changing the ultimate direction in which that stream flows. There are also a few national organizations of minority women, of mixed class composition, which have played a progressive role in their effect on the bourgeois groups and been able to voice the concerns of their constituencies in Washington. Left-wing feminist groups have been, for the most part, localist and short-lived, and have deliberately turned away from traditional modes of political work. While their emphasis on integrating the personal and political has led to innovative tactics, radical insights, and the development of a number of strong women with leadership experience, left-wing feminists have been unable to create a national organization or even sustained national campaigns. They have consequently had less impact on society as a whole than they could if their ideas were not all filtered through media and organizations controlled by bourgeois women.

During the late 1960s and early 1970s, a new socialist movement grew out of the civil rights, student, and antiwar movements. Unlike the left-wing feminist movement, it has largely abandoned its early stress on decentralization and participatory democracy in favor of more traditional party forms of organization—to the degree that it is still a movement, many of its members having succumbed to the stresses of age and history. What remains is a number of national political organizations, most of which are somewhat multinational (meaning they are mainly but not entirely white), though a few grew out of Third World groups and are still predominantly minority.

These political organizations fall into two broad categories: social-democratic (or democratic-socialist, if you prefer) and communist; for purposes of brevity I will use the latter term to cover all those who would define themselves as such, from members of the old Communist Party U.S.A. to Trotskyites to Marxist-Leninist organizations.[5] While the communist groups differ extraordinarily from each other in their political ideas, they all tend to take a position on the international situation as their starting point and deduce their positions on domestic questions from that. Many of them have not developed a detailed position on the oppression of women because they have not considered the question a high priority. The social-democratic groups have tended in some cases to follow the lead of the bourgeois feminists, in others to join with the left-wing feminists, in order to be where the action is. Many communist groups have seen no difference between one feminist and another and have attacked all with equal vehemence as "petty bourgeois." These attacks have sometimes been moderated and even reversed at the height of a rectification campaign, but by and large, in a movement where sectarianism in general is so utterly out of control, it would be unrealistic to expect a good understanding of the need for united front work among women. It is possible, and one may hope, that the severity of the present economic and political crisis will bring forward a new spirit of unity and increase the amount of attention given by the left to the oppression of women; this would be a happy departure from the general experience of the past decade.

Throughout the 1970s, the left wing of the feminist movement was plagued by its own contradictions. These were often seen purely in terms of their material origins and described as splits between gay and straight women, minority and white women, mothers and women without children, etc. While such objective differences are significant, only when discussion centers on the theoretical and strategic positions that can derive from them is the resulting struggle likely to push the movement forward. Because the feminist movement has seldom argued in concrete strategic terms, its battles have often been muddy ones, oscillating between personal anecdote and grand theory, and leading to unnecessary splits which were perceived as natural inevitabilities.

With such problems of sectarianism in their own movement, left-wing feminists have often responded to socialist attacks by avoiding further contact with "the male left," or even by becoming anticommunist. Such responses are neither productive nor permanent, since feminists with a Marxist analysis are continually drawn to the socialist movement by the need to connect their work with the things it connects to in real life: economic causes, racial and national contradictions, questions of class and power, international crises. The same issues come up year after year: We can't work for women's liberation in a way that cuts us off from the unions, the black liberation movement, and the Vietnam War. But on the other hand: We can't work with these people if they think we should abandon our own demands, our own organizations, our own movement!

Of course unity doesn't and shouldn't mean that. Only a women's movement that has its own demands, organizations, and leadership is in a position to unite with anybody else—a rather strong position, in the current state of general disarray.

But what kind of women's liberation movement does that mean we should build? Though the slogan "an autonomous women's movement" was not originally intended to mean autonomous from the class struggle or from battles against U.S. imperialism, by the 1970s it came to mean just that. The concerns of left-wing feminists became compartmentalized in a way that damaged both the women's liberation movement and the other struggles. Women's concerns were seldom taken up in more than a token manner by socialist organizations, and at the same time, the autonomous women's movement less and less took positions on anything but "women's issues"—abortion but not the war, the economy, or racism. Surely we don't want to return to the nineteenth century doctrine of a separate sphere for women, where women can make decisions about a limited range of female concerns and men can make decisions about everything else. We should not have to choose, as individuals or as organizations, between commitment to the class struggle, the national liberation movements, and women's liberation. It is a deformation in the political life of this country that so many people through the years have felt they had to do so.

The Illinois Woman's Alliance represents a crossroads in our history, where one road opened up into several diverging ones, each larger and more significant than the original path in all but promise. In its early, small, and primitive way the Illinois Woman's Alliance held within it a prophecy of all that could be achieved if the socialist movement, the labor movement, and the united front of women could work together. Without such unity today, Marxists have found it difficult to address the problems of women consistently. Left-wing feminists have found it impossible to capture leadership of the women's movement from bourgeois organizations that are utterly unable to give it the vitality and consciousness it needs. The labor movement, sunk in conservatism, has repeatedly demonstrated that nothing short of a revolution in its ranks will get its leadership to reach out to the millions of unorganized women.

Yet never has the need for unity and for a newly energetic approach to organizing been more clear. The situation of women is a sign of the general political crisis. In recent years, women have been pushed out of their jobs, lost affirmative action programs, seen public childcare virtually eliminated, and the public health and education systems reduced to the point of incapacity. In the name of strengthening the traditional family, a new antifeminist movement has blocked the ERA, viciously attacked gay rights, eaten away the right to abortion (while sterilization abuse continues), and attempted to block access to sex education and birth control information for minors. Wages have fallen far behind the cost of living, and women's wages were low to begin with. A tide of political reaction seems to be rising in both domestic and foreign policy.

Who will fight off this onslaught? Who will put forward the alternatives for women? The bourgeois women's organizations have time and again proven their inability to do so effectively. Like the suffrage movement they claim as their exemplar, they are locked into single-issue strategies and cannot build the kind of broad unity around a militant program that is needed to win substantial demands and keep them won. The record on abortion is enough to demonstrate that. The left wing of the feminist movement is only just beginning, in a few places, to try to build united fronts around specific demands; it still has little organizational strength and needs more experience in struggling around programs in a way that advances the movement rather than splits it. The socialist and national liberation movements are hard-pressed and divided, with many urgent concerns, and do not in general make the backlash against women's rights a high priority. The labor movement is also beleaguered; weakened by decades of compromise, it lacks the kind of force and sweep it has only when it is moved by real social vision and is reaching out to enlist large numbers of new workers. So the question remains what it was a hundred years ago: Who will organize the women? And when?

In Charlotte Perkins Gilman's poem about the socialist and the suffragist, the world finally awakens and tells both: "Your work is all the same; / Work together or work apart, / Work, each of you, with all your heart— / Just get into the game!"[6] The socialist, labor, and women's liberation movements have been separate now for more than one lifetime. We have seen how this occurred; it is harder to see how to reverse the process. Yet I believe it can ultimately be reversed if we pay attention to our own history and experience as well as to that of the rest of the world. Though we women did not create our own misery, only we can end it—but we can't end it alone. Women need to be part of both a women's liberation movement and a general movement to change society. And if persistent, careful efforts at unity around specific issues don't come from us, where will they come from? Do others see the need more clearly? Are others stronger?

Langston Hughes says,

> Freedom
> Is just frosting
> On somebody else's
> Cake—
> And so must be
> Till we
> Learn how to
> Bake.[7]

Women have been baking cakes for thousands of years. It's time to sum up what we know about mixing and sifting and flavoring and letting yeast ferment and rise; it's time to write down our recipes and take the practical knowledge of our hands out of the kitchen to where it will do some good; it's time and past time.

Notes

Preface

1. Recent surveys include: Rosalyn Baxandall, Linda Gordon, and Susan Reverby, eds., *America's Working Women* (New York: Random House, 1976); Philip S. Foner, *Women and the American Labor Movement* (New York: Free Press, 1979); and Barbara Mayer Wertheimer, *We Were There: The Story of Working Women in America* (New York: Random House, 1977). Recent work on the Women's Trade Union League includes: Nancy Schrom Dye, "The Women's Trade Union League of New York, 1903–20," Ph.D. dissertation, University of Wisconsin, 1974; Nancy Schrom Dye, "Creating a Feminist Alliance: Sisterhood and Class Conflict in the New York Trade Union League," *Feminist Studies* 2, no. 2/3 (1975); Nancy Schrom Dye, "Feminism or Unionism? The New York Women's Trade Union League and the Labor Movement," *Feminist Studies* 3, no. 1/2 (Fall 1975); Robin Miller Jacoby, "The Women's Trade Union League and American Feminism," *Feminist Studies* 3, no. 1/2 (Fall 1975); Alice Kessler-Harris, "Where Are the Organized Women Workers?" *Feminist Studies* 3, no. 1/2 (Fall 1975); Alice Kessler-Harris, "Organizing the Unorganizable: Three Jewish Women and Their Union," *Labor History* 17, no. 1 (Winter 1976).

Part I: The United Front of Women

1. Theresa Malkiel, *Women and Freedom* (New York: Socialist Literature Company, 1915), p. 4.
2. Elizabeth Gurley Flynn, "The I.W.W. Call to Women," *Solidarity* 31 July 1915.
3. Alice Henry, "Editorial," *Life and Labor* 1, no. 1 (January 1911), inside cover.
4. See, for instance, Joan Kelly-Gadol, "The Social Relation of the Sexes: Methodological Implications of Women's History," *Signs* 1, no. 4 (Summer 1976), p. 817.
5. Karl Marx and Frederich Engels, *Manifesto of the Communist Party* (Peking: Foreign Languages Press, 1975), p. 43.
6. John B. Andrews and W. D. P. Bliss, *History of Women in Trade Unions*, Bureau of Labor, Report on Conditions of Women and Child Wage-Earners in the United States, vol. 10 (Washington, D.C.: Government Printing Office, 1911), pp. 17–18.
7. Editorial, "Among Ourselves," *Progressive Woman* 6, no. 64 (October 1912), p. 15.
8. Even after World War I, when there was no longer a substantial feminist movement to encourage attention to women in the community as well as the workplace, at least half of the active women socialists were still housewives. The Communist Party U.S.A. devoted more attention to workplace organizing than the Socialist Party and the percentage of working women in its ranks was higher than that of the Socialist Party in 1912. In 1933 the Communist Party U.S.A.'s membership was 19 percent female; slightly over half these women

worked full time outside the home and a number of those who registered as housewives had part-time jobs as well. (Anna Damon, "Experience in Work Among Women," *Party Organizer* 6, no. 8/9 [August–September 1933], p. 62). This percentage was twice that of women in the general population who worked full time. (William H. Chafe, *The American Woman: Her Changing Social, Economic, and Political Roles, 1920–1970* [New York: Oxford University Press, 1972], p. 54 and note). This fact would seem to indicate some success in recruiting women at the workplace along the lines of classical Marxist theory. Still, half the women members remained housewives, indicating that many still came to Marxism, not through direct participation in workplace struggles, but through their family and friendship networks, through party work being done in their communities, or because of issues involving their oppression as women.

Part II: "Chicago Will Be Ours!"

Chapter 1. "There Must Be Something Wrong"

1. Philip S. Foner, ed., *The Factory Girls* (Chicago: University of Illinois Press, 1977), p. 91. This was a favorite poem of Leonora O'Reilly's.
2. Leo Huberman, *We, The People* (New York: Monthly Review Press, 1932), p. 217.
3. Henry David, *The History of the Haymarket Affair* (New York: Farrar and Rinehart, 1936), p. 13. This top 1 percent got nearly one quarter of the national income at this time, while the bottom half of the population got barely one fifth of it. Similarly, in 1953 the richest *tenth* of the nation got 27 percent of the national income, while the lowest *half* got only 23 percent. I am indebted to Hal Benenson for this statistic, which is from Ferdinand Lundberg, *The Rich and the Super-Rich* (New York: Lyle Stuart, Inc., 1968).
4. Richard O. Boyer and Herbert M. Morais, *Labor's Untold Story* (New York: United Electrical, Radio, and Machine Workers of America, 1970), p. 222.
5. Robert W. Smuts, *Women and Work in America* (New York: Schocken Books, 1971), p. 19.
6. Abraham Bisno, *Union Pioneer* (Madison: University of Wisconsin Press, 1967), p. 212.
7. See Helen L. Sumner, *History of Women in Industry in the United States,* Bureau of Labor, Report on Conditions of Women and Child Wage-Earners in the United States, vol. 9 (Washington, D.C.: Government Printing Office, 1910), p. 246; and Women's Bureau, U.S. Department of Labor, *The Occupational Progress of Women,* Bulletin No. 27 (Washington, D.C.: Government Printing Office, 1922), p. 8.
8. Women's Bureau, *The Occupational Progress of Women,* pp. 8, 26.
9. Philip S. Foner, *History of the Labor Movement in the United States,* vol. 3 (New York: International Publishers, 1964), p. 25.
10. U.S. Department of Labor, *Summary of Report on Conditions of Women and Child Wage-Earners,* Bulletin of the U.S. Bureau of Labor Statistics, no. 175 (Washington, D.C.: Government Printing Office, 1916).
11. The Women's Trade Union League explained the "utter impossibility of living on $6 a week" in a pamphlet which gave a sample budget, drawn from thousands submitted to the New York Factory Investigating Commission, the

National Consumers' League, and the Women's Trade Union League of Chicago:

Weekly Expenditure:	
One half of furnished room	$1.50
7 breakfasts, rolls and coffee, at 10¢	.70
7 dinners at 20¢	1.40
7 luncheons, coffee and sandwich, at 10¢	.70
Carfare	.60
Clothes at $52 a year—weekly	1.00
Total	$5.90

The remaining 10¢ to cover laundry, dentist, doctor, newspapers, church, and recreation. 10¢ a week for 52 weeks, makes $5.20. But the girl works only 40 weeks. She must live 52 weeks. HOW?

(Some Facts Regarding Unorganized Working Women in the Sweated Industries [Chicago: National Women's Trade Union League, 1914]: Leonora O'Reilly Papers, Box 8, File 374, Schlesinger Library, Radcliffe College, Cambridge, Mass.

12. Smuts, *Women and Work in America*, p. 19.
13. U.S. Department of Labor, *Summary of Report,* p. 28.
14. Preamble of the People's Party, drafted by Ignatius Donnelly, quoted in Boyer and Morais, *Labor's Untold Story,* pp. 111–112.
15. The AFL's lack of enthusiasm for organizing women is discussed, among other places, in: Foner, *History of the Labor Movement in the United States,* vols. 2 and 3 (New York: International Publishers, 1955, 1964); Alice Henry, *The Trade Union Woman* (New York: D. Appleton & Co., 1915); and *Women and the Labor Movement* (New York: George H. Doran Co., 1923); Theresa Wolfson, *The Woman Worker and the Trade Unions* (New York: International Publishers, 1926); Barbara Mayer Wertheimer, *We Were There: The Story of Working Women in America* (New York: Pantheon Books, 1977); and the material on the Women's Trade Union League cited in footnote 1, preface. Useful documentary material can be found in Rosalyn Baxandall, Linda Gordon, and Susan Reverby, eds., *America's Working Women* (New York: Random House, 1976).
16. For discussion of this period in Gomper's development and in that of the labor movement see: Samuel Gompers, *Seventy Years of Life and Labor* (New York: Dutton, 1925); Charles McArthur Destler, *American Radicalism 1865–1901* (Chicago: Quadrangle Books, 1966); William A. Dick, *Labor and Socialism in America: The Gompers Era* (Port Washington, N.Y.: Kennikat Press, 1972); Foner, *History of the Labor Movement,* vol. 2; Gerald N. Grob, *Workers and Utopia* (Chicago: Quadrangle Books, 1969); and John Laslett, *Labor and the Left* (New York: Basic Books, 1970).
17. Dick, *Labor and Socialism in America*, p. 21.
18. Foner, *History of the Labor Movement,* vol. 2, p. 29. This was the preamble of the Federation of Organized Trades and Labor Unions, a group superseded by the AFL, which took over its constitution.
19. Ray Ginger, *Altgeld's America: The Lincoln Ideal versus Changing Realities* (New York: Funk & Wagnalls Company, 1958), p. 280.

20. Bisno, *Union Pioneer,* pp. 154–155.
21. The most notable instance of this was the case of the Swedish Union of Special Order Workers, a federation of three largely female and woman-led garment workers in Chicago, which was destroyed by the United Garment Workers and the Teamsters in 1904–1905. See John B. Andrews and W. D. P. Bliss, *History of Women in Trade Unions,* Bureau of Labor, Report on Conditions of Women and Child Wage-Earners in the United States, vol. 10 (Washington, D.C.: Government Printing Office, 1911), pp. 164–167; Margaret Hoblitt, "A Labor Tragedy," *The Commons* 9 (1905), pp. 273–280; and the file entitled "Strikes" in the National Women's Trade Union League papers in the Schlesinger Library, Radcliffe College, Cambridge, Mass.
22. Foner, *History of the Labor Movement,* vol. 3, p. 224.
23. August Bebel, *Woman Under Socialism,* trans. Daniel De Leon (New York: Schocken Books, 1971), pp. 186–187.

Chapter 2. *"Shouting Amazons"*

1. Dorothy Richardson, "Trades Unions in Petticoats," *Leslie's Monthly Magazine* 57 (March 1904), pp. 489, 496.
2. Jane Addams, *Twenty Years at Hull House* (New York: The MacMillan Company, 1912), pp. 98–100.
3. Lizzie Swank Holmes, "Women Workers of Chicago," *American Federationist* 12 (August 1905), p. 509.
4. Philip S. Foner, *The Great Labor Uprising of 1877* (New York: Monad Press, 1977), p. 154.
5. Henry David, *The History of the Haymarket Affair* (New York: Farrar and Rinehart, 1936), p. 57.
6. "Work of the Sex," *Chicago Times,* 2 September 1894.
7. Ibid.
8. Holmes, "Women Workers of Chicago," p. 508.
9. Ibid.
10. Lizzie J. Holmes [*sic*], "The Days of Our Infancy: A Reminisence," *Progressive Woman* 5 (August 1911), p. 7.
11. Carolyn Ashbaugh, *Lucy Parsons, American Revolutionary* (Chicago: Charles H. Kerr, 1976), pp. 13–29.
12. "Mrs. Rogers Replies," *Knights of Labor* (Chicago), 5 March 1887, p. 2.
13. "Work of the Sex."
14. Barbara Mayer Wertheimer, *We Were There: The Story of Working Women in America* (New York: Pantheon Books, 1977), p. 80.
15. "Work of the Sex."
16. Allen F. Davis, "Alzina Parsons Stevens," *Notable American Women,* vol. 3 (Cambridge: Harvard University Press, 1971), p. 368.
17. "Work of the Sex."
18. Ibid. In the political jargon of the times, "independent political action" is a code phrase meaning revolution brought about by election.
19. Ashbaugh, *Lucy Parsons,* p. 34.
20. Ibid., p. 35.
21 Holmes, "Women Workers of Chicago," p. 509.
22. "Work of the Sex."

23. Quoted in Eleanor Flexner, *Century of Struggle: The Women's Rights Movement in the United States* (New York: Atheneum, 1968), p. 196.
24. "Mrs. Rogers Replies."
25. Quoted in Philip S. Foner, *History of the Labor Movement in the United States,* vol. 2 (New York: International Publishers, 1955), p. 190.
26. Eugene Staley, *History of the Illinois State Federation of Labor* (Chicago: University of Chicago Press, 1930), p. 95.
27. Ralph Scharman, "Elizabeth Morgan, Crusader for Labor Reform," *Labor History* 14 (Summer 1973), p. 340.
28. "Work of the Sex."
29. The most comprehensive account is David's *The History of the Haymarket Affair.*
30. "Shouting Amazons," *Chicago Tribune,* 3 May 1886.
31. Ibid.
32. David, *Haymarket,* p. 376.
33. Quoted in Richard O. Boyer and Herbert M. Morais, *Labor's Untold Story* (New York: United Electrical, Radio, and Machine Workers of America, 1970), p. 101.
34. Foner, *History of the Labor Movement,* vol. 2, p. 76.
35. Holmes, "Women Workers of Chicago," p. 510.
36. "Mrs. Rogers Replies."
37. "Thanks 'The Times,'" August 1888, unidentified clipping in Thomas J. Morgan Collection, Book 2, Illinois Historical Survey, Urbana, Illinois.
38. "To Help Working Women," May 1889, unidentified clipping in Morgan Collection, Book 2. See also the article on Mrs. Rogers in Davis, *Notable American Women.*
39. Holmes, "Women Workers of Chicago," p. 510.

Chapter 3. Mary Kenney and the Ladies' Federal Labor Union

1. Unidentified clipping, 1897, Thomas J. Morgan Collection, Book 2, Illinois Historical Society, Urbana, Illinois. The Morgan papers consist of scrap books of newspaper clipping complied by Elizabeth Morgan, who identified some of the clippings by date but few by source. Book 2 of the collection is the principal source of information on the Illinois Woman's Alliance.
2. Philip S. Foner, *History of the Labor Movement in the United States,* vol. 2 (New York: International Publishers, 1955), p. 190.
3. Unidentified clipping, June 1888, Morgan Collection, Book 2. This clipping is signed Hannah M. Morgan, the name Foner attributes to her. Although the principal name she used was Elizabeth Morgan, she was on occasion referred to as Eliza or Hannah.
4. Foner, *History of the Labor Movement,* vol. 2, p. 190.
5. Mary Kenney O'Sullivan, manuscript autobiography, Schlesinger Library, Radcliffe College, Cambridge, Mass., p. 16.
6. Ibid., p. 32.
7. Ibid., p. 42.
8. Ibid., p. 32.
9. Ibid., p. 34.
10. Mary Kenney O'Sullivan, "Organization of Women," *Age of Labor,* 1 January 1893. I am indebted for this reference to Rosemary Scherman.

11. O'Sullivan, manuscript autobiography, p. 38.
12. Ibid., p. 39.
13. Ibid., p. 37.
14. Ray Ginger, *Altgeld's America: The Lincoln Ideal Versus Changing Realities* (New York: Funk & Wagnalls Company, 1958), p. 245.
15. O'Sullivan, manuscript autobiography, p. 62.
16. Ibid., p. 63.
17. Ibid.
18. Ibid., p. 64. Abraham Bisno of the cloakmakers union thought that the spirit of the women at Hull House was similar to that of the Narodniks in the Russian populist movement, despite their greater primness and gentility:

> My acquaintance with the people at Hull House was an eye-opener for me. People who did not belong to our class took an interest in our lot in life. This was very new to me. I had heard of such people when lectures were held in our club on the subject of the Russian revolutionary movement. There, I was told, young members of the Russian nobility and rich members of the aristocracy, [the Narodniks] had thrown their lives in with those of the poor, and went around as crusaders for democracy and the abolition of private land-owning. They . . . were arrested, held in jail, exiled to Siberia, even killed in a great many cases, all on the altar of their missionary spirit to help the poor and abolish despotism, to overthrow the Czar, assault the authority of the army and give the people a voice in determining their political and economic status in life. . . . In this country, the venture on the part of Jane Addams and her colleagues was something new, and while I did not agree with their Anglo-Saxon estimate of the nature of the social movement, I appreciated cordially the nobility of their characters, the integrity of their effort.

(Abraham Bisno, *Union Pioneer* [Madison: University of Wisconsin Press, 1967], p. 119).
19. "Mary Kenney is Invited In," in Allen F. Davis and Mary Lynn McCree, *Eighty Years at Hull House* (Chicago: Quadrangle Books, 1969), p. 35. A number of radicals in this period, notably Ella Reeve Bloor, were involved in experiments in communal living—a natural outgrowth of their desire for a political family and their need as women activists to share housework.
20. Samuel Gompers, *Seventy Years of Life and Labor* (New York: Dutton, 1925), p. 481.
21. Mary Kenney O'Sullivan to Alice Henry, no date, National Women's Trade Union League papers, Box 28, Library of Congress.
22. O'Sullivan, manuscript autobiography, p. 81.
23. O'Sullivan, manuscript autobiography, p. 81–82. Gertrude Barnum, a judge's daughter, later became active in the Women's Trade Union League, where she got into similar confrontations. See Part III, Chapter 5.
24. Foner, *History of the Labor Movement*, vol. 2, p. 194.
25. Dorothy Richardson, "Trades-Unions in Petticoats," *Leslie's Monthly Magazine* 57 (March 1904), p. 491.

Chapter 4. The Illinois Woman's Alliance

1. This poem is in a mimeographed sheaf of poems edited by Samuel Freedman for the Socialist Committee on Youth Education, no date, File D105, Tamiment Library, New York University.
2. Other books and articles that discuss the Illinois Woman's Alliance are: Philip S. Foner, *History of the Labor Movement in the United States,* vol. 2 (New York: International Publishers, 1964); Philip S. Foner, *Women and the American Labor Movement* (New York: Free Press, 1979); Barbara Mayer Wertheimer, *We Were There: The Story of Working Women in America* (New York: Pantheon Books, 1977); Ralph Scharman, "Elizabeth Morgan, Crusader for Labor Reforms," *Labor History* 14 (Summer 1973); and especially Ann Doubilet, "The Illinois Woman's Alliance, 1888–1894," M.A. dissertation, Northern Illinois University, 1973.
3. "To Help the Slave Girls," unidentified clipping, 18 August 1888, Thomas J. Morgan Collection, Book 2, Illinois Historical Survey, Urbana, Illinois. Elizabeth Morgan kept scrapbooks of clippings on various subjects, most of those on the Alliance are unidentified except by date. Although I have footnoted only direct quotations, almost all my information about the Illinois Woman's Alliance comes from Film 6 of clipping book 2, hereafter referred to as Morgan Collection, Book 2.
4. "Thanks 'The Times,'" *Chicago Times,* August 1888, unidentified clipping, Morgan Collection, Book 6.
5. "To Help the Slave Girls," Morgan Collection, Book 2.
6. "Thanks 'The Times'" Morgan Collection, Book 2.
7. Member organizations of the Illinois Woman's Alliance included the Cook County Suffrage Society; the Miriam Chapter of the Order of the Eastern Star; the Sunshine Mission; the Presbyterian Ladies' Aid; the Single Tax Club; the Ladies' Federal Labor Union Local No. 2703; the Vincent Chatauqua Circle; the Chicago Trades and Labor Assembly; the Hopkins Metaphysical Association; the Ladies' Union of the Ethical Society; the Methodist Ladies' Aid; the Woodlawn Reading Club; the Glencoe Library; the Ladies of the Grand Army of the Republic; the Woodlawn branch of the Women's Christian Temperance Union; the Women's Physiological Society; the Anthony Club; the Knights of Labor Local Assembly No. 1789; Ryder Chapel; the South End Flower Mission; the Woman's Press Association; the Illinois Women's Medical Sanitary Association; the Working Women's Protective Association; the Women's Federation of Labor; the Moral Educational Society; the Lady Washington Masonic Chapter; the Glencoe Literary Club; Land and Labor Club No. 1; the Drexel Kindergarten Association; the Working Women's Club; and the Women's Homeopathic Medical Society.
8. "City Slave Girls," 2 October 1888, Morgan Collection, Book 2.
9. H., "Chicago Letter," *Alarm,* 11 August 1888. The "iron law" referred to is the Lassallean "iron law of wages," an erroneous economic theory which was influential in this period. According to the iron law, workers could not improve their lot through trade unionism because any rise in wages would be immediately followed by an exactly corresponding rise in prices.
10. "Women's Alliance Meeting," October 1889, Morgan Collection, Book 2.
11. "Numerous Reforms Suggested," *Chicago News,* 4 April 1891; "The Woman's Alliance," 4 April 1891, Morgan Collection, Book 2.
12. "Police Court Abuses," June 1890, Morgan Collection, Book 2.

13. "After the Vampires," July 1890; "Police Justice Fees," May 1890, Morgan Collection, Book 2.

14. "Work of the Sex," *Chicago Times*, 2 September 1894.

15. "Numerous Reforms Suggested," *Chicago News*, 4 April 1891; "The Woman's Alliance," 4 April 1891, Morgan Collection, Book 2.

16. "To Enforce the School Law," 18 December 1888, Morgan Collection, Book 2.

17. "Woman Wit[h]in School," 5 June 1889, Morgan Collection, Book 2.

18. Ibid.

19. Gertrude Breslau-Hunt, *Memorial—Corinne Stubbs Brown* (pamphlet in Chicago Historical Society, no publisher, no date).

20. "The Women's Alliance," 28 January 1889, Morgan Collection, Book 2.

21. "Report of Trade and Labor Assembly Delegates to the Woman's Alliance," 17 March 1889.

22. "End of a Big Splurge," *Chicago News*, 2 May 1889.

23. "Report of Delegates to the Woman's Alliance," 13 July 1889, Morgan Collection, Book 2.

24. "Women Wit[h]in School," 5 June 1889, Morgan Collection, Book 2.

25. "No Women Need Apply," May 1889, Morgan Collection, Book 2.

26. "Concerning Educational Matters," 18 January 1889, Morgan Collection, Book 2.

27. "Stewart's Bad Break," 13 January 1889, Morgan Collection, Book 2.

28. "The Women Are Working," May 1890, Morgan Collection, Book 2.

29. "Ladies Become Sarcastic," May 1890, Morgan Collection, Book 2.

30. "Woman's Alliance," February 1891, Morgan Collection, Book 2.

31. "Women As Inspectors," 26 July 1889, Morgan Collection, Book 2.

32. "Women Want War," October 1889, Morgan Collection, Book 2.

33. "The Woman's Alliance," 10 October 1889, Morgan Collection, Book 2.

34. "In the 'Sweat Shops,'" *Em. Journal [sic]*, 20 August 1891, Morgan Collection, Book 2.

35. Ibid.

36. Chicago Trades and Labor Assembly, *The New Slavery; Investigation Into the Sweating System as Applied to the Manufacture of Wearing Apparel* (Chicago: Detwiler Print, Rights of Labor Office, 1891). Morgan Collection, File 16.

37. Ibid., p. 20

38. Abraham Bisno, *Union Pioneer* (Madison: University of Wisconsin Press, 1967), pp. 147–148.

39. "A Workingwoman's Society of Philadelphia. . ." March 1889, Morgan Collection, Book 2.

40. Dorothy Rose Blumberg, *Florence Kelley: The Making of a Social Pioneer* (New York: Augustus M. Kelley, 1966), p. 127. While the contributions of settlement workers and reformers to the struggle for protective legislation were extremely important, particularly on the federal level, the fact that they, rather than labor leaders, wrote books has tended to leave the impression that they were the only ones involved. Hull House was founded in 1889 and did not become involved in the sweatship issue or sponsor legislation on it until Florence Kelley came there late in 1891. The Illinois Women's Alliance and the Chicago Trades and Labor Assembly had by then done three years of work on the question. If one were forced to rely only on Jane Addams' discussion of the campaign, however, one would not know that any groups beyond Hull House were involved. In a speech Addams made in 1892, for

instance, she credited "a resident" with the work exposing the board of education and putting pressure on the city for more schools that was actually done by the Alliance. (See "The Objective Value of a Social Settlement," *The Social Thought of Jane Addams,* Christopher Lasch, ed. [New York: Bobbs-Merrill Company, Inc., 1965], p. 57.)

41. "To Stop Sweating," *Chicago Inter-Ocean,* 20 February 1893, I am indebted to Rosemary Scherman for this reference.
42. "Illinois Woman's Allaince," May 1889, Morgan Collection, Book 2.
43. "Think They Are Unfairly Treated," 5 November 1891, Morgan Collection, Book 2.
44. "Fattening on Misery," August 1891, Morgan Collection, Book 2.
45. "Talked of Marriage and Divorce," 1892, Morgan Collection, Book 2.
46. "Florence Kelley Comes to Stay," in Allen F. Davis and Mary Lynn McCree, *Eighty Years at Hull House* (Chicago: Quadrangle Books, 1969), p. 40.
47. "Think They Are Unfairly Treated," 5 November 1891, Morgan Collection, Book 2.
48. "Illinois Woman's Alliance," 1894, Morgan Collection, Book 2.
49. "Talks to Toilers," 22 March 1894, Morgan Collection, Book 2.
50. "Going to Pieces," 1894, Morgan Collection, Book 2.
51. Ibid.
52. "Talks to Toilers," 22 March 1894, Morgan Collection, Book 2.
53. "They Will Unite," October 1894, Morgan Collection, Book 2.
54. The women unionists who remained with the AFL decided to form their own labor organization too. In November 1895 the *American Federationist* announced the formation in Chicago of the Dorcas Federal Labor Union, whose president was Alzina Stevens, then a resident at Hull House. The Dorcas Union met there twice a month and had a membership of perhaps fifty "working girls and the wives of trade unionists." According to Jane Addams it was represented in the Chicago Trades and Labor Assembly and later helped to found the Women's Union Label League. The mainstream of the female labor movement had thus come to rest securely under the wing of Hull House, where it was to remain, ideologically at least, for many years, no longer disturbed by an excess of radicalism. As Jane Addams described this development:

> In what we considered a praiseworthy effort to unite it [the Dorcas Union] with other organizations, the president of a leading Woman's Club [Ellen Henrotin] applied for membership. We were so sure of her election that she stood just outside the drawing-room door. . . . To our chagrin she did not receive enough votes to secure her admission, not because the working girls, as they were careful to state, did not admire her, but because she "seemed to belong to the other side." Fortunately, the big-minded woman so thoroughly understood the vote and her interest in working women was so genuine, that it was less than a decade afterward when she was elected to the presidency of the National Woman's Trade Union League. The incident and the sequel registers, perhaps, the change in Chicago towards the labor movement, the recognition of the fact that it is a general social movement concerning all members of society and not merely a class struggle.

("Chicago Labor Notes," *American Federationist* 2, no. 9 [November 1895], p. 468; Jane Addams, *Twenty Years at Hull House* [New York: The MacMillan Company, 1912], p. 213).

Part III: Fragmentation

1. Lizzie Swank Holmes, "Women Workers of Chicago," *American Federationist* 12 (August 1905), p. 509.
2. Dorothy Richardson, "Trades-Unions in Petticoats," *Leslie's Monthly Magazine* 57 (March 1904), pp. 489, 496.
3. John B. Andrews and W. D. P. Bliss, *History of Women in Trades Unions*, Bureau of Labor, Report on Conditions of Women and Child Wage-Earners in the United States, vol. 10 (Washington, D.C.: Government Printing Office, 1911), p. 148.
4. Ibid., p. 146.
5. Ibid., p. 150.
6. Alice Kessler-Harris, "Where Are the Organized Women Workers?" *Feminist Studies* 3, no. 1/2 (Fall 1975), p. 95.

Chapter 5. Leonora O'Reilly and the Women's Trade Union League

1. *Life and Labor* 2, no. 5 (May 1912), p. 153.
2. The first officers were Mary Morton Kehew of the General Federation of Women's Clubs as president; Jane Addams as vice-president; Mary Kenney O'Sullivan as secretary; and Mary Donovan of the Lynn, Massachusetts, Central Labor Union as treasurer.
3. *Life and Labor* 2, no. 3 (March 1912), back cover.
4. Mary Wolfe to Mary Dreier, no date, Leonora O'Reilly papers, Box 1, Schlesinger Library, Radcliffe College, Cambridge, Mass.
5. Ibid.
6. Eleanor Flexner, *Century of Struggle* (New York: Atheneum, 1968), p. 207.
7. Ibid., p. 208.
8. O'Reilly Papers, Box 13, File 299.
9. The Society addressed a verse appeal, "Shop Early," to shoppers in 1886: "O woman, tender hearted, / Who shared the negroes' throes, / Whose gentle tears are started, / By dogs' and horses' woes; / Who feel a sister's pity / For women far away / For slaves in your own city / We ask your help today / . . . The hearts of masters soften, / They see the havoc wrought, / But women will too often / Shop later than they ought / . . ." O'Reilly Papers (Microfilm IV, 13, 1905).
10. See Alice Henry, *The Trade Union Woman* (New York: D. Appleton & Co., 1915), pp. 43–44.
11. Maggie Finn to Leonora O'Reilly, 9 July 1912, O'Reilly Papers, Box 6, File 51.
12. Louisa Perkins to Leonora O'Reilly, 25 January [1895], O'Reilly Papers, Box 4, File 30.
13. Leonora O'Reilly to H. M., 1 January 1896, O'Reilly Papers (Microfilm 1, 2).
14. Louisa Perkins to Leonora O'Reilly, 28 January 1898, O'Reilly Papers (Microfilm 1, 4).
15. R. L. Duffus, *Lillian Wald, Neighbor and Crusader* (New York: The MacMillan Company, 1938), p. 66.
16. 29 July 1894, O'Reilly Papers, Box 4, File 29.
17. Its record in New York is documented in Nancy Schrom Dye, "The Women's Trade Union League of New York, 1903–20," Ph.D. dissertation, University of Wisconsin, 1974. For one example of UGW destruction of a female union,

see Chapter 2, note 12. The Amalgamated Clothing Workers of America was born in 1915 out of the scandal of the UGW.

18. O'Reilly Papers (Microfilm 1, 4).
19. Ibid.
20. Dye, "The Women's Trade Union League," p. 34.
21. Typescript of proceedings of National Women's Trade Union League Convention, 1915, p. 100, in the National Women's Trade Union League papers, Schlesinger Library, Radcliffe College, Cambridge, Mass.
22. Ibid., p. 113.
23. Women's Trade Union League, *Labor Songs*, no date, O'Reilly Papers, Box 16, File 378.
24. Proceedings, League Convention, 1915, p. 108.
25. Alice Henry, *Women in the Labor Movement* (New York: George H. Doran Company, 1923), pp. 99–100.
26. Elizabeth Gurley Flynn, "Women and Unionism," *Solidarity*, 27 March 1911.
27. Samuel Gompers, *Seventy Years of Life and Labor* (New York: Dutton, 1925).
28. Examples include the Swedish Special Order Workers in Chicago, smashed by the United Garment Workers in 1904; the Illinois shoe workers who were not permitted to join the International in 1900; the candy workers organized in Philadelphia by Pauline Newman in 1918, who finally fell apart after repeated rejections by their International; and the women printers in New York in 1920. For further discussion, see Henry, *Women in the Labor Movement;* Dye, "The Women's Trade Union League"; and Alice Kessler-Harris, "Where Are the Organized Women Workers?" *Feminist Studies* 3, no. 1/2 (Fall 1975).
29. Jane Addams, "The Settlement as a Factor in the Labor Movement," *Hull House Maps and Papers* (New York: T. Y. Crowell & Co., 1895), p. 202.
30. Working-class women in the early days of the League included Louisa Mittelstadt and Myrtle Whitehad of the Brewery Workers; Rose Schneiderman, Pauline Newman, and Fania Cohen of the ILGWU (all socialists); Josephine Casey of the Elevated Railroad Clerks; Agnes Nestor of the Glove Workers; Melinda Scott of the Hat Trimmers; Elizabeth Maloney of the Hotel and Restaurant Employees; Hilda Swenson of the Commercial Telegraphers; Nellie Quick of the Bindery Workers; Mary Anderson, Emma Steghagen, Mary McEnery and Mary Haney of the Boot and Shoe Workers; and Sarah Conboy of the United Garment Workers. Alice Bean, Mabel Gillespie, and Helen Marot were all members of the Bookkeepers, Stenographers, and Accountants Union, but the latter at least was a college graduate who joined only after she became staff at the League's New York office.
31. Dye's thesis has a detailed picture of this development; for a condensed version, see "Feminism or Unionism? The New York Women's Trade Union League and the Labor Movement," *Feminist Studies* 3, no. 1/2 (Fall 1975).
32. Pauline Newman to Rose Schneiderman, no date, in the Rose Schneiderman papers, Tamiment Library, New York University.
33. Raymond Robins to Mary Dreier, 12 November 1913, in the Raymond Robins papers, Wisconsin Historical Society, Madison, Wisconsin, Box 5, File 5.
34. In the first strike aided by the League, the 1905 strike of textile workers in Fall River, Massachusetts, Barnum developed the novel strategy of getting the strikers jobs as maids in Boston, thus attempting to solve at one blow the financial problems of the strikers and the servant problems of the Boston society women who were interested in the League. "The experiment was

encouraged on the ground that housework, with all the valid objections to it, might prove better than mill-work under existing conditions." Gertrude Barnum, "Fall River Mill Girls in Domestic Service," *Charities* 12 (4 March 1904), p. 550.

35. Gertrude Barnum, "National Organizer's Report," 1905, National Women's Trade Union League papers, Library of Congress, Box 1, Vol. 1.

36. Mildred Moore, "A History of the Women's Trade Union League of Chicago," M.A. dissertation, University of Chicago, 1915, p. 22.

37. *Life and Labor* 2, no. 4 (April 1912), p. 99.

38. Laura Elliot to Leonora O'Reilly, no date [March 1911] O'Reilly papers, Box 5, File 47.

39. June 1908, O'Reilly papers, Box 4, File 43.

40. "To the Executive Board of the National Women's Trade Union League," no date, signed Agnes Burns, Leora Lipshitz, Lily Brzostek, May Gordon Thompson, Florence Adesska, and Julia S. O'Connor. National Women's Trade Union League papers, Library of Congress, Box 1, Vol. 2.

41. Helen Marot, *American Labor Unions* (New York: Henry Holt & Co., 1914), p. 67.

42. Women's Trade Union League of New York, *Annual Report 1907–1908,* in O'Reilly papers, Box 8, File 388.

43. One of the ways Mary Dreier supported the New York League was by settling an annuity–not included on the balance sheet–upon her close friend Leonora O'Reilly in 1908. This enabled O'Reilly to work full time for the League for some years. Dreier wrote Winifred O'Reilly, Leonora's mother, at that time: "You know dear Mother O'Reilly how difficult it is to keep a free spirit under pressure—whether it is industrial, political, class—whatever it may be—and when you see one and know her for a friend, you know how you want to set her free—as far as our old civilization permits—free to live her life for the people as she wants to. And that is what I hope has come to Leonora—the freedom to use her gifts for the people in her own way. . . . Leonora and I will doubtless have different opinions frequently, that seems inevitable—and people never could agree on all things—but never could that make a particle of difference in our sense of freedom—nor in our love." 16 January 1908, O'Reilly papers, Box 4, File 42.

44. Pauline Newman to Rose Schneiderman, 9 December 1911, Rose Schneiderman papers, Tamiment Library, New York University.

45. "Minutes of Executive Board of National Women's Trade Union League," 18 March 1909, typescript, O'Reilly papers, Box 16, File 364.

46. O'Reilly's notes on the back of a letter from William English Walling, 17 December 1903, O'Reilly papers, Box 4, File 38.

47. Dye, "The Women's Trade Union League," p. 93.

48. Gertrude Barnum to Leonora O'Reilly, 8 December 1905, O'Reilly papers, Box 4, File 41.

49. O'Reilly papers, no date, Box 10, File 168.

50. Gertrude Barnum to Leonora O'Reilly, 13 February 1906, O'Reilly papers, Box 4, File 41.

51. Margaret Dreier Robins to Leonora O'Reilly, 19 July 1914, O'Reilly papers, Box 6, File 57.

52. Mary Dreier to Leonora O'Reilly, 31 August 1915, O'Reilly papers, Box 6, File 57.

53. Theresa Wolfson, *The Woman Worker and the Trade Unions* (New York: International Publishers, 1926), pp. 13, 123.
54. "National Work," January 1912, National Women's Trade Union League papers, Library of Congress, Box 1, Vol. 2. Forming cooperatives was a rather frequent response to lockouts and lost strikes in the early U.S. labor movement, and one especially favored by the Knights of Labor. These cooperatives seldom lasted long, being unsuited to survival in a capitalist system of production and distribution.
55. Dye, "The Women's Trade Union League," p. 424.
56. William O'Neill, *Everyone Was Brave* (Chicago: Quadrangle Press, 1969), p. 220.
57. National Women's Trade Union League papers, Library of Congress, Box 26.
58. Leonora O'Reilly to Mary Dreier, 6 September 1915, O'Reilly papers, Box 6, File 57.
59. Margaret Dreier Robins to Leonora O'Reilly, 27 July 1915, O'Reilly papers, Box 6, File 57.
60. Mary Wolfe to Mary Dreier, no date, O'Reilly papers, Box 1.

Chapter 6. Rebel Girls and the IWW

1. Joyce L. Kornbluh, ed., *Rebel Voices: An I.W.W. Anthology* (Ann Arbor: University of Michigan Press, 1968), p. 145. This is one of a number of invaluable background sources on the IWW which I used in preparing this book. See also Paul F. Brissenden, *The I.W.W.: A Study of American Syndicalism* (New York: Columbia University Press, 1919); Joseph Conlin, *Bread and Roses Too* (New York: Greenwood Publishers, 1969); Melvin Dubofsky, *We Shall Be All* (Chicago: Quadrangle Books, 1969); Philip S. Foner, *History of the Labor Movement in the United States*, vol. 4 (New York: International Publishers, 1965); Patrick Renshaw, *The Wobblies* (New York: Doubleday and Co., 1967); Fred Thompson, *The I.W.W.: Its First Fifty Years* (Chicago: I.W.W., 1955); Robert Tyler, *Rebels of the Woods* (Eugene, Oregon: University of Oregon Press, 1967).
2. Kornbluh, *Rebel Voices*, pp. 12–13.
3. Dubofsky, *We Shall Be All*, p. 176.
4. Foner, *History of the Labor Movement*, vol. 4, p. 127.
5. "All Along the Coast," *Solidarity*, 25 June 1910.
6. See William E. Trautmann, "Hammond Strike Won," *Industrial Worker*, 5 February 1910; "Women Active in Lumber Strike," *Industrial Worker*, 18 April 1912; "California Fishermen Strike and Win," *Solidarity*, 14 October 1916; Foner, *History of the Labor Movement*, vol. 4, pp. 223, 297.
7. Rheta Childe Dorr, "As a Woman Sees It," *Solidarity*, 23 September 1916.
8. "California Fishermen Strike and Win," *Solidarity*, 14 October 1916.
9. "Problems in Organizing Women," *Solidarity*, 15 July 1916.
10. Sophie Beldner, "Work for Women in Industrial Unionism," *Industrial Union Bulletin*, 3 August 1907.
11. "Cheerful Note from Joe Hill," *Solidarity*, 19 December 1914.
12. Elizabeth Gurley Flynn to Anna Strunsky Walling, no date, William English Walling papers, Wisconsin Historical Society, Madison, Wisconsin, Box 1, File 1.

13. "Tenth I.W.W. Convention," *Solidarity*, 16 December 1916.
14. Sophie [Beldner] Vasilio, "Women in the I.W.W.," *Industrial Union Bulletin*, 25 April 1908.
15. Ibid.
16. "From a Woman Toiler," *Solidarity*, 25 June 1910.
17. Charles Ashleigh, "The Floater," in Kornbluh, *Rebel Voices*, pp. 80–81.
18. Frank S. Hamilton, "A Screed and a Suggestion," *Solidarity*, 21 November 1914.
19. Sin Bad, "Some Weaknesses of the Western Wobbly," *Solidarity*, 16 January 1915.
20. Frank Jakel, "Wanted Women Organizers on Pacific Coast," *Solidarity*, 9 December 1916.
21. Jane Street, "Denver's Rebel Housemaids," *Solidarity*, 1 April 1916.
22. "'We Have Got Results': A Document on the Organization of Domestics in the Progressive Era," Daniel T. Hobby, ed., *Labor History* 17, no. 1 (Winter 1976), p. 104. This document is a letter from Jane Street to Mrs. Elmer F. Buse of Tulsa, Oklahoma, written in 1917 and intercepted by the U.S. Post Office, which forwarded it to the Justice Department to help its campaign of repression against the IWW. It is cited as Department of Justice Record Group 60, File 18701–28, in the National Archives.
23. "Housemaids From Union in Denver," *Solidarity*, 1 April 1916.
24. Ibid.
25. Mildred Morris, "Housemaids' Union Plots Revenge," reprinted in *Solidarity*, 29 July 1916.
26. "The Maids' Defiance," *Solidarity*, 6 May 1916.
27. C. W. Sellars, "The Domestic Workers' Union," *Solidarity*, 11 November 1916.
28. Press Committee, Local 614, "Rebel Girl Defenders," *Solidarity*, 26 November 1913.
29. "Denver Housemaids' List Stolen," *Solidarity*, 11 November 1916.
30. "We Have Got Results," pp. 106–107.
31. "Song Makes Hit," *Solidarity*, 1 July 1916; Mildred Morris, "Housemaids' Union Plots Revenge"; Mort E. Warshavsky, "The Domestics' Industrial Union," *Solidarity*, 15 November 1916; "In Other Women's Homes," *Solidarity*, 1 July 1916; "Seattle Houseworkers Organize," *Solidarity*, 28 October 1916.
32. "We Have Got Results," pp. 106–107.
33. For a thorough and illuminating discussion of the left and "the sex question," see chapter 9 of Linda Gordon, *Woman's Body, Woman's Right* (New York: Grossman Publishers, 1976).
34. Abraham Bisno, *Union Pioneer* (Madison: University of Wisconsin Press, 1967), pp. 224–226.
35. Harriet Knowles Snowden, "The Socialist Girl and 'Advanced Theories,'" *New York Sunday Call*, 5 November 1911.
36. Floyd Dell, *Homecoming* (New York: Farrar and Rinehart, 1933), pp. 288–289.
37. "Men and Women," 1915 manuscript notes in the Flynn papers in the American Institute for Marxist Studies, New York.
38. Mrs. Floyd Hyde, "Is There a Woman's Question in the Revolutionary Movement?" *Solidarity*, 28 December 1912.
39. Ibid.
40. Mrs. Floyd Hyde, "The Woman Question Again," *Solidarity*, 25 January 1913.
41. Elizabeth Gurley Flynn, "Men and Women." American Institute for Marxist Studies.

42. Elizabeth Gurley Flynn, *I Speak My Own Piece* (New York: Masses and Mainstream, 1955), pp. 271. Unless otherwise cited, the biographical information in this section comes from Flynn's autobiography, which has been republished under the title *The Rebel Girl* (New York: International Publishers, 1978). For other biographical information, see also Rosalyn Baxandall, "Elizabeth Gurley Flynn: The Early Years," *Radical America* 9, no. 1 (January–February 1975).
43. Inez Haynes Irwin, manuscript autobiography, pp. 414–415, Inez Haynes Irwin papers, Box 3, Schlesinger Library, Radcliffe College, Cambridge, Mass. See also "Marriage Customs and Taboos Among the Early Heterodites," a parody of the anthropological work of fellow-member Elsie Clews Parsons, Irwin papers, Box 2. The Irwin papers also contain a photograph album presented to Marie Jenney Howe in 1920, with pictures and autographs of all the members of the Heterodoxy Club. These include Stella Comen, Mary Ware Dennet, Agnes DeMille, Crystal Eastman, Zona Gale, Susan Glaspell, Charlotte Perkins Gilman, Fannie Hurst, Elizabeth Irwin, Paula Jacobi, Gertrude B. Kelley, Fola LaFollette, Inez Milholland, Alice Duer Miller, Elsie Clews Parsons, Grace Potter, Ida Rauh, Doris Stevens, Rose Pastor Stokes, Rose Strunsky, Mary Heaton Vorse, and Gertrude Marvin Williams.
44. Gladys Vera Lamb, "Prayer of a Tired Housewife," scrapbook, Flynn papers, American Institute for Marxist Studies, New York.
45. Matilda Robbins' autobiographical papers contain the following anecdote about a woman apparently modeled on Margaret Prevey, an Ohio socialist:

> Monday morning always found her over two wooden washtubs on a bench near the kitchen sink. The breakfast dishes were washed, the kitchen clean and warmed by the coal stove black and shiny with its nickel trim. Here Tess would stand and rub clothes on a washboard and drop them into the steaming wash boiler on the stove and lift them out with a smooth round stick and rinse and dip the soap water out of the tub into the sink and then lift the tub with the remainder of the water and pour it out. Back breaking work. Thousands of workers' wives were doing the same thing all over this happy land.
>
> The clothes were on the line before noon. There was the midday dinner to be gotten for Dan and the boys and after that more dishes, cleaning, mending, in the winter keeping fires going, sifting ashes to retrieve every bit of coal; innumerable household chores. Dan went to meetings perhaps four nights a week, or else meetings were held at the house. Always it meant that supper had to be on time and early, dishes washed, the boys' clothes looked after; there was mending and sewing. . . .
>
> One morning we sat in the kitchen folding leaflets and talking. . . . Tess dwelt at some length on E. F.'s stay with them; the fine speeches she made; the enthusiasm she aroused. And then surprisingly she said, "But you know, I'm sorry for her."
>
> I was rather startled. "Sorry, sorry for E. F.?"
>
> "Yes. You see she is so dependent for everything. She can't do a thing for herself. So helpless. She can't make a bed, nor wash a pair of stockings, nor mend a rip, nor make a cup of coffee—nothing. Oh, sure, she's a wonderful speaker and all that. If I had a girl I would be very proud to have her do the work E. F. does. Still I would want her to know how to take care of herself. I would want her to know some other

kind of work besides organizing and speaking. It seems somehow more in keeping with the things we believe in that those who talk to workers should know how to work"

(Matilda Robbins, "These I Have Known," pp. 4–5, Robbins papers, Wayne State University, Detroit, Michigan).

46. Flynn, *I Speak*, pp. 41–42.
47. Edward Bellamy's *Looking Backward* was a utopian novel describing a future after a socialist (which he called Nationalist) revolution; it was one of the sacred texts of the populist movement. Sinclair Lewis's *The Jungle* was a sensational—and socialist—exposé of the Chicago meatpacking industry. Mary Wollstonecraft was the mother of modern feminism. August Bebel was a leader in the German socialist party; his *Woman and Socialism* was, with Engels' *Origins of the Family, Private Property and the State*, one of the two major theoretical books on the oppression of women produced by the socialist movement of this period.
48. Elizabeth Gurley Flynn, "Men and Women" manuscript, Flynn papers, American Institute for Marxist Studies, New York.
49. Scrapbook, Flynn papers, American Institute for Marxist Studies, New York.
50. Flynn, *I Speak*, p. 176.
51. Ibid., pp. 76–77.
52. Ibid., pp. 94–95.
53. James Wilson, "Modern Slave Traders," *Industrial Union Bulletin*, 24 October 1908.
54. Dubofsky, *We Shall Be All*, p. 176.
55. Flynn, *I Speak*, p. 97.
56. Ibid., p. 98.
57. "Miss Flynn Tells of Jail Experiences," *New York Call*, 13 December 1909.
58. Flynn, *I Speak*, p. 103.
59. Ibid., p. 113.
60. Elizabeth Gurley Flynn, "Problems Organizing Women," manuscript draft in Flynn papers, American Institute for Marxist Studies, of the article that appeared in a somewhat altered form in *Solidarity*, 15 July 1916.
61. Elizabeth Gurley Flynn, "Women and Unionism," *Solidarity*, 27 May 1911.
62. Ibid.
63. Elizabeth Gurley Flynn, manuscript outline, no date, Flynn papers, File 5, American Institute for Marxist Studies.
64. Flynn, "Problems."
65. Kate O'Hare, "Birth Control and Pellagra," *National Ripsaw* 12, no. 10 (December 1915), p. 6.
66. Gordon, *Woman's Body*, p. 238.
67. Elizabeth Gurley Flynn, "The Case of Margaret Sanger," *Solidarity*, 22 January 1916.
68. Margaret Sanger, *An Autobiography* (New York: W. W. Norton and Co., 1938), p. 96.
69. Eliza Burt Gamble, "Race Suicide in France," *International Socialist Review* 9, no. 7 (January 1909); Caroline Nelson, "Neo-Malthusianism," *International Socialist Review* 14, no. 4 (October 1913).
70. Sanger, *Autobiography*, p. 108.
71. David S. Kennedy, *Birth Control in America* (New Haven: Yale University Press, 1970), p. 22.
72. *The Woman Rebel* 1, no. 1 (March 1914), p. 1.

73. Margaret Sanger, "The Militants in England," *The Woman Rebel* 1, no. 4 (June 1914), p. 25.
74. Margaret Sanger, "To My Friends and Colleagues," 5 January 1915, Margaret Sanger papers, Library of Congress.
75. Margaret Sanger, "Suppression," *The Woman Rebel* 1, no. 4 (June 1914), p. 25.
76. Margaret Sanger, *Family Limitation* (5th edition, New York 1916), Margaret Sanger papers, Sophia Smith Collection, Smith College, Northampton, Mass.
77. Sanger, *Autobiography*, p. 117.
78. Margaret Sanger, *My Fight for Birth Control* (New York: Farrar and Rinehart, 1913), p. 127.
79. Elizabeth Gurley Flynn to Margaret Sanger, no date, Sanger papers, Library of Congress.
80. Flynn, "Problems."
81. Robert Tyler, *Rebels of the Woods* (Eugene, Oregon: University of Oregon Press, 1967), p. 139.

Chapter 7. Socialists and Suffragists

1. Crystal Eastman, "Feminism," in *On Woman and Revolution*, Blanch Wiesen Cook, ed. (New York: Oxford University Press, 1978), p. 51.
2. Ellen Carol DuBois, *Feminism and Suffrage: The Emergence of an Independent Women's Movement in America 1848–1869* (Ithaca: Cornell University Press, 1978), pp. 17–18.
3. Ibid., pp. 174–175.
4. Mari Jo and Paul Buhle, eds., *The Concise History of Woman Suffrage* (Urbana, Illinois: University of Illinois Press, 1978), pp. 29–30.
5. Eleanor Flexner, *Century of Struggle* (New York: Atheneum, 1968), pp. 217–218.
6. Quoted in William L. O'Neill, *Everyone Was Brave: The Rise and Fall of Feminism in America* (Chicago: Quadrangle Books, 1969), p. 36.
7. Editorial, June 1917, in William O'Neill, ed., *The Woman Movement*, pp. 188–189.
8. Aileen Kraditor, ed., *Up From the Pedestal* (Chicago: Quadrangle Books, 1970), p. 260.
9. Ibid., p. 170.
10. Quoted in Flexner, *Century of Struggle*, p. 250.
11. Ibid., p. 251.
12. Ibid., p. 52.
13. Quoted in Ronald Schoffer, "The New York City Woman Suffrage Party, 1909–19," *New York History* 43 (July 1962), p. 275.
14. Ibid.
15. Leonora O'Reilly wrote Mary Hay of the Woman Suffrage Party in 1913: "The little Wage Earners group, such as it is, remembers very distinctly that it was through the activity of Mary Beard and the Woman's Suffrage Party that they were brought into being, at all." 13 May 1913, O'Reilly papers (Microfilm 1, 18) Schlesinger Library, Radcliffe College, Cambridge, Mass.
16. Unidentified clipping, 11 April 1911, O'Reilly papers, Box 15, File 357.
17. Monday, 13 November 1911, O'Reilly papers (Microfilm 1, 18).
18. O'Reilly to A. F. Brody, 13 January 1914, O'Reilly papers, Box 6, File 54.
19. Mary Beard to O'Reilly, no date, O'Reilly papers, Box 6, File 50 (1912).

20. Leaflet, O'Reilly papers, Box 15, File 357.
21. O'Reilly to Brody, no date, O'Reilly papers, Box 6, File 50 (1912).
22. Leaflet, O'Reilly papers, Box 15, File 357.
23. Ibid.
24. Leonora O'Reilly, introduction to Margaret Hinchey, "Thirty Days," *Life and Labor* 3, no. 9 (September 1913), p. 264.
25. "Suffrage in Bowery Hotel," *New York Times,* 5 May 1915.
26. Maggie Hinchey to Leonora O'Reilly, "Thursday, 29th," no date, O'Reilly papers, Box 6, File 52.
27. Maggie Hinchey to Leonora O'Reilly, no date, O'Reilly papers, Box 6, File 51.
28. Maggie Hinchey to Leonora O'Reilly, no date [1918], O'Reilly papers, Box 6, File 52.
29. Paula Scheier, "Clara Lemlich Shavelson," *Jewish Life* 8, no. 95 (November 1954), p. 10.
30. Mary Beard to O'Reilly, 1 January 1912, O'Reilly papers, Box 6, File 51.
31. Beard to O'Reilly, 21 July 1912, O'Reilly papers, Box 6, File 51.
32. Rose Wortis to Elizabeth Gurley Flynn, 6 June 1951, Flynn papers, American Institute for Marxist Studies, New York.
33. Scheier, p. 11.
34. Elizabeth Gurley Flynn, "Women," manuscript dated 21 December 1909, Flynn papers, American Institute for Marxist Studies, New York.
35. Anna Tewksbury, "Woman and Industrial Unionism," *Solidarity,* 12 February 1910.
36. Ben Williams, "'Votes' and 'Women's Wages,'" *Solidarity,* 22 February 1913.
37. Charles Ashleigh, "Women in the I.W.W.," *Industrial Union Bulletin,* 25 April 1908.
38. J. E. [Justus Ebert], "Women and Labor," *Solidarity,* 1 July 1916.
39. Flynn, "The I.W.W. Call to Women," *Solidarity,* 31 July 1915.
40. Flynn, "Men and Women," unpublished 1915 speech, Flynn papers, American Institute for Marxist Studies, New York.
41. Elizabeth Gurley Flynn, "Problems Organizing Women," *Solidarity,* 15 June 1916.
42. Marie Equi to Margaret Sanger, 20 October 1916, Margaret Sanger papers, Library of Congress, Box 2.
43. Ira Kipnis, *The American Socialist Movement 1897–1912* (New York: Columbia University Press, 1952), p. 247.
44. Charlotte Perkins Gilman, "The Socialist and the Suffragist," *The Forerunner* 1, no. 12 (October 1910), p. 25.
45. Mari Jo Buhle, "Women and the Socialist Party, 1909–1914," *Radical America* 4, no. 2 (February 1970), p. 38. See also Bruce Dancis, "Socialism and Women in the United States, 1900–1917," *Socialist Revolution* 6, no. 1 (January–March 1976).
46. Mari Jo Buhle, "Women and the Socialist Party," p. 41.
47. Hebe [Meta Stern], "The Socialist Party and Women," *Socialist Woman* 2, no. 14 (June 1908), p. 9.
48. Articles on women by Clara Zetkin which have been translated into English include "Lenin on the Women Question," in V.I. Lenin, *The Emancipation of Women* (New York: International Publishers, 1966); "Surrender of the Second International in the Emancipation of Women," *Communist International* 6, no. 9–10 (April 1929); "Some Critical Remarks on the Draft Programme," *Communist International* 5, no. 15 (1 August 1928). Recent work

discussing Zetkin's organizing career include Jean H. Quataert, "Unequal Partners in an Uneasy Alliance: Women and the Working Class in Imperial Germany," in Marilyn J. Boxer and Jean H. Quataert, eds., *Socialist Women: European Socialist Feminism in the Nineteenth and Early Twentieth Centuries* (New York: Elsevier North-Holland, Inc., 1978); Karen Honeycutt, "Clara Zetkin: A Socialist Approach to the Problem of Woman's Oppression," *Feminist Studies* 3, no. 3/4 (Spring 1976); Werner Thönnessen, *The Emancipation of Women: The Rise and Decline of the Women's Movement in German Social Democracy 1863–1933*, trans. by Joris de Bres (London: Pluto Press, 1973).

49. Josephine C. Kaneko, "Are the Interests of Men and Women Identical?" *Socialist Woman* 1, no. 12 (May 1908), p. 5.

50. "The National Convention on the Woman Question," *Socialist Woman* 2, no. 12 (June 1908), p. 3.

51. May Wood Simons, "Work in Chicago After the Convention," *Chicago Daily Socialist*, 13 June 1908.

52. Mila Tupper Maynard, "Women in the Locals," *New York Call*, 15 March 1909.

53. *Proceedings of the National Convention* (Chicago: Socialist Party, 1912), pp. 205, 207; "Among Ourselves," *Progressive Woman* 6, no. 64 (October 1912), p. 15.

54. *Proceedings of the National Convention*, 1912, p. 207.

55. Clara Zetkin, "The Limited Woman Suffrage Fight in England," *Socialist Woman* 2, no. 15 (August 1908), p. 6.

56. Anita C. Block, "Socialism and the Suffrage Movement Once More," *New York Sunday Call*, 2 January 1910.

57. Anita C. Block, "The Conference and Its Significance," *New York Sunday Call*, 19 December 1909.

58. See Part IV, Chapter 8, "The Uprising of the Thirty Thousand."

59. *Proceedings of the National Congress of the Socialist Party*, (Chicago: Socialist Party, 1910), p. 180.

60. Ibid., p. 181.

61. Ibid., p. 185.

62. Ibid., p. 186.

63. Ibid., p. 191.

64. Ibid., p. 192.

65. Victor Berger, "Let Us Not Sidestep Too Much," *Social-Democratic Herald* (Milwaukee), 17 July 1909. In 1912 Pauline Newman made some bitter observations about the strength of the Socialist party's committment to woman suffrage:

> Surely the Socialist Party stands for woman suffrage, it has always stood—still. It has not done much in that direction.
>
> It is one thing to have a plank in a platform and another thing to advocate it. Don't you know, brother Socialist, that with the exception of one or two speakers of the Socialist party all the rest ignore that plank. . . . Only recently a Philadelphia revolutionist was speaking on the contemporary social revolution to a large open air meeting, and when asked by a woman passerby as to what the Socialist party's stand was on woman suffrage, answered: "We don't bother with such nonsensical questions!" ("A Task for Women of the Socialist Party," *New York Call*, 1 November 1912.)

66. "To the Local Secretaries of the Socialist Party," no date, Socialist Party papers, Milwaukee Historical Society, Milwaukee, Wisconsin.

67. Janet Korngold, "Work for Women," *American Socialist*, 19 July 1915.
68. Letter from May Wood Simons, *American Socialist*, 9 January 1915.
69. Theresa Malkiel, "More Serious Than Funny," *American Socialist*, 24 April 1915.
70. Josephine C. Kaneko, "Abolishing the Woman's Department," *American Socialist*, 10 July 1915.
71. Kate Richards O'Hare, "The Eternal Feminine," *New York Call*, 7 June 1915.
72. "Report of the Women's National Committee, Majority Report," *National Committee Session of May, 1915* (Chicago: Socialist Party, 1915), p. 1.
73. Agnes H. Downing, "Votes for Women," *New York Call*, 13 May 1915.
74. Mary S. Oppenheimer, "The Suffrage Movement and the Socialist Party," *New Review* 3, no. 9 (December 1915), p. 359.
75. Julius Gerber to Jessie Ashley, 23 April 1912, 4 May 1912; Jessie Ashley to Julius Gerber, 11 February 1912, 25 April 1912; Anita Block to Julius Gerber, 28 February 1914, New York Socialist Party papers, Microfilm 2, Tamiment Library, New York University.
76. William Z. Foster, *American Trade Unionism* (New York: International Publishers, 1947), p. 66.
77. Eastman, "Alice Paul's Convention," in Cook, *On Woman and Revolution*, p. 63.
78. Sherna Gluck, "Socialist Feminism Between the Two World Wars: Insights from Oral History," paper delivered at the Fourth Berkshire Conference on the History of Women, August 1978, p. 18.
79. In the 1920s lawyers believed that the courts would use the ERA to void all protective legislation that did not cover men as well as women and children. Today most believe that the precedents set under Title VII could be used to extend protective legislation to men if the ERA were passed, except in cases where its effects are clearly discriminatory against women; such laws would be made void.

Part IV: Case Studies

Chapter 8. The Uprising of the Thirty Thousand

1. *The Voice of Labor*, Women's Trade Union League songbook, Leonora O'Reilly papers, Box 15, File 349, Schlesinger Library, Radcliffe College, Cambridge, Mass.
2. As quoted in the *New York Call*, 28 November 1909.
3. Ladies' Waist Makers' Union, *Souvenir History of the Strike* (New York: Ladies' Waistmakers' Union, 1910), pp. 11–12.
4. Paula Scheier, "Clara Lemlich Shavelson," *Jewish Life* 8, no. 95 (November 1954), p. 8.
5. Ibid., p. 9.
6. M. B. Sumner, "Spirit of the Strikers," *Survey* 23 (22 January 1910), p. 554.
7. Scheier, "Clara Lemlich Shavelson," p. 9.
8. Ibid.
9. Louis Levine, *The Women's Garment Workers, A History of the International Ladies Garment Workers' Union* (New York: B. W. Heubsch, Inc., 1924), pp. 146–147.
10. The cutters were not members of Local 25, the shirtwaist makers' local, but of Local 30. They generally had higher wages and worked shorter hours than the women. Two days after the general strike began, 500 members of Local 30 struck in solidarity.

11. Ladies' Waist Makers' Union, *Souvenir History*, pp. 2–3.
12. Woods Hutchinson, M.D., "The Hygienic Aspects of the Shirtwaist Strike," *Survey* 23 (22 January 1910), p. 545.
13. Ibid.
14. The number of working women who were hired as organizers or union staff in this period could be easily counted on one person's fingers. Among them were Rose Schneiderman, Pauline Newman, Gertrude Barnum, and Josephine Casey.
15. Helen Marot, "A Woman's Strike—An Appreciation of the Shirtwaist Makers of New York," in *Proceedings of the American Academy of Political Science, City of New York* 1 (1910), p. 122. Out of the thirty thousand strikers, Marot estimates that six thousand were Russian men, two thousand Italian women, one thousand American women, and twenty-one thousand Russian women.
16. Ladies' Waist Makers' Union, *Souvenir History*, p. 4.
17. Quoted in Levine, *The Women's Garment Workers*, p. 148.
18. Ladies' Waist Makers' Union, *Souvenir History*, p. 2.
19. Sumner, "Spirit of the Strikers," p. 554.
20. *New York Call*, 28 September 1909.
21. *New York Call*, 5 October 1909.
22. Marot, "A Woman's Strike," p. 120.
23. Levine, *The Women's Garment Workers*, p. 152.
24. *New York Call*, 23 October 1909.
25. *New York Call*, 5 November 1909.
26. Sue Ainslie Clark and Edith Wyatt, "Working Girls' Budgets: The Shirtwaist Makers and Their Strike," *McClure's Magazine* 36 (November 1910), p. 81.
27. Marot, "A Woman's Strike," p. 135.
28. Woods Hutchinson, "The Hygienic Aspects," p. 545.
29. Marot, "A Woman's Strike," p. 126.
30. Ibid, p. 124.
31. Clark and Wyatt, "Working Girls' Budgets," p. 82.
32. Levine, *The Women's Garment Workers*, p. 159.
33. Rose Schneiderman, with Lucy Goldthwaite, *All for One* (New York: Paul S. Ericksson, Inc., 1967), p. 93.
34. *New York Call*, 4 December 1909.
35. William Mailly, "How Girls Can Strike," *Progressive Woman* 3, no. 33 (February 1910), p. 6.
36. Grace Potter, "Women Shirt-Waist Strikers Command Sympathy of Public," *New York Call*, 12 December 1909.
37. Levine, *The Women's Garment Workers*, p. 166.
38. Marot, "A Woman's Strike," pp. 123–124.
39. Ibid., pp. 122–123.
40. National Women's Trade Union League, *Proceedings of the Third Biennial Convention* (1911), p. 19.
41. Mary White Ovington, *Half a Man* (New York: Longmans, Green and Company, 1911), pp. 144, 150.
42. Ibid., pp. 161–163.
43. Philip S. Foner, *Women and the American Labor Movement* (New York: Free Press, 1979), pp. 339–340.
44. Mary White Ovington, *The Walls Come Tumbling Down* (New York: Schocken Books, 1970), p. 43.
45. "Woman's Sphere," *New York Call*, 4 January 1910.

46. Alfred T. White, "Shirtwaist Makers' Union," *Survey* 23 (29 January 1910), p. 588.
47. Margaret Dreier Robins, "Shirtwaist Makers' Union," *Survey* 23 (19 February 1910), p. 788.
48. Foner, *Women and the American Labor Movement,* p. 341.
49. *New York Call,* 22 December 1909.
50. Minutes, Executive Board, 21 May 1910, National Women's Trade Union League papers, Library of Congress.
51. The lingerie manufacturers in the white goods shops tried to use black workers as strikebreakers as they had used them in the white goods general strike of 1913. This failed partly because the strikers threw "missiles" at them, and partly because they were unskilled at the trade. Hyman Berman, "The Era of the Protocol," Ph.D. dissertation, Columbia University, 1956, p. 189.
52. See the National Women's Trade Union League papers, Library of Congress and Mildred Rankin's letters to Margaret Dreier Robins, Robins papers, University of Florida, Gainesville, Florida.
53. Levine, *The Women's Garment Workers,* p. 165.
54. Ibid., p. 163.
55. *New York Call,* 28 December 1909.
56. Marot, "A Woman's Strike," p. 29.
57. *Proceedings of the . . . Convention* (1911), p. 18.
58. "The League and the Strike of the Thirty Thousand," *Annual Report of the Women's Trade Union League of New York, 1909–1910,* p. 3.
59. *New York Call,* 20 December 1909.
60. Aileen S. Kraditor, *The Ideas of the Woman Suffrage Movement, 1890–1920* (New York: Anchor Books, 1971), p. 225.
61. *New York Call,* 21 December 1909.
62. *New York American,* 29 December 1909.
63. Theresa Serber Malkiel, *Diary of a Shirtwaist Striker* (New York: Cooperative Press, 1910), pp. 40–41.
64. *New York Call,* 4 January 1910.
65. Minutes, National Executive Board Meeting, National Women's Trade Union League, 20 May 1910, National Women's Trade Union League papers, Library of Congress.
66. *New York Daily Tribune,* 22 January 1910.
67. Raymond Robins to Margaret Dreier Robins, 5 February 1910, Raymond Robins papers, Wisconsin Historical Society, Box 1, File 1.
68. Raymond Robins to Margaret Dreier Robins, 3 February 1910, Raymond Robins papers, Wisconsin Historical Society, Box 1, File 1.
69. Theresa Malkiel, Metal Stern, and Antoinette Konikow, "Socialist Women and the Shirtwaist Strike," *New York Call,* 8 February 1910.
70. Ibid.
71. Ibid.
72. Levine, *The Women's Garment Workers,* p. 165; *New York Call,* 15 February 1910.
73. Leon Stein, *The Triangle Fire* (New York: J. B. Lippincott Company, 1962), p. 168.
74. Martha Bensley Bruere, "The Triangle Fire," *Life and Labor* 1, no. 5 (May 1911), p. 137.
75. Schneiderman, *All for One,* p. 100.
76. *Solidarity,* 15 April 1911.
77. Levine, *The Women's Garment Workers,* p. 218.

78. *Proceedings of the . . . Convention* (1911), p. 18.
79. 13 May 1911; quoted by Nancy Schrom Dye, "The Women's Trade Union League of New York, 1903–1920," Ph.D. dissertation, University of Wisconsin, 1974, p. 182. As the ILGWU continued to call general strikes to organize various branches of the garment industry, the League lost patience, particularly when the strikers included "American girls." Mary Dreier wrote Margaret Dreier Robins on the occasion of the lingerie workers' strike in 1912:

> This strike seems to be as unorganized as the shirtwaist workers—there are some American girls out, very promising material for organization, but the Union has not yet asked our help, though we tooted up to see if we cd help. . . . I wish we had the authority to go straight into any strike situation and make them obey us—I mean of course in these unorganized strikes. It wd be much better all around. (4 January 1912, Margaret Dreier Robins papers, University of Florida, Gainesville).

80. Dye, "The Women's Trade Union League," p. 205. It appears that Leonora O'Reilly, Mollie Schepps, Helen Marot, Melinda Scott, and Maggie Hinchey were against the protocol. Rose Schneiderman and Pauline Newman were presumably for it.
81. Levine, *The Women's Garment Workers*, p. 224.
82. Ibid., pp. 224–225.
83. Ibid., p. 301.
84. Ibid., p. 313.
85. Ibid., pp. 315–316.
86. Ibid., p. 301.
87. Ibid., p. 303.
88. Quoted in Dye, "The Women's Trade Union League," p. 234.
89. Helen Marot, *American Labor Unions* (New York: Henry Holt & Co., 1914), p. 75.
90. *Solidarity*, 26 February 1916.
91. Berman, "The Era of the Protocol," p. 370.
92. The same discrimination against women exists today in the ILGWU, complicated by racial and ethnic factors. In 1970 one-third at the very least of the union's membership were black, Latin, or Asian, but there was only one minority member on the executive board. Women made up 80 percent of the union membership and in 1970 they too had only one member on the executive board. The union's president, Louis Stolberg, told the *Wall Street Journal,* "Women are very peculiar. I once tried to promote one. She went off and married a man. What the hell can I do?" *Wall Street Journal,* 30 December 1970.
93. Scheier, "Clara Lemlich Shavelson," p. 8.

Chapter 9. Lawrence, 1912

1. Joyce Kornbluh, ed., *Rebel Voices: An I.W.W. Anthology* (Ann Arbor: University of Michigan Press, 1964), p. 196.
2. *The Strike at Lawrence, Massachusetts, Hearings Before the Committee on Rules of the House of Representatives, 1912,* 62nd Congress, 2nd Session, House Document 671 (Washington, D.C.: Government Printing Office, 1912), p. 32. Hereafter cited as *Hearings.*

3. Philip Foner, *History of the Labor Movement in the United States,* vol. 4 (New York: International Publishers, 1965), p. 313.

4. *Solidarity,* 19 October 1912.

5. Foner, *History of the Labor Movement,* vol. 4, p. 308.

6. Kornbluh, ed., *Rebel Voices,* p. 181.

7. Elizabeth Gurley Flynn, *I Speak My Own Piece* (New York: Masses and Mainstream, 1955), pp. 124–125.

8. Ibid., p. 117.

9. Elizabeth Shapleigh, "Occupational Diseases in the Textile Industry," *New York Call,* 29 December 1912.

10. William D. Haywood, "On Ettor and Giovannitti" (speech made at Cooper Union, New York, 21 May 1912), (n.p.: IWW, n.d.), in IWW papers, Wayne State University, Detroit, p. 5.

11. Ibid.

12. *Solidarity,* 18 March 1911; "James P. Thompson's Report," *Solidarity,* 19 October 1912.

13. *Solidarity,* 18 March 1911.

14. "James P. Thompson's Report," *Solidarity,* 19 October 1912.

15. Ibid.

16. Ibid.

17. Kornbluh, ed., *Rebel Voices,* p. 159.

18. Haywood, "Ettor," p. 4.

19. Fred Beal, "Strike!", in Kornbluh, ed., *Rebel Voices,* p. 178.

20. Haywood, "Ettor," pp. 6–7.

21. Melvin Dubofsky, *We Shall Be All* (Chicago: Quadrangle Books, 1969), p. 245.

22. Mary Heaton Vorse, *A Footnote to Folly* (New York: Farrar and Rinehart, Inc., 1935), p. 7.

23. Flynn, *I Speak,* p. 125.

24. Ibid., p. 126.

25. *Boston Evening Transcript,* quoted in Donald Cole, *Immigrant City: Lawrence, Massachusetts, 1845–1921* (Chapel Hill: University of North Carolina Press, 1963), p. 182.

26. *Hearings,* pp. 112–113.

27. This refers to an alleged attack by strikers on the trolley line, which derailed two cars on Jan. 16. The IWW claimed this was done by two detectives dressed as workers. *Hearings,* p. 292.

28. Haywood, Moyer and Pettibone, all active in the Western Federation of Miners, were kidnapped in Denver in February 1906 by the Idaho State Police to be framed for the murder of Idaho's Governor Stuenenberg. Clarence Darrow defended them in a celebrated trial. They were acquitted.

29. Flynn, *I Speak,* p. 121.

30. Vorse interview in the Columbia Oral History Collection, Columbia University, New York, April 1957, p. 2. Copyright 1975 by The Trustees of Columbia University and used with permission.

31. Flynn, *I Speak,* p. 126.

32. Vorse, *Footnote,* pp. 13–14.

33. *Report on Strike of Textile Workers in Lawrence, Massachusetts in 1912,* 62nd Congress, 2nd Session, Senate Document 870 (Washington, D.C.: Government Printing Office, 1912), p. 12.

34. "U.S.A. vs. William Haywood, et al," stenographic record of testimony 5

August 1918. There is a transcript of the trial in the IWW papers at Wayne State University, Detroit.

35. Haywood, "Ettor," pp. 11–12.
36. "Statement on behalf of the Lawrence Textile Workers' Strike Committee, issued on March 24, the day on which it went out of existence," *Survey* 28 (6 April 1912), pp. 79–80.
37. Vorse, *Footnote*, p. 14.
38. William D. Haywood, "The Battle of Butte," *International Socialist Review* 15, no. 4 (October 1914), p. 225.
39. *Solidarity*, 2 March 1912.
40. Fred Beal, *Proletarian Journey* (New York: Hillman-Curl, Inc., 1937), p. 44.
41. Flynn, *I Speak*, p. 122.
42. Elizabeth Gurley Flynn, "The I.W.W. Call to Women," *Solidarity*, 31 July 1915.
43. H. E. Fosdick, "After the Strike in Lawrence," *Outlook*, 15 June 1912; reprinted in *Solidarity*, 6 July 1912.
44. Flynn, *I Speak*, pp. 125–126.
45. *Hearings*, p. 32.
46. Other IWW strikes had used this tactic before on a smaller scale, such as the strike in the Irwin coal fields in December 1910. *Solidarity*, 4 December 1910.
47. Before she became a birth control militant, Sanger was active in the Socialist Party in New York City and was at this time head of its women's committee. She was also an IWW sympathizer.
48. 12 February 1912; Mary Heaton Vorse papers, Wayne State University, Detroit.
49. *Hearings*, pp. 227–228.
50. *Hearings*, p. 46.
51. Foner, *History of the Labor Movement*, vol. 4, p. 326.
52. *Solidarity*, 2 March 1912.
53. Leslie Marcy and Frederick Sumner Boyd, "One Big Union Wins," *International Socialist Review* 12, no. 10 (April 1912), p. 625.
54. Ibid.
55. *Hearings*, p. 302.
56. *Solidarity*, 16 March 1912.
57. Vorse, *Footnote*, pp. 13–14.
58. Marcy and Boyd, "One Big Union Wins," p. 629.
59. Ibid., p. 630.
60. *Hearings*, p. 89.
61. "James P. Thompson's Report," *Solidarity*, 19 October 1912.
62. Mary Kenney O'Sullivan, "The Labor War in Lawrence, *Survey* 28 (6 April 1912), p. 74.
63. Elizabeth Glendower Evans to Margaret Dreier Robins, 25 March 1912, Elizabeth Glendower Evans papers, Schlesinger Library, Radcliffe College, Cambridge, Mass.
64. Ibid.
65. Sue Ainslie Clark to Margaret Dreier Robins, no date, Rose Schneiderman papers, Tamiment Library, New York University.
66. See, for instance, Robert Dvorak, "The Garment Workers Strike Lost: Who Was To Blame," *International Socialist Review* 11, no. 9 (9 March 1911).

67. Minutes, Executive Board, 19 April 1912, National Women's Trade Union League papers, Library of Congress, Box 25.
68. Elizabeth Glendower Evans to Margaret Dreier Robins, 25 March 1912.
69. Haywood, "Ettor," p. 2.
70. William Haywood, "Socialism, the Hope of the Workers," *International Socialist Review* 12, no. 8 (February 1912), pp. 467–469.
71. Unidentified clipping, Socialist Party papers, Milwaukee Historical Society, Milwaukee, Wisconsin. In March 1912 Elizabeth Gurley Flynn made a fund-raising tour for the strike and stopped in Milwaukee, where she had high hopes of a warm reception since Milwaukee was a stronghold of conservative socialism, with a socialist mayor, Emil Seidel, and a socialist congressional representative, Victor Berger. She was disappointed. Seidel told her that he was a candidate for re-election and that he could lose his candidacy if he broke state electoral rules by making a contribution. Even worse,

> he could never run for office again; all this if he as much as slipped me one little lonesome dime for the starving women and children of Lawrence! . . . He went on to say that traps of this sort had been laid for him before and he had to be very careful. The insinuation that I was simply [trying] to lay a trap for him is indeed worth of the type who look upon the world movement for emancipation as a job-[getting] institution for themselves. . . . I was mad clear through. I didn't say much. What could I say to this complacent, self-satisfied individual, who read me laws for a half hour, as to why he couldn't help workers! Who never asked, "How is the strike? What are its prospects? Are you successful in your efforts? . . ." I had all the "comradeship" I could stand for one day. It's a brand that will make Milwaukee famous, alright. (*Solidarity,* 16 May 1912.)

72. "The National Convention," *International Socialist Review* 12, no. 12 (June 1912), p. 826.
73. James Conlin, *Bread and Roses Too* (New York: Greenwood, 1970), p. 125.
74. Quoted in Ben Williams, "Strike Tactics," *Solidarity,* 2 August 1913.
75. Ibid.
76. Samuel Lipson to Victor Berger, 29 April 1912, Socialist Party papers, Milwaukee County Historical Society, Box 5.
77. *Industrial Worker,* 10 October 1912.
78. Flynn, *I Speak,* p. 139.
79. *Solidarity,* 2 November 1912.
80. Ibid.
81. Dubofsky, *We Shall Be All,* p. 259.
82. *Industrial Worker,* 10 October 1912.
83. Dubofsky, *We Shall Be All,* p. 257.
84. *Solidarity,* 15 February 1913.
85. *Solidarity,* 9 January 1915.
86. Foner, *History of the Labor Movement,* vol. 4, pp. 347–348.
87. Phillips Russell, "Cells of a New Society," *International Review* 13, no. 10 (April 1913), p. 725.

Part V: Practical Conclusions

1. *Selected Works of Mao Tse-Tung,* Vol. 1 (Peking: Foreign Languages Press, 1967), pp. 304–305.
2. "Some Critical Remarks on the Draft Programme," *Communist International* 5, no. 15 (August 1928), p. 374.
3. *American Trade Unionism* (New York: International Publishers, 1947), p. 66.
4. I would consider the National Organization for Women (NOW) and the National Women's Political Caucus (NWPC) both, like NAWSA, bourgeois women's organizations in that their program for women could be comfortably assimilated by either of the bourgeois political parties. Indeed, this is their goal. This does not mean these organizations, both of which are large, are made up only of ruling-class people and politicians; NOW, at least, has a heterogeneous membership and some of its local chapters are quite different in both composition and politics from the national leadership. They have little effect on the organization's policy, however, which is set with an increasingly firm hand from Washington.

   Minority women's organizations have, on the national scale, included the National Organization of Black Feminists, Women of All Red Nations, and the Third World Women's Alliance; most minority women's groups, however, have been local ones comprised of Afro-American, Chicana, Puerto Rican, Asian-American, and Native American women. Left-wing feminist organizations have all been local and most have lasted only a few years; examples would include Bread and Roses in Boston, the Chicago Women's Liberation Union, the New Haven Feminist Union, and a host of socialist-feminist groups.
5. As this is being written, the main social-democratic organization is the Democratic Socialist Organizing Committee (DSOC); the old Socialist Party still exists as well, and some would include the New American Movement (NAM) among these groups. Social-democratic politics are frequently represented in the newspaper *In These Times.* Then there is the Communist Party U.S.A. and the various Trotskyist splits from it and from the Socialist Workers Party (SWP); these include International Socialists (IS), International Socialist Organization (ISO), the Spartacist League, Workers World Party and its youth affiliate, Youth Against War and Fascism (YAWF), as well as many others. Progressive Labor (PL), which split from the CPUSA at the time of the Sino-Soviet rift, has grown increasingly to resemble its predecessors.

   There is a large and ever-growing number of new Marxist-Leninist groups (as self defined), most of which are oriented towards China or Albania, though a few look more to Cuba. A fairly up-to-date list would include the Central Organization of U.S. Marxist-Leninists (COUSML), the Communist Labor Party, the Communist Party Marxist-Leninist (CPML), the Communist Workers Party, El Comite (MINP), the League of Revolutionary Struggle, the National Network of Marxist-Leninist Clubs, the Proletarian Unity League (PUL), the Philadelphia Workers Organizing Committee (PWOC) and its Organizational Committee for an Ideological Center (OCIC), the Revolutionary Communist Party (RCP), and the Revolutionary Workers Headquarters (RWH). Revolutionary organizations that are predominantly Third World include the All-African Peoples Party, the Republic of New Africa (RNA), and the Puerto Rican Socialist Party (PSP). A number of organizations that were previously only Third World have merged with others to become multinational, while some have been destroyed by police repression.

6. Charlotte Perkins Gilman, "The Socialist and the Sist," *The Forerunner* 1, no. 12 (October 1910), p. 25.

7. Langston Hughes, "Frosting," *The Panther and the Lash* (New York: Alfred E. Knopf, 1974), p. 84.

Index